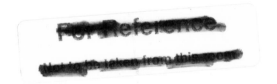

EXPLORERS &
DISCOVERERS

EXPLORERS & DISCOVERERS

From Alexander the Great to Sally Ride

Volume
Hi-Pi

Peggy Saari
•
Daniel B. Baker

AN IMPRINT OF GALE RESEARCH INC.,
AN INTERNATIONAL THOMPSON PUBLISHING COMPANY

I(T)P

NEW YORK • LONDON • BONN • BOSTON • DETROIT • MADRID
MELBOURNE • MEXICO CITY • PARIS • SINGAPORE • TOKYO
TORONTO • WASHINGTON • ALBANY NY • BELMONT CA • CINCINNATI OH

Explorers and Discoverers

From Alexander the Great to Sally Ride

Peggy Saari and Daniel B. Baker

Staff

Carol DeKane Nagel, *U·X·L Developmental Editor*
Thomas L. Romig, *U·X·L Publisher*

Shanna Heilveil, *Production Associate*
Evi Seoud, *Assistant Production Manager*
Mary Beth Trimper, *Production Director*

Pamela A. E. Galbreath, *Page and Cover Designer*
Cynthia Baldwin, *Art Director*

Margaret A. Chamberlain, *Permissions Supervisor (Pictures)*

The Graphix Group, *Typesetter*

This book is printed on acid-free paper that meets the minimum requirements of American National Standard for Information Sciences—Permanence Paper for Printed Library Materials, ANSI Z39.48-1984.

ISBN 0-8103-9787-8 (Set)
ISBN 0-8103-9798-6 (Volume 1)
ISBN 0-8103-9799-4 (Volume 2)
ISBN 0-8103-9800-1 (Volume 3)
ISBN 0-8103-9801-X (Volume 4)
Printed in the United States of America

Published simultaneously in the United Kingdom
by Gale Research International Limited
(An affiliated company of Gale Research Inc.)

I(T)P™   U•X•L is an imprint of Gale Research Inc.,
an International Thomson Publishing Company.
ITP logo is a trademark under license.

Contents

Chronology of Exploration

Explorers by Place of Birth

Index

Volume 2: Ch-He

Volume 4: Po-Z

Chronology of Exploration 875

Explorers by Place of Birth 883

Index xli

Preface

Explorers and Discoverers: From Alexander the Great to Sally Ride features biographies of 171 men, women, and machines who have expanded the horizons of our world and universe. Beginning with ancient Greek scholars and travelers and extending to twentieth-century oceanographers and astronauts, *Explorers and Discoverers* tells of the lives and times of both well-known and lesser-known explorers and includes many women and non-European explorers whose contributions have often been overlooked in the past. Who these travelers were, when and how they lived and traveled, why their journeys were significant, and what the consequences of their discoveries were are all answered within these biographies.

The 160 biographical entries of *Explorers and Discoverers* are arranged in alphabetical order over four volumes. Because the paths of these explorers often crossed, an entry about one explorer may refer to other explorers whose biographies also appear in *Explorers and Discoverers*. When this occurs, the other explorers' names appear in bold letters and are followed by a parenthetical note to see the appropriate entry for further information. The 176 illustrations and maps bring the subjects to life as well as provide geographic details of specific journeys. Additionally, 16 maps of major regions of the world lead off each volume, and each volume concludes with a chronology of exploration by region, a list of explorers by place of birth, and an extensive cumulative index.

Comments and Suggestions

We welcome your comments on this work as well as your suggestions for individuals to be featured in future editions of *Explorers and Discoverers*. Please write: Editors, *Explorers and Discoverers,* U·X·L, 835 Penobscot Bldg., Detroit, Michigan 48226-4094; call toll-free: 1-800-877-4253; or fax: 313-961-6348.

Introduction

Explorers and Discoverers: From Alexander the Great to Sally Ride takes the reader on an adventure with 171 men and women who have made significant contributions to human knowledge of the earth and the universe. Journeying through the centuries from ancient times to the present, we will conquer frontiers and sail uncharted waters. We will trek across treacherous mountains, scorching deserts, steamy jungles, and icy glaciers. We will plumb the depths of the oceans, land on the moon, and test the limits of outer space. Encountering isolation, disease, and even death, we will experience the exhilaration of triumph and the desolation of defeat.

Before joining the explorers and discoverers, however, it is worthwhile to consider why they venture into the unknown. Certainly a primary motivation is curiosity: they want to find out what is on the other side of a mountain, or they are intrigued by rumors about a strange new land, or they simply enjoy wandering the world. Yet adventurers often—indeed, usually—embark on a journey of discovery under less spontaneous circumstances; many of the great explorers were commissioned to lead an expedition with a specific mission. For instance, Spanish and Portuguese states sent **Christopher Columbus, Vasco da Gama,** and the sixteenth-century *conquistadors* on voyages to the New World in search of wealth.

Explorers also receive support from private investors. Prince **Henry the Navigator** financed expeditions along the coast of Africa. The popes of Rome sent emissaries to the Mongol khans. The Hudson's Bay Company, through the development of fur trade, was largely responsible for the exploration of Canada. **Joseph Banks** and the Royal Geographical Society backed the great nineteenth-century expeditions to the African continent. In each of these cases the explorer's discoveries resulted in lucrative trade routes and increased political power for the investor's home country.

Religion has been another strong motivating force for exploration. Famous Chinese travelers such as **Hsüang-tsang,** who was a Buddhist monk, went to India to obtain sacred Buddhist texts. **Abu Abdallah Ibn Battutah,** a Muslim, explored the Islamic world during a pilgrimage to Mecca. The medieval travel writer and rabbi **Benjamin of Tudela** investigated the state of Jewish communities throughout the Holy Land. Later, Christian missionaries **Johann Ludwig Krapf, Annie Royle Taylor,** and **Susie Carson Rijnhart** took their faith to the indigenous peoples of Asia and Africa.

Explorers have been inspired, too, by the quest for knowledge about the world. **Alexander von Humboldt** made an expedition to South America that collected a wealth of scientific information, while **James Cook** is credited with having done more than any other explorer to increase human knowledge of world geography. **Charles Darwin**'s famous voyage to South America aboard the Beagle resulted in his revolutionary theory of evolution.

Perhaps the foremost motivation to explore, however, is the desire to be the first to accomplish a particular feat. For instance, for nearly three centuries European nations engaged in a competition to be the first to find the Northwest Passage, a water route between the Atlantic and Pacific oceans, which the Norwegian explorer **Roald Amundsen** successfully navigated in 1903. Similarly, in the 1950s the United States and the Soviet Union became involved in a "space race," which culminated in 1969 when **Neil Armstrong** became the first human to walk on the moon.

Sometimes the spirit of cooperation can also be an incentive. During an 18-month period of maximum sunspot activity, from July 1957 through December 1958, 67 nations joined together to study the solar-terrestrial environment. Known as the International Geophysical Year, the project resulted in several major scientific discoveries along with the setting aside of Antarctica as a region for purposes of nonmilitary, international scientific research.

Although daring individuals throughout history have been driven by the desire to be first, the achievement began to take on special meaning with the increasing participation of women in travel and exploration during the nineteenth century. Pioneering women such as **Hester Stanhope, Mary Kingsley,** and **Alexandra David-Neel** broke away from rigid social roles to make remarkable journeys, but their accomplishments have only recently received the recognition they deserve. Since the advent of the aviation age in the early twentieth century, however, women have truly been at the forefront of exploration. **Amelia Earhart, Amy Johnson,** and **Beryl Markham** achieved as many flying "firsts" as their male colleagues; Soviet cosmonaut **Valentina Tereshkova** and U.S. astronaut **Sally Ride,** the first women in space, have made important contributions to space exploration.

By concentrating on biographies of individual explorers in this book we seem to suggest that these adventurers were loners who set out on their own to singlehandedly confront the unknown. Yet possibly the only "one-man show" was **René Caillié,** the first Westerner to travel to the forbidden city of Timbuktu and return alive. As a rule, explorers rarely traveled alone and they had help in achieving their goals. Therefore, use of an individual name is often only shorthand for the achievements of the expedition as a whole.

Famous explorers of Africa like **Richard Burton, John Hanning Speke, David Livingstone,** and **Henry Morton Stanley,** for instance, were all accompanied by large groups of servants and porters. In fact, the freed African slave **James Chuma,** who was the caravan leader for Livingstone and several other explorers, has been credited with the success of more than one expedition. Similar stories occur in other areas of exploration. For example, **Robert Edwin Peary** is considered to be the first person to reach the North Pole, yet he was accompanied by **Matthew A. Henson,** his African American assistant, and four Inuit—Egingwah, Seeglo, Ootah, and Ooqueah.

Explorers and Discoverers tells the stories of these men and women as well as others motivated by a daring spirit and an intense curiosity. They ventured forth to rediscover remote lands, to conquer the last frontiers, and to increase our knowledge of the world and the universe.

A final note of clarification: When we say that an explorer "discovered" a place, we do not mean she or he was the first human ever to have been there. Although the discoverer may have been the first from his or her country to set foot in a new land, most areas of the world during the great periods of exploration were already occupied or their existence had been verified by other people.

Picture Credits

The photographs and illustrations appearing in *Explorers and Discoverers: From Alexander the Great to Sally Ride* were received from the following sources:

On the cover: John Smith; **The Granger Collection, New York:** Beryl Markham and Matthew A. Henson.

UPI/Bettmann: pages 1, 129, 306, 375, 406, 489, 555, 611, 657, 699, 733, 742, 817, 856; **Norwegian Information Service:** page 14; **NASA:** pages 26, 30, 31, 34, 351, 400, 588, 723, 779, 844, 847; **The Granger Collection, New York:** pages 43, 44, 52, 61, 81, 86, 107, 122, 133, 141, 144, 145, 150, 164, 179, 187, 193, 209, 225, 282, 285, 311, 321, 325, 330, 334, 336, 345, 355, 359, 393, 424, 428, 433, 449, 460, 474, 499, 508, 512, 524, 560, 578, 589, 632, 638, 704, 744, 757, 772, 783, 806, 811, 830, 836, 852, 864; **The Bettmann Archive:** pages 169, 176, 268, 303, 341, 464, 494, 528, 623, 653, 695, 735, 767, 809, 828, 867; **Novosti Press Agency, Moscow:** page 378; **Hulton Deutsch Collection Limited:** page 418; **AP/Wide World Photos:** pages 538, 800;

Maps

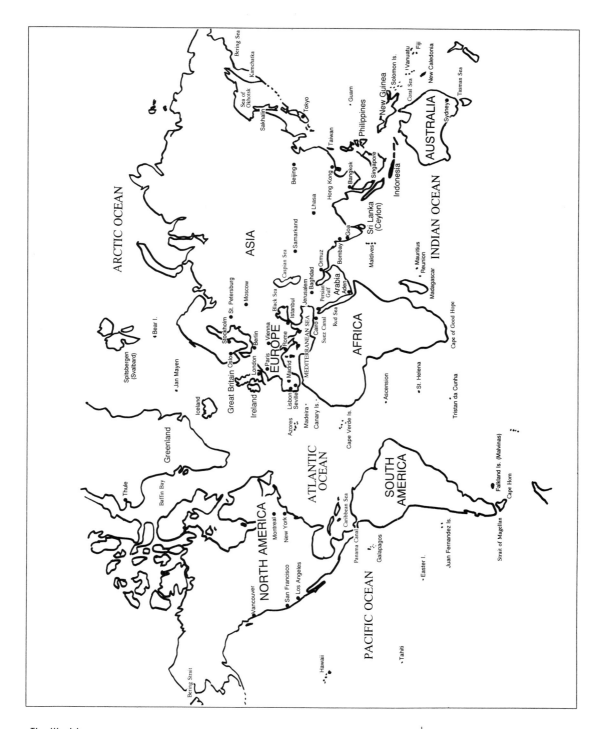

The World

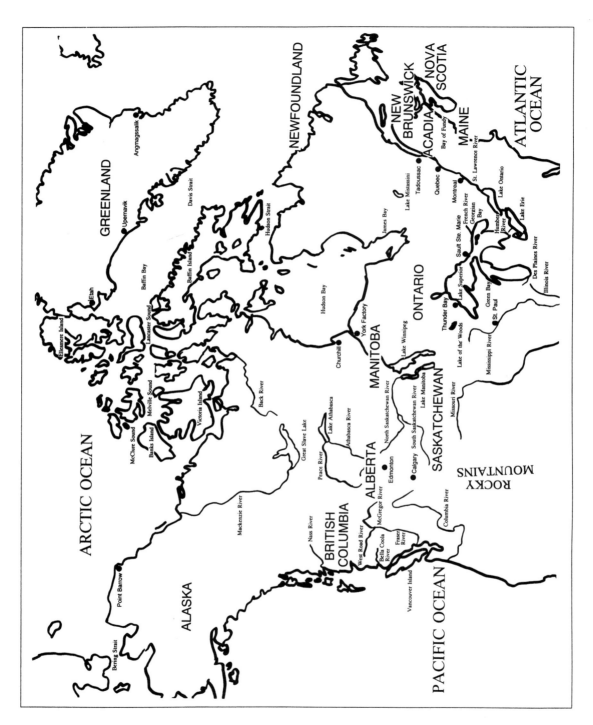

Americas–Canada.

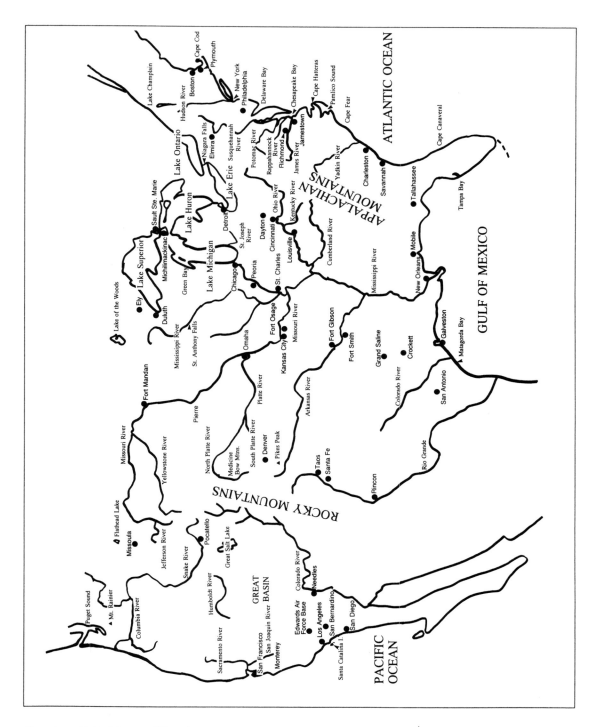

Americas—United States of America.

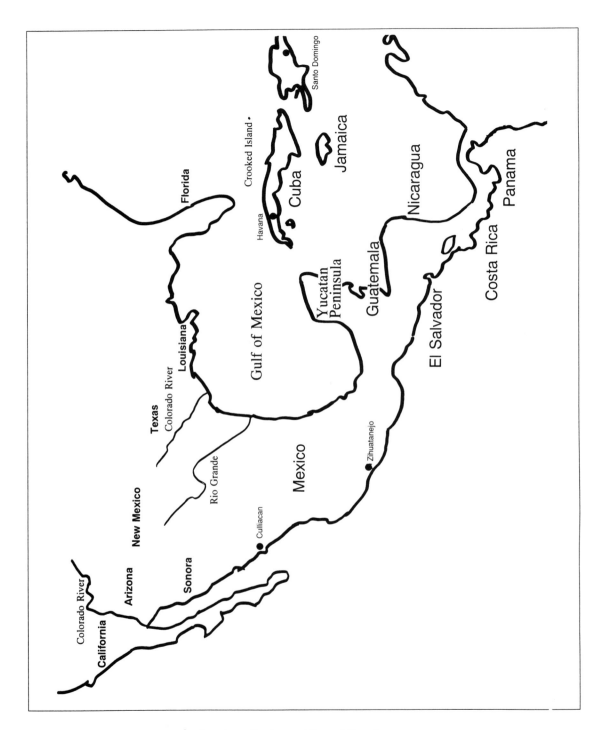

Americas—Mexico and Central America.

Americas—South America.

Africa and the Middle East—Northwest Africa.

Africa and the Middle East—The Middle East and Arabia.

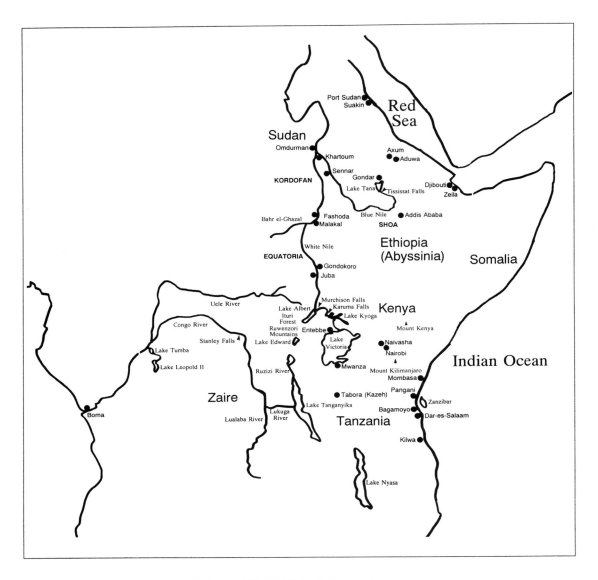

Africa and the Middle East—Eastern Africa.

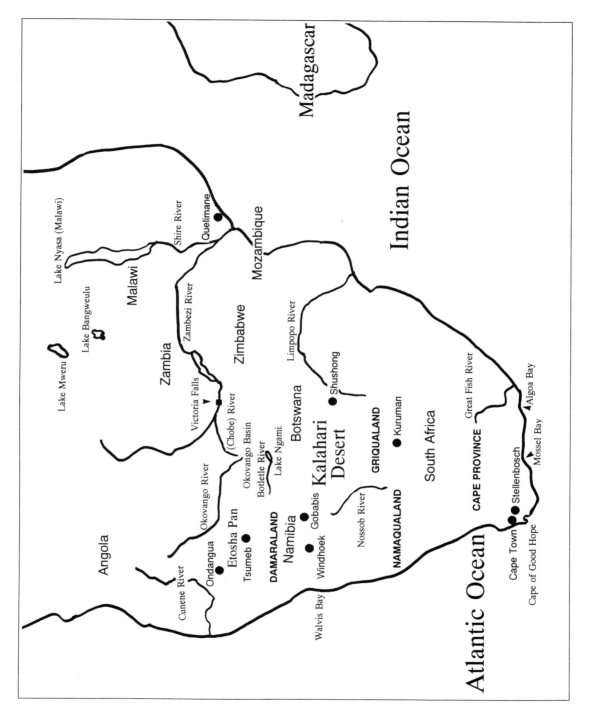

Africa and the Middle East—Southern Africa.

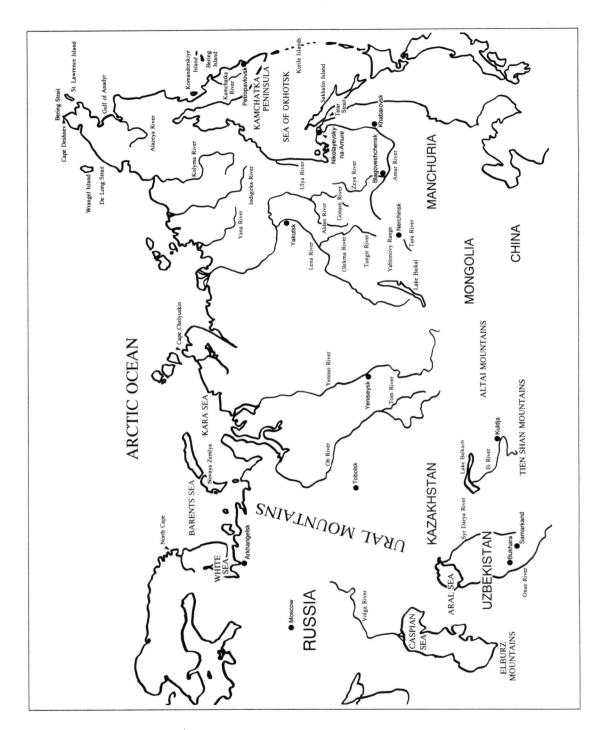

Asia–Siberia.

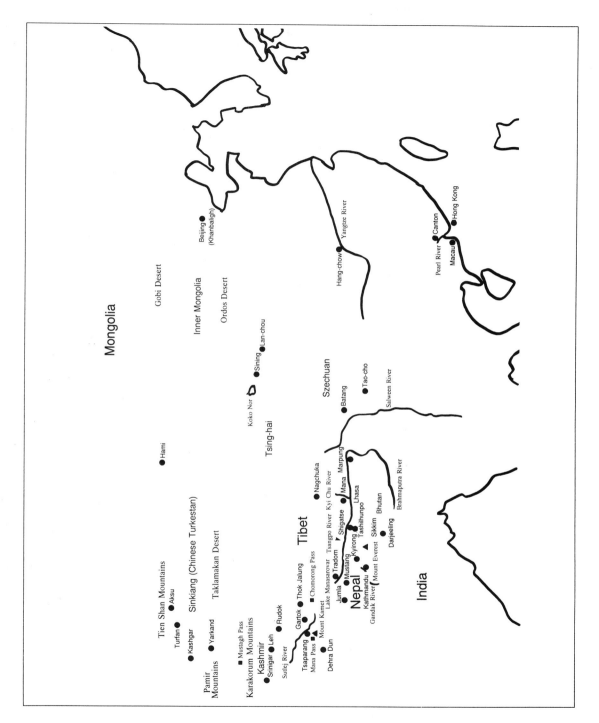

Asia—China and Tibet.

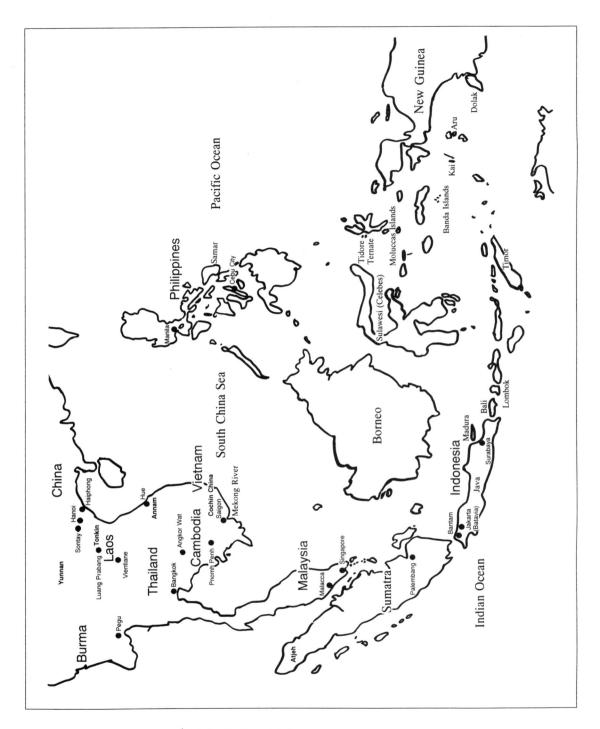

Asia–Southeast Asia.

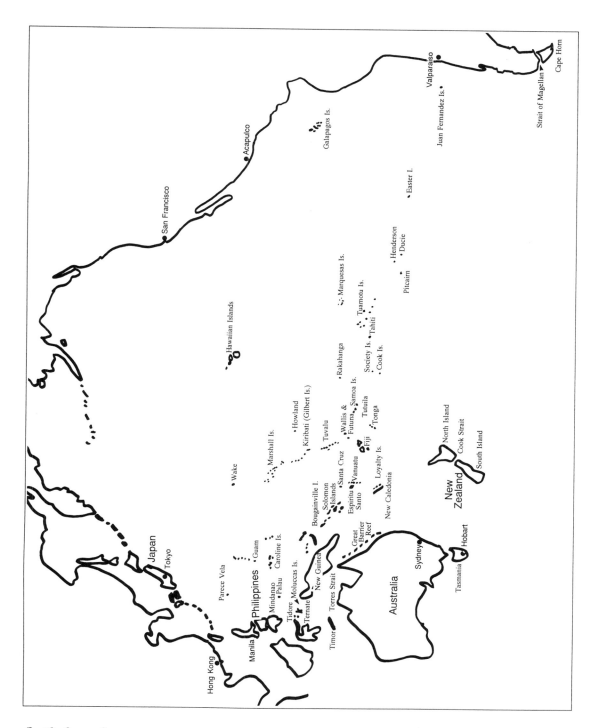

Pacific Ocean—Oceanea.

Pacific Ocean—Australia.

Arctic Region.

Antarctic Region.

EXPLORERS &
DISCOVERERS

Edmund Hillary

Born July 20, 1919,
Auckland, New Zealand

Edmund Hillary and Tenzig Norgay ▶

dmund Hillary was born in Auckland, New Zealand, on July 20, 1919. He grew up on a farm in the small town of Tuakau, 40 miles south of Auckland, and commuted to Auckland Grammar School. At 16 he saw mountains and snow for the first time on a school trip to Mount Ruapehu, a volcano in Tongariro National Park on New Zealand's North Island. He attended college for two years but quit to work as a beekeeper on his father's farm. At the start of World War II he decided not to volunteer in the New Zealand armed forces because of religious convictions. He then took a trip to the Southern Alps on New Zealand's South Island to think over his decision. The trip resulted in Hillary's interest in mountain climbing, which guided his later life.

New Zealander Sir Edmund Hillary was the first person to climb Mount Everest, the highest mountain peak in the world; he also led an expedition to the South Pole.

Pursues interest in mountain climbing

When New Zealand instituted conscription later in the war, Hillary decided to volunteer for the Royal New Zealand

Air Force. He spent much of his time climbing mountains around the air base where he was stationed, scaling his first tall mountain, Mount Tapuaenuku, at 9,465 feet. While at navigation school he climbed Mount Egmont (8,260 feet), New Zealand's "Mount Fuji." Hillary spent the end of the war as an airplane navigator flying near the islands of the South Pacific. He was seriously injured when his plane crashed in the ocean near a small atoll.

Climbs Mount Cook

Hillary returned to New Zealand and again climbed in the Southern Alps, where he met a famous mountaineer, Harry Ayres, who gave the self-taught Hillary his first formal training in the techniques of mountain climbing. Together they climbed Mount Cook, at 12,349 feet New Zealand's highest peak; then, a few years later, they climbed its southern face, becoming the first to do so. Hillary returned to the family's bee farm, which he eventually bought from his father. When the family traveled to Europe for his sister's wedding, Hillary climbed in the Austrian and Swiss Alps for the first time.

Prepares for Mount Everest climb

Next Hillary was invited to take part in the first all-New Zealand expedition to the Himalayas. He and three colleagues traveled to India in May 1951 and then to Nepal. They conquered 23,760-foot Mukut Parbat on the Nepal-Tibet border in August 1951. On their return to India, Hillary and another mountaineer were invited to join a British expedition led by Eric Shipton that was making a reconnaissance of Mount Everest, which at 29,028 feet is the highest mountain in the world. In October the mountaineers made several climbs up various faces of the mountain to try to determine the best approach. Hillary returned to New Zealand in December 1951 and soon was invited by Shipton to join an expedition in 1952 to climb Cho Oyu (26,870 feet) in preparation for a full-scale Everest expedition in 1953.

The British expedition ran into impassable ice fields that stopped them from reaching the summit of Cho Oyu. But the experience proved invaluable as many of the members, including Hillary, were invited to participate in the 1953 expedition headed by Colonel John Hunt of the British army. Several Sherpa guides and porters, who were Nepalese and lived in the Himalayas near Mount Everest, were recruited for their expert knowledge of the mountains. Tenzing Norgay, an experienced climber who had been part of two Swiss expeditions in 1951 and 1952, joined this group.

Begins assault on Everest

Hillary took charge of setting up the base camp on Khumbu Glacier, at 17,900 feet, which he completed on April 12, 1953. Hillary and Tenzing became climbing partners; Tenzing saved Hillary's life when Hillary, who was standing on a piece of overhanging ice that collapsed, fell into a deep crevasse. Hillary and Tenzing left the base camp to set up an advance base, and experimented with the expedition's oxygen system. They were given three days to accomplish this task but completed it in one. On May 7 the assault on Everest began in earnest. On May 26 two members of the expedition left from Camp VIII and reached 28,700 feet, the highest ever climbed, but the beginning of darkness and an insufficient oxygen supply kept them from the top. Their exhaustion forced them to be sent down the mountain.

Reaches peak

On the morning of May 28, 1953, a team of five climbers made it up to 27,900 feet where they set up a tent and some supplies. Hillary and Tenzing spent the night in the tent. They went to bed at 6 P.M. and awoke at 3:30 A.M. on the morning of May 29. After eating and preparing their equipment, they departed at 6:30 A.M. Hillary fell at one point and suggested going back but decided against it. They reached the South Peak of Mount Everest at 9:00 A.M. and then followed along a descending ridge that led up to the mountain's peak. At the ridge's end they had to climb up a "chimney" 40 feet high leading to the summit. The two men reached the summit at 11:30 A.M., Hillary first followed by Tenzing. They stayed on the peak for about 30 minutes. Hillary took a picture of Tenzing at the top, but Tenzing was unable to photograph Hillary because he did not know how to operate the camera. It took them the rest of the day to return to the advance camp. The following day they climbed down to the rest of the expedition; news of the triumph was radioed to the world.

On June 2, 1953, Queen Elizabeth II was crowned in London. One of the highlights of the coronation celebration was the successful climbing by a British team of the highest point in the world, a feat first attempted in 1924. As one of her first official acts, the queen knighted Hillary for his achievement, while the local Nepalis proclaimed Tenzing a hero. Hillary was besieged by members of the world press to tell his story. In Katmandu the British climbers were greeted by the king and queen of Nepal. In London, Hillary was received by Queen Elizabeth in a private ceremony. Hillary returned to New Zealand in August 1953, stopping in Sydney to propose to Louise Rose, who married him the next month. After the wedding Hillary began lecture and personal appearance tours in Europe and in the United States.

In 1954 Hillary led a New Zealand expedition to the Himalayas that ended in disaster. One man fell into a crevasse and Hillary broke three ribs trying to rescue him. Then at the camp at 22,000 feet Hillary came down with pneumonia and had to be evacuated to a hospital.

Joins Antarctica expedition

In June 1955 Hillary was invited to join **Vivian Fuchs**'s (see entry) expedition to cross Antarctica by way of the South Pole. Hillary reached Scott Base on the Ross Ice Shelf in January 1956 and helped establish the New Zealand base before returning to New Zealand for more supplies. Hillary returned to Antarctica in December 1956, setting up supply depots for the trip across the continent.

According to the original plan, the New Zealanders under Hillary were to serve as the British support team. The Fuchs team was to reach the South Pole from the opposite side of the continent at Shackleton Base, and then use the supply depots set up by Hillary to continue across Antarctica. As it happened, the New Zealanders made much better progress than the British, arriving at the South Pole on January 4, 1958, two weeks before Fuchs. He was the first person to reach the pole by using gas-powered vehicles and the first there since Robert Scott in 1912. Hillary and Fuchs then traveled together to Scott Base in time to catch the supply ship on March 2 before it was forced to leave by encroaching ice.

Searches for Abominable Snowman

In 1960 Hillary led an expedition to Nepal to search for Yeti, the so-called Abominable Snowman, and to conduct research in the Himalayas. While there, Hillary built a school for the local Sherpa population, the first of 17 schools and two hospitals that he was to build in northern Nepal. The projects were funded through income Hillary earned through product endorsements, lecture tours, and writings.

The Abominable Snowman

The Abominable Snowman is said to be a humanlike creature covered with long, dark hair. Some people who claim to have seen the creature say it is about 6 feet 8 inches tall; its tracks have also reportedly been found in the snow. In North America the snowman is known as Bigfoot or Sasquatch. It is known as Yeti in the Himalaya Mountains, where it supposedly originated. Although Sir Edmund Hillary's search for Yeti in 1960 gave support to the theory that the Abominable Snowman exists, most experts reject it as fantasy.

Makes other Antarctic discoveries

In 1967 Hillary led an expedition to Antarctica in which two New Zealand climbers scaled 11,000-foot Mount Herschel, one of the highest mountains on the continent. The expedition collected geological samples later used to support the theory that Antarctica had once been linked to Australia. Hillary continued his extensive travels, returning every year to Nepal to build a new school. On one trip, in 1975, his wife and teenage daughter were killed in an airplane crash. Also in 1975, he wrote an account of his adventurous life in *Nothing Venture, Nothing Win*. In 1977 Hillary led an expedition from the mouth of the Ganges River to its headwaters in the Himalayas. He then retired and now lives on his bee farm outside of Auckland.

Cornelis de Houtman

Born c. 1540,
North Holland

Died 1599,
Sumatra, Indonesia

Cornelis de Houtman was a Dutch merchant who led the first Dutch trading expedition to the area that is now Indonesia.

Cornelis de Houtman's trip to the East Indies is always called "The First Voyage" because it was the beginning of the Dutch East India Company and the Dutch empire in Indonesia. Little is known about Houtman's early life except that he was a merchant from the Dutch province of North Holland. His father was a brewer from the famous cheese-making town of Gouda.

Sent to Lisbon

In the summer of 1592 Houtman went to Lisbon, Portugal, in the employ of his wealthy cousin Reynier Pauw. It has long been thought by some historians that he was sent to Lisbon specifically to serve as a commercial spy. According to this theory, his mission was to bring back maps and sailing instructions on the Portuguese route to the East Indies (modern Indonesia) in order to break the Portuguese monopoly on the spice trade. Other historians have claimed, however, that he was in Lisbon on legitimate business and that any information he brought back was incidental. The Dutch had many other relations with Portugal, and men such as Jan Huyghen van Linschoten had also brought back valuable data. In any case, Houtman returned to Holland in 1594 with a plan to sail to the East.

Dutch East India Company founded

On Houtman's return seven wealthy Amsterdam merchants invested in a new enterprise called the Compagnie van Verre, which was an example of a Dutch financial innovation that was later to spread throughout the world: each person invested a certain amount in a venture and then was subject to risks or rewards in relation to the amount invested. The Compagnie was the beginning of the joint stock company, or corporation. The enterprise eventually became the famous Dutch East India Company, which bought four ships, outfitted them, and hired 248 crew members. The head of navigation was Pieter de Keyzer, and Houtman was the "chief merchant"; they sailed on the *Mauritius*. Houtman's younger brother Frederik, who was given the title of "junior merchant," sailed on the *Hollandia*.

Embarks on first venture

On April 2, 1595, the fleet sailed from Texel at the northern tip of the province of Holland. At first the party made good time: by April 19 they had passed the Canary Islands off the coast of the western Sahara, and they reached the Cape Verde Islands on April 26. Then the Dutch ships ran into the "doldrums," a nautical condition that results when the wind and sea are both still. They did not sight the coast of Brazil, where Portuguese ships altered course to the east, until June 27. Many of the men were sick with scurvy, and the navigators had a hard time steering according to the unfamiliar constellations of the Southern Hemisphere. When they sighted the island of Tristan da Cunha, however, they were able to adjust their course toward the Cape of Good Hope at the southern tip of Africa. The fleet landed at the Cape on August 2, 1595, but took another two months to reach the island of Madagascar. By the time they arrived, there were 71 corpses on the ships. The dead crewmen were buried in a small bay that was named Holland Cemetery.

Encounters problems on the ships

The ships stayed in the bay for several months while the surviving men recovered. The party was forced to set sail in February 1596 when the islanders grew tired of their problems and drove them away. By this time, the Dutchmen were in constant battle with each other. It did not help that they had set sail after the favorable monsoon winds had passed, and it took them four months to cross the Indian Ocean. When the fleet sighted some of the outlying islands of the Indonesian archipelago, Houtman had the chief merchant on one of the other ships arrested for mutiny.

Anchors at Bantam

On June 23, 1596—15 months after they had left Holland—the four Dutch ships anchored off the port of Bantam on the northwest coast of Java with a much smaller crew. Bantam was the chief port in the East Indies at the time, and the sultan was happy to have new trading partners. He welcomed the Dutchmen and gave them a house to use as a headquarters in the town. Houtman, who fancied himself a clever trader, quickly alienated the townspeople by refusing to pay the going price for spices. The Portuguese on the island naturally tried to eliminate their rivals by claiming the Dutch were pirates. When the Dutch ships began to take soundings of the harbor, the sultan suspected they were spies. He ordered that all supplies, including water, be cut off.

Encounters more problems

Houtman and some of the Dutch merchants stayed in the town while the ships under de Keyzer sailed across the Sunda Strait to Sumatra in order to get food and water. During the trip, de Keyzer died under mysterious circumstances; according to reports at the time, he had been poisoned. Moreover, by the time de Keyzer's ships had returned to Bantam, Houtman and the other Dutchmen had been arrested. In retaliation, the ships bombarded the town and some of the boats in the harbor. Relations were temporarily restored when Houtman was released. The truce did not last long, however: soon word was spread along the coast of Java that the Dutch were thieves and pirates.

Refusing to deal for spices in Bantam, Houtman headed east along the coast of Java with the aim of reaching the Moluccas, which were the actual source of the spices being traded at that time. At the port of Sidayu, near what is the modern city of Surabaya, open hostilities broke out between the two sides; 12 men from one of Houtman's ships were killed, including the captain and one of the merchants. When the Dutch reached the island of Madura off the east coast of Java, one of the local kings came out to greet them. The nervous Europeans mistook his intentions and fired on his canoes, killing the king and several islanders. This incident ruined their welcome elsewhere as well.

Forced to return to Holland

Only 94 of the men who had started on the voyage were now still alive. Many wanted to turn back, but Houtman continued on to the Moluccas. When one of the captains opposed him, the man was soon found dead. One eyewitness wrote, "A child could tell he had been poisoned." Houtman was accused of murder and arrested; the crew put him in chains. He was released when he agreed to return to Holland. The Dutch burned one of their ships and divided the crew among the remaining three. The party stopped at the island of Bali, which they proclaimed to be an island paradise, thus contributing to a reputation that continues to this day. Bali was so appealing that two of the sailors deserted.

The Dutch ships left Bali on February 26, 1597, sailing along the south coast of Java. As far as is known, this route had never been taken by another European ship. Since the return trip was much easier, they arrived in Holland on August

14, 1597. Eighty-nine men were still alive, but seven of them died a short time after the return. Because of Houtman's stubbornness, the cargo of spices was quite small and apparently did not bring enough profit to cover expenses. Nevertheless the party was received enthusiastically because they had pioneered the route to the East Indies and had shown it was possible to break the Portuguese stranglehold on the spice trade.

Dutch voyages continued to the East

Soon after Houtman's return Amsterdam investors equipped a larger fleet of eight ships and sent it east. Other investors soon followed, and in 1598 a total of 22 Dutch ships left Holland headed for the East. Nine of the ships tried to reach Indonesia by sailing west through the Strait of Magellan. A ship commanded by Captain Oliver van Noort successfully negotiated the straits, becoming the first Dutch vessel to circumnavigate the world. Ships that reached Java returned with cargoes that earned enormous profits.

Amazingly, Houtman and his brother Frederik were chosen to command two of the ships that sailed east in 1598 on another expedition. The Houtmans were employed by a group of merchants from the town of Middelburg in the southern province of Zeeland; also in their party was an Englishman, John Davis, who had been sent to spy on the Dutch. The brothers sailed from Middelburg in mid-March 1598. Once again, they got stuck on the coast of Madagascar, where memories of their previous visit were still vivid. Rather than going back to Java, where they knew they would not be welcome, the Houtmans sailed toward the island of Sumatra.

Finds success in Sumatra

Encountering better luck in Sumatra, the Houtmans were able to trade profitably for the pepper for which the island was renowned. In June 1599 they arrived in the Kingdom of Atjeh at the northern end of Sumatra, the stronghold of Islam in Indonesia. The sultan welcomed them and asked them to take part in a campaign against his enemy the sultan of Johore across the Strait of Malacca in what is now Malaysia. When the Dutch captains refused, their ships were stormed and Cornelis de Houtman was killed. Frederik de Houtman was captured and put in prison for two years, where he was continually threatened with being executed. While in prison, he wrote the first Malay-Dutch dictionary and composed a prayer book in the Malay language.

Hsüan-tsang

Born 602,
Chin-liu, China

Died 664,
Sian, China

Hsüan-tsang, a Chinese Buddhist monk, made an overland trip to India and then traveled throughout the subcontinent.

Hsüan-tsang was born the youngest of four sons in the town of Chin-liu, China. His father was a member of the Mandarin class of officials who governed China. It is said that Hsüan-tsang started reading the sacred Buddhist texts at the age of eight. Impressed by Hsüan-tsang's studiousness, one of his older brothers, a Buddhist monk, had him brought to the monastery in Luo-yang, a city on the Yellow River. Hsüan-tsang did so well that he was one of only 14 students in China awarded a scholarship to come to the monastery to study Buddhist texts.

Journey across Asia

At the fall of the Sui dynasty in 618, China experienced a period of strife and upheaval. In order to escape this, Hsüan-tsang went to the new capital of the T'ang dynasty (618-906) at Ch'ang-an. Unable to find the peace he sought, he traveled on to the monastery at Ch'eng-tu, located in the Szechwan province in south-central China, where he found serenity and prosperity. Fully ordained as a monk at the age of 20, he then returned to Ch'ang-an. Conditions in the country had begun to improve as the T'ang emperor established control. Taking advantage of the freer environment, Hsüan-tsang decided to follow the example of Fa-Hsien—a Chinese Buddhist monk who made an epic voyage to India to collect religious texts—and travel to India to discuss Buddhist texts with learned men. In an account he wrote years later, he said his aim was to "travel to the countries of the west [in Asia] in order to question the wise men" on the points that were troubling his mind.

Beginning his trip from the city of Sian in 629, Hsüan-tsang traveled to Liang-chou, where he served as a guest lecturer at a monastery. When he was told by the governor that he could not travel to India, he ignored the order and slipped out of town with the aid of two monks. On several occasions Hsüan-tsang was stopped by border guards at the frontier. Each time, however, they allowed him to pass, telling him about a detour around the last and most dangerous guard post. The detour sent him and his horse into the southern Gobi Desert, where he lost his way and dropped his water bag. According to his chronicles, he traveled four nights and five days without water until his horse found a spring. They eventually reached Ha-mi, an oasis in western China.

From Ha-mi Hsüan-tsang was escorted by an honor guard sent by the king of Turfan (now in Chinese Turkistan). The king was a devout Buddhist and wanted to keep the eminent monk at his court. When Hsüan-tsang declined the offer, the king supplied him with horses, provisions, money, and letters of introduction to the countries he planned to visit. Proceeding westward by way of the oases of Kharashahr and Kucha the following spring, Hsüan-tsang crossed the Tien Shan range and descended to Issyk-Kul, a lake in what is now the Republic of Kyrgyzstan on the border of China. There he met the khan of the western Turks, who was pleased to receive the Chinese monk. Moving on, Hsüan-tsang traveled through the khan's capital at Tashkent, the city of Samarkand, and then through the Iron Gates gorge to Bactria (modern Afghanistan).

In Bactria he visited the city of Balkh, where he saw many relics of the Buddha.

Arrival in India

Crossing the Hindu Kush Mountains, Hsüan-tsang arrived in Bamian, where he saw a figure of the Buddha that was carved out of stone and stood 140 to 150 feet high. During the summer of 630, he traveled down the Kabul River through present-day Pakistan into the cities of Peshawar and Taxila (which is now in ruins near the Pakistani capital at Islamabad). From there Hsüan-tsang journeyed to Srinagar, the capital of Kashmir, where, according to his chronicle, he was greeted by the king, his ministers, and 1,000 monks. Hsüan-tsang stayed in Srinagar until early 633, studying Buddhist texts with nine monks who were experts in various fields.

In the Punjab, a region in northwest India and Pakistan, Hsüan-tsang and his party were assaulted by 50 bandits, and they escaped only because Hsüan-tsang was able to slip away to get help. They traveled on to the headwaters of the Ganges, the sacred river of India, and then stopped at Kannauj. Hsüan-tsang stayed in Kannauj for three months to study with a famous Buddhist master and to study Sanskrit, the language in which the Buddhist texts were written. He then sailed down the Ganges to Kanpur. During the voyage Hsüan-tsang's boat was captured by pirates who wanted to sacrifice him to their god. As he was preparing to die, the pirate boats were hit by a cyclone and destroyed. To avoid an even worse fate, the pirates released Hsüan-tsang immediately.

Visit to Buddha's homeland

In the vicinity of Allahabad and Varanasi in northern India, Hsüan-tsang visited the sacred sites where the historical Buddha lived (in an area then controlled by the kingdom of Magadha). At the village of Kasia he saw the place where the Buddha had entered Nirvana—a state of bliss and release from suffering that is the religious goal of Buddhism. Hsüan-tsang stayed there for five years, from 633 to 637, studying the sacred texts at the great monastery of Nalanda.

After leaving the monastery, Hsüan-tsang continued down the Ganges to the port of Tamralipti. From there he sailed down the eastern coast of India and visited southern India and Maharashtra in west-central India. Turning north, he stopped again near Nalanda to study nonreligious subjects, such as mathematics and geography, with a famous teacher. Next he went farther northeast to Gauhati to convert the king to Buddhism. Finally, in 643, after taking leave of the monks at Nalanda, Hsüan-tsang headed back toward his native country, crossing the Thar Desert and the Indus River. Although he was able to cross the Indus safely on the back of an elephant, the monk who followed him was swept away by the current. The monk had been carrying Hsüan-tsang's manuscripts and a collection of rare seeds; he survived but his cargo was lost.

Return to China

Crossing the high mountains into central Asia, Hsüan-tsang faced many hazards. He survived blizzards and storms and the death of his elephant, who drowned while fleeing an attack by bandits. Hsüan-tsang reached Kashgar, in what is now the westernmost part of China, and then proceeded to Hotien, the capital of the Buddhist kingdom of Khotan, where the king came out to greet him. Hsüan-tsang spent seven or eight months in Khotan lecturing about the knowledge he had acquired during his pilgrimage.

In the spring of 645, after a journey of 40,000 miles, he finally returned to Sian, to which he brought 150 Buddhist relics, 6 statues, and more than 650 religious texts, 73 of which he had translated from Sanskrit. At the order of the emperor, Hsüan-tsang wrote about his experiences. He had completed his book, *Ta-T'ang Si-Yu-Ki* ("Memoirs on Western Countries"), by the time he died in 664.

Hubble Space Telescope

Launched April 24, 1990

The Hubble Space Telescope is the first optical observatory to be launched into space.

The Hubble Space Telescope (HST) was named for Edwin P. Hubble, the first astronomer to prove the existence of galaxies beyond Earth's galaxy, the Milky Way. Launched from the United States space shuttle *Discovery* in 1990, the HST is the most powerful telescope in the world. The spacecraft is orbiting 380 miles above Earth and is scheduled to remain in space for 15 years. Although it has been plagued by problems since it was put into orbit, the HST has nevertheless provided scientists with valuable information about the stars and the universe.

Telescopes have been used by astronomers since the seventeenth century. The Dutch inventor Hans Lippershey reportedly built the first telescope in 1608; the Italian scientist Galileo made the first astronomical studies with the instrument in 1610 when he discovered the craters on Earth's moon as well as the moons of Jupiter and the rings of Saturn. Galileo also determined that the Milky Way was not a "heavenly cloud" but rather a cluster of stars "so numerous as to be beyond belief."

These early telescopes were called refractors because they worked with lenses—an outside lens collects and focuses light and the eyepiece lens magnifies the image—a design that is still in use today. In the 1660s Isaac Newton, the English scientist, invented a telescope called a reflector, which uses mirrors to reflect an image to the magnifying eyepiece. Since Newton's time telescopes have become bigger and more powerful; for instance, the Hale reflector on Mount Palomar in California measures 200 inches in diameter and can photograph stars that are 15 million times fainter than those seen by the naked eye. These giant modern telescopes rely on Newton's basic reflector design.

HST provides new perspective

Although telescopes built in the twentieth century have helped astronomers piece together a fairly comprehensive picture of the universe, they are not powerful enough to answer important questions: How large is the universe? Do other stars beyond Earth's galaxy have planets? The HST was developed to provide this kind of information. While it is only 94 inches in diameter, the HST can see even farther than the Hale reflector and other powerful telescopes because it has a unique perspective—it is located in space.

Telescopes that are located on Earth must look through the air, or the atmosphere, which naturally dims and distorts star images and which is made even more dense by pollution and city lights. For this reason most observatories are located as far above the atmosphere as possible, on mountain tops or other high elevations. Yet there is no site on Earth that can be free of the atmosphere. Only outer space, where there is no air, can offer the best view of the stars.

Expected to be revolutionary

In 1977 the National Aeronautics and Space Administration (NASA) began the HST project, with assistance from the European Space Agency. The goal was to put into space an unmanned observatory that would orbit outside Earth's atmosphere and send back photographs of stars and galaxies. It was to become the most expensive instrument ever developed for astronomical research, eventually costing over $2.1 billion.

Considered the most significant development in astronomy since the invention of the telescope, the HST was designed to assist scientists in determining the structure, age, and future of the universe. It would help to discover planets around distant stars; the faint-object camera would photograph planets and the fine-guidance sensors could detect "wobbles" in stars, which indicate whether planets are pulling apart.

Another important function would be the study of quasars and black holes. Having the appearance of a star, a quasar is a distant object that generates more energy than an entire galaxy. A quasar can contain an invisible object called a black hole, which pulls in nearby adjacent stars and gas; this process releases great amounts of energy as the stars and gases are destroyed.

Access to the HST would not be limited to NASA and its partner. Astronomers who worked on the project would be permitted to use the telescope for their own projects; astronomers throughout the world could compete for use of the observatory by submitting proposals to the Space Telescope Science Institute.

Project delayed

Weighing 12.8 tons, the HST is equipped with a high-quality mirror that can detect a lighted candle over 250,000 miles away; other features include a faint-object camera that can photograph dim objects and fine-guidance sensors that can determine the exact location of stars. The HST also carries computers that can receive commands from two data-gathering sites, the NASA Space Flight Center outside Washington, D.C., and the Space Telescope Institute in Baltimore, Maryland.

The HST was designed to be put into space by a manned space shuttle that would take it to a distance of 370 miles above Earth. Once the HST was aloft, a mechanical arm on the shuttle would release the observatory to orbit Earth alone. The HST was originally scheduled for launching in 1983, but construction problems moved the launch date to 1985 and then to 1986. The longest delay occurred when the shuttle *Challenger* exploded in space on January 28, 1986, killing the seven crew members aboard. Although the *Challenger* project was unrelated to the HST, the disaster caused delays in all space shuttle programs until the reason for the accident was discovered. After investigators determined that faulty O-rings, elastic gaskets used for sealing, were not properly designed, NASA changed several features on the space shuttle.

Flaws found

The HST was finally launched on April 24, 1990, aboard the shuttle *Discovery*. Within two months, however, engineers discovered major flaws in the mirror: because of faulty manufacturing procedures it was shaped incorrectly and therefore was not able to form sharp images in visible light; vibration problems also developed. They estimated that as much as 40 percent of astronomers' work would be lost. In July 1990 NASA appointed a commission to study repair procedures for the observatory.

In spite of these difficulties, however, the HST produced impressive results. It was able to send back pictures of such quasars as the Einstein Cross, which is eight billion light-years away; it also detected a white spot on Saturn, which turned out to be a storm system at least three times the size of Earth. Because computers could compensate for fuzzy images, the HST has provided remarkable details about supernovas (exploding stars), the motion and composition of celestial objects, the formation and merging of galaxies, the activity of black holes, the composition of binary stars, and the physical processes surrounding shock waves.

Repairs made

In December 1993 astronauts aboard the space shuttle *Endeavour* completed repairs to the HST during five space walks over a period of ten weeks. Using an apparatus called the Corrective Optics Space Telescope Axial Replacement

(COSTAR), they installed corrective mirrors the size of quarters on the primary mirror; they also put in a new main camera and made other repairs. A month after the repairs astronomers reported that virtually full vision had been restored to the HST; the spacecraft's first discovery was a globular cluster that consists of a large population of aging white dwarf stars in a dense field of other stars. In January 1994 HST embarked on an ambitious mission to search for black holes. By the following May it had reportedly been successful in locating a massive black hole that promised to be a significant discovery.

Photographs comet crashes on Jupiter

In July 1994 the HST took hundreds of pictures as 20 large chunks of the comet Shoemaker-Levy 9 smashed into Jupiter, raising fireballs more than 1,200 miles wide and scarring the planet with a black dot about half the size of Earth. Taken after the impact points had rotated into view as seen from Earth, the images have helped astronomers learn more about the composition of comets and Jupiter and the dynamics of celestial crashes.

Henry Hudson

Born c. 1565,
England
Disappeared 1611,
Atlantic Ocean

Nothing is known about the early life and career of Henry Hudson. He undertook his first recorded voyage in 1607, when he was hired by the Muscovy Company of England to search for the Northeast Passage, a sea route around the northern coast of Siberia to China. Hudson explored the coast of the Svalbard Islands in the Arctic Ocean and sighted Jan Mayen Island east of Greenland, but he did not find a sea passage to China. In 1608 he ventured out to try again, but when his ship encountered heavy ice, he was forced to turn back without making any new discoveries.

In 1609 Hudson was hired by the Dutch East India Company to look for the Northeast Passage once again. He set out with the ship *Half Moon* and a mixed crew of English and Dutch sailors. Beyond the North Cape, located off the northern coast of Norway in the Arctic Ocean, the ship ran into heavy ice, and Hudson's crew refused to go any farther. Instead of returning to Holland, however, Hudson decided to try to find the Northwest Passage to Asia. He turned the *Half*

Henry Hudson, an English navigator, led two expeditions to North America and explored what came to be known as the Hudson River and Hudson Bay. He disappeared after his rebellious crew mutinied and set him adrift in the waters of the North American wilderness.

Moon west, heading for the coast of North America. His friend **John Smith** (see entry), the English explorer who had colonized Virginia, may have given Hudson this idea when he reportedly mentioned a large bay that might lead to a Northwest Passage.

Exploration of the Hudson River

Hudson and his crew reached the coast of Nova Scotia in July 1609, traveling as far as Chesapeake Bay before turning north to explore Delaware Bay. Continuing north, Hudson and his crew reached Sandy Hook, a peninsula at the entrance to New York Harbor, on September 12, 1609. The Italian explorer **Giovanni da Verrazano** (see entry) had already discovered the entrance to the harbor in 1524 but had not gone inland. Hudson sailed up the wide river that now bears his name to the site of present-day Albany; some of his crew members then rowed a boat even farther north.

During his voyage up and down the river, Hudson noted the richness of the land and recognized the opportunity for a prosperous fur trade. (His report inspired the Dutch to form a new company, The Dutch West India Company, which founded the colony of New Netherland, later New York, along the Hudson and Delaware rivers in 1614.) Hudson and his party had a few unfriendly encounters with Native Americans along the way. During a particularly violent skirmish, one of his crew members was killed by an arrow through the throat. Relations improved, however, when Hudson began trading European goods for food. Before heading back across the Atlantic, the *Half Moon* stayed for several days in New York Harbor on what Hudson described as "that side of the river that is called Manna-hata"—a Native American word for the island now called Manhattan.

Voyage to Hudson Bay

On its return to Europe, the *Half Moon* stopped in the

When Hudson entered Hudson Bay via Davis Strait, he mistakenly believed he had found the Northwest Passage. ▶

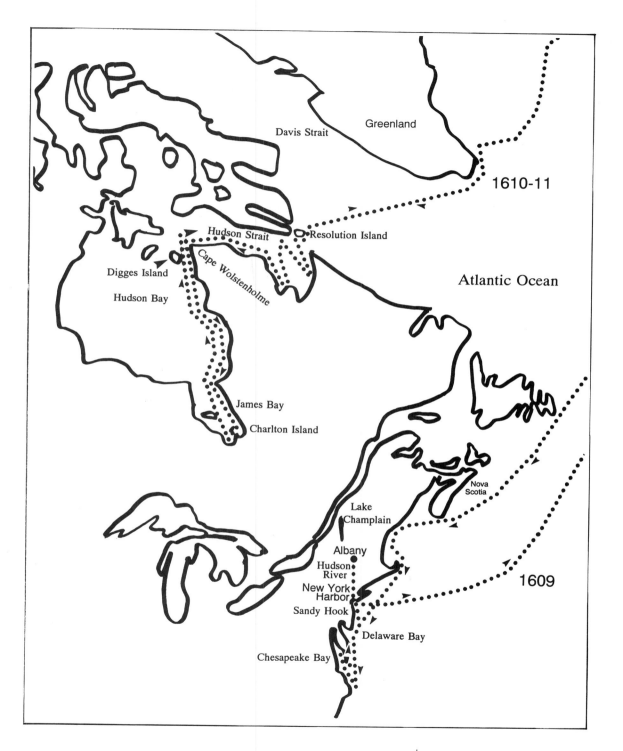

Davis Strait

Greenland

1610-11

Hudson Strait

Resolution Island

Cape Wolstenholme

Digges Island

Hudson Bay

Atlantic Ocean

James Bay

Charlton Island

Nova Scotia

Lake Champlain

Albany

Hudson River

New York Harbor

Sandy Hook

Delaware Bay

1609

Chesapeake Bay

English port of Dartmouth on November 7, 1609. The authorities took Hudson and all the English crew members off the ship, forbidding them to work for a foreign country again. Hudson would not be discouraged, however, and he soon interested a group of English investors in supporting an expedition to renew the search for the Northwest Passage. This time he planned to explore farther north than on his previous voyage.

Hudson set sail for North America on April 17, 1610, in the ship *Discovery*. Almost immediately there were signs of trouble among the crew members, and Hudson apparently could not control the men. Nonetheless, they reached North America, and in June they sighted Resolution Island, which separates Davis Strait from what is now called Hudson Strait in northeastern Canada. The strait had already been discovered by Martin Frobisher, the English navigator, in 1578, but Hudson was the first to sail through it—a voyage that took six weeks.

Hudson and his crew then rounded Cape Wolstenholme, named after one of the backers of the voyage, and entered Hudson Bay. At this point Hudson believed he had sailed from the Atlantic to the Pacific. He soon recognized his mistake when the *Discovery* turned south into what is now known as James Bay, the southern extension of Hudson Bay, and he found they were landlocked.

By this time it was October and the bay was beginning to freeze, so the Englishmen were forced to spend the winter there. Because of Hudson's lack of foresight, he and his crew did not have enough food and other necessities. Although they had made contact with nearby Native Americans, efforts at trading with them had failed. Everyone aboard the *Discovery* suffered through a very difficult winter, and there was frequent fighting among the crew members.

Banishment in the Atlantic

On June 12, 1611, the ice had melted enough for the *Discovery* to sail toward home. When the ship reached Charlton Island in the southern part of James Bay on June 23, the crew mutinied against Hudson. The following morning they put Hudson, his 19-year-old son, John, and six of the weaker crew members on a small boat and set them adrift. Hudson and his party were never seen or heard from again.

The *Discovery* continued north through Hudson Bay, piloted by Robert Bylot, and anchored at Digges Island at the entrance to Hudson Bay. During a battle with a party of Inuit, the ringleader of the mutiny, Henry Greene, and several other crewmen were killed. The ship finally landed in southern Ireland, where the crew was rescued and taken to London; only eight men survived the voyage back across the Atlantic. No one was ever convicted of any charges connected with the mutiny or with the banishment of Hudson, his son, and the other crew members.

Alexander von Humboldt

*Born September 14, 1769,
Berlin, Germany*

*Died May 6, 1859,
Berlin, Germany*

Alexander von Humboldt, a German scientist, made an expedition to South America with his companion Aimé Bonpland that included a trip up the Orinoco River and across the Andes; they collected a wealth of scientific information.

A generation before **Charles Darwin** (see entry), Alexander von Humboldt made an expedition to South America with Aimé Bonpland, during which the two men collected data on the natural history and geography of the region. They discovered Casiquiare Canal, the world's only natural canal, connecting the Amazon and Orinoco river systems.

Friedrich Wilhelm Karl Heinrich Alexander von Humboldt was born in Berlin, then the capital of Prussia, on September 14, 1769, within a year of the birth of several other great Europeans—Napoléon Bonaparte, the Duke of Wellington, and Ludwig von Beethoven. Humboldt's father was a nobleman and a major in the army of Frederick the Great, king of Prussia. His mother came from a wealthy family descended from French Huguenots who had escaped from France during the persecutions of Protestants by King Louis XIV. Humboldt's father died in 1779 and left the education of his sons, Alexander and Wilhelm, to the judgment of his wife, who hired private tutors, envisioning that her sons would someday hold public positions.

Becomes interested in botany

As a child, Humboldt suffered from poor health and he was a weak student. He attended the University of Frankfurt-an-der-Oder for six months before transferring to the University of Berlin. At the university he developed a passionate interest in botany and spent his time collecting and classifying plant specimens. After a year in Berlin, Humboldt joined his older brother Wilhelm, who was to become a famous linguistics scholar, at the University of Göttingen. He boarded in the same house as Prince Clemens von Metternich, a future chancellor of Austria. He studied under Georg Forster, who had been a naturalist on the second expedition led by the British explorer **James Cook** (see entry). While at Göttingen Humboldt made his first scientific expedition, a field trip up the Rhine River. He also accompanied Forster on a trip to England, where he met the most famous political and scientific men of the day.

In 1790 Humboldt entered the School of Mines in Freiburg in southern Germany. He developed the ability to work long hours, which would serve him well during his explorations. Although he did not graduate, he was able to secure employment in the mining department of the Prussian government where he worked for five years. He traveled to the Alps and the Carpathian Mountains and wrote reports on the mining industries of other countries. He also spent his time studying other fields of science, carrying out experiments with electricity, inventing a safety lamp, and making the acquaintance of two of Germany's greatest literary artists, Johann Wolfgang von Goethe and Friedrich Schiller.

Walks to Spain

In 1797 Humboldt was crushed when a fellow student, to whom he had a passionate attachment, got married. Shortly afterward his mother died of breast cancer, leaving her sons a large fortune. That same year Humboldt decided to dedicate himself to scientific exploration and immersed himself in study. The Napoleonic Wars prevented his participation in a number of scientific expeditions. Determined to travel to Egypt one way or another, Humboldt accidentally met Aimé Bonpland, a young French doctor and amateur botanist, who also wanted to go to Egypt. Their plan was to travel to the Mediterranean seaport of Marseilles, France, where they could catch a ship to North Africa and then travel overland to Egypt.

When they arrived in Marseilles they were unable to board the ship because Britain and France were at war and the Royal Navy was blockading French ports. They then decided to walk to Spain, where they hoped they would have success in finding transportation. Upon reaching Madrid they used Humboldt's connections to meet Spanish officials, and Humboldt had an audience with King Carlos IV in March 1799. Carlos authorized them instead to travel to Spanish America, commanding all royal officials to come to Humboldt's assistance. The Spanish overseas empire was closed to foreigners and, despite the expeditions of the French mathematician Charles-Marie de La Condamine and the Spanish botanist Hipólito Ruiz, there was little scientific knowledge of Central and South America.

Takes first expedition

Humboldt used his own wealth to finance the expedition, which would last for five years, from 1799 to 1804, and involve the two men traveling 6,000 miles in an often hostile and dangerous environment. Humboldt and Bonpland sailed from the Spanish port of La Coruña on June 5, 1799. Eleven days later they landed at Cumaná east of Caracas on the coast of what is now Venezuela. In Cumaná they were told that travel to the interior was impossible because of the rainy season. The two men spent several months collecting specimens of plant and animal life and examining traces of an earthquake that had occurred a few months previously. In November 1799 they went to Caracas, where they prepared for their expedition to the Orinoco River. Their aim was to travel to the Orinoco

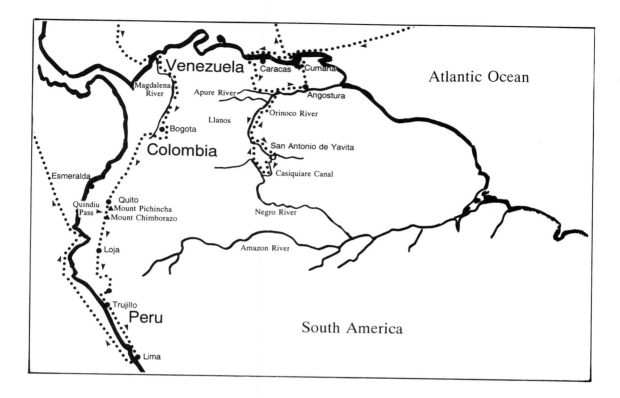

Map showing the routes of Humboldt and Bonpland through northern South America, with labels: Venezuela, Caracas, Cumaná, Magdalena River, Apure River, Angostura, Atlantic Ocean, Llanos, Orinoco River, Bogota, Colombia, San Antonio de Yavita, Esmeralda, Casiquiare Canal, Quito, Mount Pichincha, Mount Chimborazo, Quindiu Pass, Negro River, Loja, Amazon River, Trujillo, Peru, Lima, South America.

and see how it connected to the Amazon River, a phenomenon on which La Condamine had reported.

The two scientists left Caracas on February 7, 1800. To reach the Orinoco it was necessary to cross the llanos, a tropical grassland that was practically a desert during the dry season and was covered with water during the rainy season. The annual mean temperature on the llanos is 90°F, one of the highest in the world. Despite the heat and discomfort, Humboldt and Bonpland encountered many natural phenomena that they found fascinating. In the little cattle town of Calabozo, Humboldt investigated an electric fish, *Eletrophorus electricus,* which can produce currents of up to 650 volts, enough to kill a horse. Humboldt accidentally stepped on one of the fish after it had been taken from the water, receiving a jolt that produced "a violent pain in the knees, and in almost every joint" for the rest of the day. Humboldt also examined the "milk tree" or *palo de vaca,* which produces a white drinkable sap. When

During their two expeditions to Central and South America in 1799-1800 and 1801-02, Humboldt and Bonpland made several important discoveries and contributed significantly to scientific knowledge of the continent.

he returned to Europe he found that it was Artocarpus, a plant introduced by the Spaniards.

Explores the Orinoco River

In March 1800 Humboldt and Bonpland reached the town and mission station of San Fernando de Apuré on the Apuré River, a tributary of the Orinoco. On March 30 they started down the Apuré in a large dugout canoe furnished by the Capuchin monks; they reached the Orinoco in six days. They suffered terribly from hordes of insects—mosquitoes, flies, gnats, chiggers, and ants accompanied by tiny piumes, a kind of fly that stings like a wasp.

Along the way they saw flamingos, spoonbills, herons, small jet-black monkeys, stingrays, flesh-eating fish, manatees, turtles, and freshwater dolphins. On the banks they saw 20-foot-long alligators, large swimming rodents called capybara, snakes, jaguars, peccaries, and tapirs. At night they could hear the sounds of howler monkeys and parrots.

On April 6, they reached one of the three islands in the Orinoco where turtles lay their eggs in the sand. They were in time to see the turtle eggs being harvested by several hundred Native Americans, who came from great distances to collect the eggs in order to make turtle oil. Humboldt estimated that there were about 500,000 female turtles laying eggs along the Orinoco, and each one laid about 100 eggs.

Discovers Casiquiare Canal

On April 17, 1800, Humboldt and Bonpland reached the mission station of La Concepción de Urbana. By then the river had narrowed and their guides no longer knew the way. After purchasing a new canoe they took on board Father Bernardo Zea, a missionary who knew the Orinoco well and was happy to accompany the explorers. The trip increased in difficulty, with more and greater rapids. In May they reached the mission of San Antonio de Yavita. There they hired Native Americans to drag their canoe across the narrow neck of land that separated the Orinoco river system from that of the Rio Negro, a tributary of the Amazon. On their way back, Humboldt and Bonpland used the 180-mile-long Casiquiare Canal to return to the Orinoco. This location is the only one in the world where two great river systems are joined by a natural canal, and the two explorers discovered this connection.

Once back on the Orinoco, they traveled upstream to the mission station of Esmeralda—the farthest reach of Christianity. On May 23, 1800, Humboldt and Bonpland started back down the river; soon they both became ill with typhoid fever. They reached Angostura—the source of Angostura bitters, now called Ciudad Bolivar—on June 13; Bonpland's illness persisted for another month and he nearly died. Upon his recovery he fell in love with a *mestiza* woman and left Humboldt to pursue her into the interior. The two men were reunited in November. This was the end of the Orinoco expedition. Besides confirming and mapping the Casiquiare Canal, they disproved age-old rumors of a vast Lake Parima in the interior and collected 12,000 plant specimens, although a third of them had been ruined by the humidity.

Goes back to South America

Traveling over the llanos to Cumaná, Humboldt boarded a ship to take them to Cuba at the end of November 1800. They had planned to journey from there to North America but decided instead to head south again in April 1801. From the port of Cartagena, Humboldt and Bonpland embarked up the Magdalena River in April 1801. The Magdalena, which the Spanish conquistador Gonzalo Jimenez de Quesada had followed to Bogotá to conquer the Chibcha in the 1530s, was still the main route into the interior of Colombia in the early nineteenth century. It took them six weeks to reach Bogotá. As they journeyed, Humboldt surveyed the river to make a map. When they reached the point where the boat could go no farther, they rode mules and horses to cross the Andes to Bogotá. In Bogotá they visited the famous Spanish naturalist José Celestino Mutis, who showed them some of his collection of 20,000 plants and gave Humboldt 100 botanical drawings.

On September 8, 1801, they were on their way to Quito

through the snow-covered Quindio Pass. They reached Quito on January 6, 1802, and spent several months there. Humboldt decided he wanted to climb to the top of Mount Chimborazo, a volcanic mountain south of Quito that had never been climbed. Chimborazo is 20,577 feet above sea level and was practically impossible to climb in the time before oxygen equipment existed, not to mention modern mountain-climbing gear. In fact, Humboldt rightly concluded that the dizziness he and Bonpland experienced was caused by a lack of sufficient oxygen at high altitudes.

Sets record on Chimborazo

Humboldt prepared for the climb by climbing Pichincha, at 15,672 feet the smallest volcano in the Valley of Añaquito. He left for Chimborazo on June 9, 1802, and started the climb on June 23, accompanied by Bonpland and the son of the provincial governor. The first 6,000 feet of the climb posed little difficulty, but thereafter the path became steeper and more dangerous. At the snow line, 7,000 feet from the summit, their porters left them, and the three Europeans and a *mestizo* boy were left to finish the climb themselves. Their progress was impeded by snow, ice, and low-lying clouds. In addition, the climbers began to suffer from soroche, or mountain sickness—nausea, dizziness, and bleeding from the eyes, lips, and gums.

They kept climbing until, 1,000 feet from the summit, they found themselves on the brink of a vast ravine that was impossible to cross. Although they did not reach the top, Humboldt calculated they had climbed to 19,286 feet—which remained a world record for nearly 30 years. On the way back down they were hit by a hailstorm and then a blizzard. Many years later, just before his death at the age of 90, Humboldt sat for a last portrait. He asked that the background be Mount Chimborazo.

Travels to Peru

On their return from the mountain-climbing excursion, Humboldt and Bonpland decided to leave Quito and head for

Lima, Peru, in order to observe the transit of the planet Mercury across the sun. They left on horseback for the 1,000-mile trip to Lima. Along the way, they stopped to investigate Inca ruins at Cañar; Humboldt made the first accurate drawings of them, becoming the earliest archaeologist of South America.

Near Loja, Bonpland spent his time collecting specimens of the bark of the cinchona tree, which is the source of the medicine quinine—then the only known remedy for malaria. The plant was a valuable local commodity collected by hunters in the wild. Humboldt recognized that if this trade was allowed to continue without regulation the plant might one day disappear, and a major natural medicine would no longer be available. Humboldt was one of the first to recognize the need for biodiversity and the protection of species in the tropical rain forest. Fortunately, 50 years later Richard Spruce, the English botanist, was able to gather specimens and cultivate them.

Makes important discoveries

From the mountains around Loja, Humboldt and Bonpland descended to the town of Jaén on the Marañon River, the upper course of the Amazon. Humboldt used the occasion to improve on La Condamine's 50-year-old map. After 17 days on the upper Amazon the two men climbed the mountains to Cajamarca where the Inca Atahualpa had surrendered to **Francisco Pizarro** (see entry). When they descended to the coast at Trujillo, they encountered the desert that makes up the narrow coastal plain of Peru at the foot of the Andes. Humboldt started investigating the reasons the coast would be so dry. He established that it was caused by the cold current that flows north along the shores of Peru, which was named the Humboldt Current in his honor. He also identified guano, the remains of bird dropping that were to become the world's main source of phosphate fertilizers.

Humboldt and Bonpland arrived in Lima on October 22, 1802. Two weeks later they observed the transit of Mercury. On January 2, 1803, Humboldt and Bonpland boarded a ship bound for Acapulco, Mexico. They stayed in Mexico until March 1804 when they sailed to Cuba. From Cuba they sailed to the United States, where they spent three months as the guests of President Thomas Jefferson at Monticello. They sailed for France in July 1804.

Hailed as hero in France

On their arrival in Europe, Humboldt and Bonpland were received as heroes, having caught the popular imagination through the descriptions of South America Humboldt had written in letters to friends in Europe. After their return, Bonpland worked as the superintendent of the gardens of Napoléon's wife, Josephine. After her death in 1814, he went to Buenos Aires and became the director of a museum. While on a collecting expedition, he was captured by soldiers of the Paraguayan dictator José Francia and held captive for nine years. He was finally released after numerous pleas by Humboldt and others and retired to a small town in Uruguay, where he raised a family with a local woman.

Remains active in later years

After his return Humboldt lived in Paris for many years, working on the vast amount of data he had brought back from South America. He interrupted his work for a short time in 1815 to serve as a representative to the Congress of Vienna, where treaties were negotiated to end the Napoleonic Wars. Humboldt wrote 30 volumes on South America, covering an array of scientific and social discoveries. Having spent much of his fortune on the South American expedition and in publishing his books, he accepted a court appointment and returned to Berlin in 1827.

Humboldt organized one of the world's first international scientific congresses in 1828. The next year, at the age of 60, he made an expedition across Russia and Siberia to the Yenisei River. In 1845, at the age of 76, Humboldt started on *Kosmos,* a comprehensive account of the physical structure of the universe. Four volumes of the work had appeared by the time he died at the age of 90 in May 1859; a fifth volume was published after his death. He never married.

Wilson Price Hunt

Born 1782,
Hopewell, New Jersey

Died 1842,
St. Louis, Missouri

Robert Stuart

Born 1785,
Scotland

Died 1848,
Detroit, Michigan

Born in Hopewell, New Jersey, in 1782, Wilson Price Hunt moved to St. Louis in 1804. Five years later he went to work for John Jacob Astor, a wealthy New York businessman who was trying to organize the fur trade with the Pacific Northwest. In 1810 Astor sent Hunt to Montreal to engage trappers for an expedition to the Columbia River to trap for furs. After completing his mission, Hunt returned to Missouri with his men, who were dubbed the "Overland Astorians." They spent the winter of 1810-11 at a camp near present-day St. Joseph, Missouri, before embarking up the Missouri River in the spring.

Hunt pioneers Oregon Trail

In June 1811 Hunt's party of 61 men reached the villages of the Arikara tribe, where they acquired 82 horses from the Spanish trader Manuel Lisa. They left the Arikara villages the following month. Avoiding the dangerous Blackfoot country

American Wilson Price Hunt and Canadian Robert Stuart were two employees of John Jacob Astor's fur company who pioneered the route through the northwestern United States that was to become known as the Oregon Trail.

Wilson Price Hunt
Robert Stuart

to the north, Hunt led the party due west through the area that is now South Dakota into southeast Montana, across Wyoming to the Wind River, then over the Rocky Mountains near Jackson Hole, Wyoming, to the headwaters of the Snake River in Idaho.

When Hunt reached the Snake, he decided to let the horses go and to float down the river by raft. But this plan proved impossible because of the numerous rapids and obstructions, so the party was forced to walk overland, splitting up into smaller groups along the way. As a result they almost starved to death and had to live on skins and roots. In January of 1812 several members of the party reached Astoria, a trading post founded by Robert Stuart, at the mouth of the Columbia River. Hunt himself did not show up until February 15. In spite of their difficulties, however, they had pioneered the western part of the route that was to become the Oregon Trail.

After his successful trip to the Northwest, Hunt became involved in trading ventures by sea with the Russians to the north in Alaska and with traders in Hawaii and China. In 1814 he returned to St. Louis, where he was active in business and politics until his death in 1842.

Stuart discovers South Pass

In the meantime, another Astor employee, Robert Stuart, had reached Astoria by sea. A native of Scotland, Stuart had moved to Montreal in 1807. He arrived in Astoria in 1811 on board the *Tonquin* and built the post that Hunt found when he stumbled out of the forest. Stuart was chosen to lead the trip back overland, in the reverse direction that Hunt had come, at the head of the party that was called the "Returning Astorians."

Stuart left Astoria with six men on June 29, 1812, crossing over the Blue Mountains of eastern Oregon to the Snake River; like Hunt, they found the Snake difficult to navigate. By the time Stuart and his party had traveled over the Grand Tetons to Jackson Hole, they had exhausted their supply of food. So they were nearly starving to death when they found a stray buffalo that they were able to kill for food. In October, traveling south of the route Hunt had followed, they discovered the South Pass, which was the easiest means to cross the Rockies and which was to become the eastern end of the Oregon Trail.

Leaving South Pass, Stuart and his party rested by the Sweetwater River. In December they traveled to the Platte River in western Nebraska where they spent the rest of the winter. Upon their arrival in St. Louis on April 30, 1813, they received a hero's welcome. They were the first Americans to cross North America after Lewis and Clark.

After Stuart submitted a report of his expedition to Astor in New York, he was put in charge of fur-trading posts in northern Michigan. He settled in Detroit where he became one of the city's most influential citizens until his death in 1848 following a sudden illness.

Willem Janszoon

Born 1570
Died seventeenth century

Willem Janszoon was a Dutch sea captain who was the first European to sight Australia.

I n 1595 the Dutch sent out their first great trading expedition to the East Indies under the command of **Cornelis de Houtman** (see entry). The expedition was made up of four ships that were built in Amsterdam. The fourth and smallest was a three-masted "yacht" of 50 tons named the *Duifken* (Little Dove) that was destined to play a major role in history. The ships left Amsterdam in 1595 and returned on August 14, 1597. The voyage was such a commercial success for the Dutch merchants that they sent out a second fleet in 1598.

Dutch East India Company formed

The Dutch continued to enjoy a profitable sea trade and in 1601 formed the Dutch East India Company. The new company sponsored two expeditions before 1605. The *Duifken* sailed on both of these voyages; in a battle with the Portuguese off Bantam, on the west coast of Java, the small ship distinguished itself by capturing a much larger galley. The second expedition was commanded by Admiral Van der Hagen, who returned to Holland at the end of July 1606. He left behind in Bantam the two small yachts in his fleet, the *Delft* and the *Duifken,* giving them special missions: the *Delft* went on a reconnaissance trip to the east coast of India and the *Duifken* was to explore the south coast of New Guinea.

Sails for New Guinea

Willem Janszoon was put in command of the *Duifken,* which left Bantam for New Guinea on November 28, 1605. Sailing through the Banda Sea past the Kai and Aru islands, Janszoon sighted the southwest corner of New Guinea at Dolak Island. He guided the *Duifken* into what is now called the Torres Strait, where it ran into shallow water. Concluding he had encountered a body of water with no outlet, Janszoon turned southward. Following a route that would prove to be an unfamiliar one, Janszoon sailed down the west coast of the Cape York Peninsula on the east side of the Gulf of Carpentaria.

Discovers Australia

Janszoon thought they were traveling along the coast of New Guinea. The Dutch had in fact discovered Australia, a continent long sought by explorers and known for several centuries as Terras Australis, or the great southern continent. The *Duifken* thus joined the small number of European ships, including **Christopher Columbus**'s (see entry) *Niña* and *Pinta,* that sailed to an unknown continent for the first time. Janszoon's men were also the first Europeans to meet the Australian Aborigines. This encounter ended tragically, however: when the Dutch went ashore to trade with the Aborigines, nine crew members were killed.

According to some accounts a Portuguese navigator, Manuel Godhino de Eredia, sighted Australia in 1601, five years before Janszoon. Several historians, however, have verified that the Dutch party made the first visit to the continent; Janszoon is therefore generally credited with being the first European to sight Australia.

Australia remains unexplored

A few months after Janszoon's discovery, the Spanish explorer Luis Vaez de Torres sailed through the straits between Australia and New Guinea, which were later named in his honor. But the Spaniards did not sight Australia and were unaware that they had sailed between two great landmasses. When Janszoon returned to Java, he reported that the land he had found was desolate, with no opportunities for trade, which was of primary interest to the Dutch. Seventeen years later another Dutch captain, Jan Carstenszoon, retraced Janszoon's route and came back with an equally unfavorable report.

The Dutch did not return to the continent, except for accidental landings. The most important of these occurred in 1616 when Captain Dirk Hartog sailed too far east in the Indian Ocean and landed on the west coast of Western Australia. Consequently the Dutch knew there was a great landmass south of New Guinea, and they named it New Holland; yet they did not investigate the possibility that New Holland was separate from New Guinea. The continent remained unexplored for more than 150 years, until **James Cook** (see entry) claimed the fertile east coast for Great Britain in 1770.

Amy Johnson

Born 1903,
Hull, England
Died January 5, 1941,
London, England

Amy Johnson was born in the northern English seaport of Hull, where her father was a well-to-do fish merchant. She attended Sheffield University for three years. After an unhappy romance with a fellow student from Switzerland, she took a typing course and moved to London in 1927. Johnson worked first as a sales clerk and then took a position as a secretary in a lawyer's office. Her interest in flying began in 1928 when she rented a room near an airfield at Stag Lane. In order to receive reduced tuition for flying lessons, she became the volunteer secretary for the British Air League.

Pursues interest in flying

Johnson began flying lessons in the fall of 1928. Since she took twice as long as the average student to earn her license—she got lost on her first solo flight—her instructor told her she had no aptitude for flying. In the meantime, she had begun visiting the hangar at the flight school, where she

Amy Johnson was a British pilot who was the first woman to fly from Britain to Australia and who then set speed records from London to Tokyo and London to South Africa.

eventually learned to take care of aircraft engines. By December 1929 Johnson had become the first woman in Great Britain to qualify as a ground engineer.

As a result of this accomplishment, she received publicity in the popular press, where aviation was a matter of intense interest at the time. In one article she announced that she was going to fly solo to Australia—much to the astonishment of her fellow flyers. There had been only one previous solo flight from Britain to Australia. An Australian pilot, Bert Hinkler, had flown the distance in 1928 in 15 days. Johnson's goal was to beat Hinkler's time and set a new record.

Takes adventurous solo flight to Australia

Johnson began badgering well-known British personalities who were interested in flying to put up the money for her proposed expedition. She convinced her father to contribute the first £500 and Lord Wakefield, an oil magnate, to advance an additional £500. She bought a secondhand Gipsy Moth airplane, painted it bottle green, and wrote the name *Jason*—for the legendary Greek navigator—in silver on its side. When Johnson took off from Croydon Airfield on May 5, 1930, she had a total of only 75 hours in the air, her longest flight was 147 miles, and she had never flown over water. She later wrote, "The prospect did not frighten me, because I was so appallingly ignorant that I never realized in the least what I had taken on."

Johnson took two days to fly from England to Istanbul. She nearly turned back when she became nauseated while manually pumping gasoline from the storage tank to the tank in the upper wing of the plane. Throughout the flight she had to pump 50 gallons of fuel every hour. On the fourth day a sandstorm in the Iraqi desert forced her to make an emergency landing. She used her luggage to brake the plane's wheels, covered the engine and fuel tanks with canvas to keep the sand out, and sat on the wing for three hours with a revolver in hand in case she was attacked by wild animals. When she was able to take off again, she flew on to Baghdad, where one of the plane's wheel struts broke on landing. It was repaired overnight, but it broke again the next day during the landing in Oman.

Gains fame for breaking record

On the sixth day Johnson reached Karachi, Pakistan, two days ahead of the schedule Hinkler set on his record flight. She had left London with little publicity, but now the news that she had made record time to Karachi was telegraphed around the world. Suddenly, the international media were interested in this British woman pilot who was breaking aviation records.

During the flight from Karachi, Johnson ran out of fuel over the town of Jhansi; she landed on a parade ground at a British military post, scattering marching soldiers across the field, and stopped by wedging the plane between two barracks. Once again, the damage was repaired overnight so she was able to keep pace with Hinkler's record. On the flight between Calcutta and Rangoon, in India, she ran into monsoon storms. Unable to see to navigate, she landed the plane nose-down in a ditch near the Burmese Technical Institute. Students helped her repair the plane in their machine shop; however, the repair job took two days, causing Johnson to fall hopelessly behind Hinkler's schedule.

On the next leg of her trip, from Bangkok, Thailand, to Singapore, China, Johnson got lost, only to find that she had been making circles in the air. She was finally forced to land in Songkhla, Thailand. The following day she flew to Singapore, where the whole British colony turned out to welcome her.

Fails to break record but becomes a heroine

Johnson continued to encounter problems after she left Singapore. While she was flying over Java, clouds parted just in time for her to see that bamboo stakes were tearing off the bottom part of her plane's wings. Over Surabaja, Indonesia, she had engine trouble. Then while approaching the island of Timor northwest of Australia, she missed the airfield and landed in a field of ant mounds. On May 24, 1930, however, Johnson reached the northern Australian town of Darwin, having taken 19½ days, four days longer than Hinkler.

Realizing she had not broken the record, Johnson thought the flight was a failure. On the contrary, the world thought she was a heroine. In Darwin she was greeted by an ecstatic crowd and received congratulatory telegrams from the king and queen of England, the British prime minister, and famed aviator **Charles Lindbergh** (see entry). The London *Daily Mail* announced that it was awarding her £10,000.

Breaks under publicity pressure

After only one night's rest in Darwin, Johnson started out on a triumphal air tour of Australia. Physically and emotionally drained, she cried uncontrollably when she was out of public view. The crowds would leave her alone only after she crashed the *Jason* while trying to land in the Australian city of Brisbane.

Johnson returned to England by sea. The amount of publicity built up by her flight was intense. Several popular songs were written about her, among them "Queen of the Air," "Aeroplane Girl," "The Lone Dove," and "Amy, Wonderful Amy." It is estimated that a million people turned out to greet her when she arrived in London on August 5, 1930. The *Daily Mail* sent her on a tour of the country, but she lasted only a week before her health and nerves collapsed. Never having had to deal with the public before, Johnson now only wanted to escape from her fans. She conceived the idea of flying solo across Siberia to Japan. Setting out in January 1931, she was forced to give up the idea when she crash-landed in a potato field in Poland.

Marries fellow pilot

The following summer Johnson again attempted the flight to Japan, this time with fellow pilot Jack Humphreys. They set a record, flying the 7,000 miles from London to Tokyo in ten days. The flight was so uneventful that it received little publicity, much less than that of pilot Jim Mollison, who set a new record for flying from London to Australia at the same time. On her return to England, Johnson had a serious operation, then went to South Africa to recover. While she was in South Africa she was introduced to Mollison. They met again in London in May 1932 and were married in July. In the popular press they became known as the "Flying Sweethearts" and the "Air Lovers."

Competes with husband

Soon husband and wife began trying to outdo one another. Mollison set a record for flying east to west across the Atlantic in 1932; Johnson then flew solo to Cape Town, South Africa, and beat his previous record time by 11 hours. She was given an award for the most meritorious flying achievement in 1932; the next year he won the same award for flying solo across the South Atlantic. In 1933 Johnson and Mollison tried to make their first joint flying venture by setting a world long-distance record. This attempt ended with a crash landing in Bridgeport, Connecticut, that put both of them in the hospital. During Johnson's recovery, she became a close friend of **Amelia Earhart** (see entry).

Flies for Royal Air Force

In 1934 Johnson and Mollison entered another race to Australia but were forced to abandon it because of engine trouble. In 1936 Johnson set a second world aviation record on a flight from London to South Africa, a feat that once again brought her widespread popular fame. In 1938 the couple divorced. Johnson wrote *Sky Roads of the World,* a book about her adventures that was published in 1939.

When Johnson began experiencing money problems she took a job flying for an air ferry company. As Britain rearmed for World War II, she was hired by the Air Transport Auxiliary of the Royal Air Force. She seems to have enjoyed her work even though she was paid less than a man for doing the same work. On January 5, 1941, while Johnson was on a routine flight delivering an aircraft from Scotland to an airfield near London, her plane crashed in the Thames River and she drowned.

Louis Jolliet

Born 1645,
Beauport, Canada

Died 1700,
Quebec, Canada

Louis Jolliet was a Canadian-born Frenchman who was the first European to travel down the Mississippi River; he also made expeditions to Hudson Bay and the coast of Labrador.

When he discovered the upper Mississippi River, Louis Jolliet was accompanied by Father Jacques Marquette, a Jesuit missionary. On Jolliet's return trip to Quebec province (then known as New France) to present a report on the expedition, his canoe overturned and he lost all of his papers. He wrote another report entirely from memory; this narrative corresponds closely with Marquette's description, which is considered the official account of the journey.

Jolliet was born in the new colony of New France in 1645, the son of a craftsman who died while Jolliet was still a child. His mother was widowed twice before she married Jolliet's father, who was a farmer, and settled down in the town of Beauport near Quebec City.

At the age of 11, Jolliet entered the Jesuit college in Quebec, where he studied philosophy and prepared to enter the priesthood. He also studied music and played the organ at the cathedral of Quebec for many years. In 1666 he defended a

thesis before Bishop Laval of Quebec and other learned men. The bishop was so impressed by Jolliet's work that he became one of the young man's principal patrons.

Enters fur trade

In 1667 Jolliet gave up his seminary studies and borrowed money from Laval to spend a year in France. During

In 1672 the French government sent Jolliet to confirm reports from its Native American trading partners of a great river, which was later called the Mississippi.

495 | Louis Jolliet

his stay he studied hydrography, the science of charting bodies of water. On his return to Quebec he decided to enter the fur trade, which was the main business in New France. In that capacity Jolliet made at least one trip to the West, from 1670 to 1671, and was one of the signers of a document in which the French claimed possession of the Great Lakes region.

Leads search for Mississippi

In 1672 Jolliet was chosen by the two highest officials in French Canada—the intendant, Jean Talon, and the governor, the Count de Frontenac—to lead an expedition to search for the Mississippi River. The French knew of the river from reports from their Native American trading partners, but they wondered if it emptied into the Gulf of Mexico or farther west, into the Gulf of California.

On October 4, 1672, Jolliet left Quebec with his party. In early December they reached the mission and trading post at Michilimackinac, which is now the town of St. Ignace on the Mackinac peninsula between Lake Huron and Lake Michigan. Jolliet stayed at the mission for the winter. While he was there he made the acquaintance of the priest in charge of the mission, Father Jacques Marquette. Jolliet had brought instructions that Marquette was to accompany him on his voyage in order to preach among the Native American tribes along the way.

Reaches Mississippi

The exploring party left Michilimackinac in May 1673 with seven men in two canoes; of the seven men, only the names of Jolliet and Marquette are known. Since both Jolliet's and Marquette's logs of the journey were lost, their exact route is unknown; however, it is supposed that they traveled westward along the north shore of Lake Michigan to Green Bay, Wisconsin, then up the Fox River. Making a portage overland to the Wisconsin River, they descended to the Mississippi on June 15, 1673. They traveled down the Mississippi past the Missouri and Ohio rivers.

Jolliet and Marquette stopped about 450 miles south of the mouth of the Ohio River at the mouth of the Arkansas River, just north of the present boundary between the states of Arkansas and Louisiana. They stayed among the Quapaw tribe, from whom they heard reports of the Spanish approaching from the west. The unfriendliness of the Quapaws, as well as the knowledge that the Mississippi must run into the Gulf of Mexico, convinced the explorers to turn back without having reached the mouth of the Mississippi.

Returns to Quebec

In mid-July 1673 the expedition began the return trip up the Mississippi to the Illinois River, making the portage at Chicago into the southern part of Lake Michigan. Jolliet and Marquette split up at Saint Francis Xavier mission at Green Bay. Jolliet spent the winter of 1673-74 at Sault Sainte Marie in Upper Michigan, writing and copying his journal and making maps. However, he later lost all of his papers when his canoe overturned on the Lachine Rapids near Montreal. He finally reached Quebec in the fall of 1674.

Becomes active in fur trade

Once back in Quebec, Jolliet married and settled down as a fur merchant. He requested permission from the French government to establish a colony in the Illinois country, but France was reluctant to start any new ventures because its meager resources were already spread over a wide area in New France. Jolliet therefore devoted his efforts to the fur trade on the North Shore of the St. Lawrence River.

In 1679 Jolliet headed a mission to explore an overland route to the rich fur-trading regions of Hudson Bay, which were being exploited by the English. When he reached Hudson Bay he encountered English traders and was able to learn the extent of their activities. On his return to Quebec, he wrote a report saying that the French risked losing the fur trade if they allowed the English to continue trading in the area.

As a reward for his success Jolliet was given trading rights and land on the North Shore; he was also awarded the island of Anticosti in the middle of the Gulf of St. Lawrence. Although many of the details of Jolliet's life from that point onward are sketchy, it is known that he had a successful career in the fur and fish trades on the St. Lawrence. He also made several exploratory trips, including a mission to the coast of Labrador in 1689.

Explores Labrador

In 1694 Jolliet was commissioned to return to Labrador to map the coastline. Leaving Quebec April 28, he sailed along the North Shore and the coast of Labrador until he reached the settlement of Zoar in July. Jolliet drew the first maps of the area, described the landscape, and gathered information about the Inuit inhabitants. He noted that the only economic resources in Labrador were whale oil and seal oil, which could be traded with the Inuit. In October 1694 he returned to Quebec, only to discover that Anticosti Island had been seized by the British during his absence.

In 1692 Jolliet was made royal professor of hydrography at the Jesuit college in Quebec. He died during the summer of 1700.

Mary Kingsley

*Born October 13, 1862,
Cambridge, England*

*Died June 3, 1900,
Simontown, South Africa*

M ary Kingsley was born in Cambridge, England, on October 13, 1862, into a prominent British family. Her father, George, was a doctor and the younger brother of the well-known writers Charles and Henry Kingsley; Charles was the author of the popular children's book *The Water Babies*. As a child, and even as a young woman, Mary Kingsley did not have the opportunities enjoyed by other members of her family. Although her parents spared no expense in educating her younger brother, they refused to provide formal schooling for her. Like many girls of that era, she was taught to read at home and then was allowed free use of the family library.

Mary Kingsley was an Englishwoman who made two pioneering trips to West Africa and became a well-known writer on African subjects.

Secluded childhood

At an early age Kingsley was forced to take charge of the household. Her father, who frequently traveled abroad, was rarely home and her mother was an invalid. She later wrote, "The whole of my childhood and youth was spent at home, in the house and garden." Her life changed when her mother and father both died in 1892. She felt she no longer had a reason to live. At the age of 30 she found herself, as she put it, "dead tired and feeling no one had need of me any more, when my Mother and Father died within six weeks of each other in '92, and my Brother went off to the East, I went down to West Africa to die."

Trips to Africa

Kingsley did not die when she went to West Africa; in fact, the trip opened an entirely new world to her. During a previous vacation in the Canary Islands, off the coast of northwest Africa in the Atlantic Ocean, she had watched cargo vessels being loaded for a voyage to West Africa. Intrigued by images of an exotic land, she returned to England and began planning her own trip to West Africa. For her first journey in 1893, Kingsley chose an unusual mode of transportation for a lady traveling alone: a cargo ship. One of only two women on board, she spent four months on the West African coast, going from Freetown in Sierra Leone to Luanda in Angola. She also took advantage of the opportunity to learn about navigation and piloting.

Kingsley embarked on her second voyage to West Africa in late 1894. She had decided to operate as a trader in order to finance the trip, so she brought along a supply of cloth to trade for ivory and rubber. For 11 months she traveled from Gabon up the Ogooué River to the land of the Fan tribe. Although the Fan were reputed to be extremely hostile to the presence of Europeans in West Africa, they received Kingsley with great hospitality and she quickly made friends among the tribe. On this journey she had many other adventures, such as facing down two leopards and being attacked by crocodiles.

Once she undertook an expedition simply for the thrill of discovery, climbing Mount Cameroon, which at more than 13,000 feet is the tallest peak in West Africa. She scaled the mountain alone through a rainstorm and was disappointed to find, when she finally reached the top, that the rain blocked the view. Nevertheless proud of her achievement, she claimed to be "the third Englishman to ascend the Peak, and the first to have ascended it from the south-east face." On all of her trips Kingsley wore a typical Victorian lady's costume: a shirtwaist dress with stays, a long skirt, and a cap. She commented that "You have no right to go about Africa in things you would be ashamed to be seen in at home."

Return to England

Upon her return to England in 1895, Kingsley wrote a book titled *Travels in West Africa,* which was published in 1897; she also wrote a number of articles on African subjects. Because she opposed the methods the British and other Europeans were using to colonize Africa, she immediately found herself to be the center of controversy. Her views made her a hero among certain interest groups and a target for others.

Kingsley wanted to return to West Africa, but in 1899 the Boer War broke out between Great Britain and the Afrikaner republics of South Africa. She instead went as a journalist and nurse to South Africa. Soon after her arrival she became ill with typhus and died in the port of Simonstown near Cape Town on June 3, 1900, almost four months short of her thirty-eighth birthday. In her honor, the Mary Kingsley Hospital was founded in Liverpool, England, for treatment of tropical diseases, and the African Society was established for the study of African anthropology.

Johann Ludwig Krapf

Born January 11, 1810,
Tübingen, Germany

Died November 26, 1881,
Korntal, Germany

Johann Ludwig Krapf was a German missionary who was the first European to see Mount Kenya. His explorations in East Africa paved the way for the explorers who found the source of the Nile River.

During the nineteenth century mission work intensified throughout Africa. European missionaries established stations in remote locations for the purpose of bringing Christianity to native peoples through religious education and medical assistance. They were instrumental in furthering European settlement and commercial expansion in previously unknown regions. Many missionaries were also explorers; among them were such well-known figures as **David Livingstone,** the Scottish medical missionary who explored the African lake system. Another was Ludwig Krapf. In the process of seeking sites for mission stations in East Africa, Krapf made important geographical discoveries that aided **Richard Burton** and **John Hanning Speke** (see separate entries) in finding the source of the Nile River.

Johann Ludwig Krapf was born the son of a farmer in the village of Derendingen near the south German city of Tübingen on January 11, 1810. When Krapf was 11 years old the village tailor, for no apparent reason, beat him so badly that he was forced to stay in bed for six months. During his recuperation he occupied himself by reading the Bible and other religious works. From then on, his family said he was destined to become a preacher. Later he was attracted by an essay he read on the work of missionaries. At the age of 16 he went to Basel in Switzerland and applied to a missionary training school. Although he was accepted the following year, he was soon expelled for reading forbidden books. He briefly studied theology at the University of Tübingen before being readmitted to the school in Basel.

Becomes missionary in Ethiopia

After completion of his studies, Krapf wrote to the Church Missionary Society in London and asked to be sent on a mission to Ethiopia, which was then called Abyssinia; he was appointed in 1837. On a stop in Cairo during his journey to Ethiopia, he showed a talent for languages by quickly learning to speak Arabic. In Ethiopia Krapf met a fellow missionary, C. W. Isenberg, and traveled with him to Adwa, the capital of the province of Tigre. In 1839 he went to the province of Shewa, the center of Ethiopia. He was well received by the king of Shewa and accompanied him on a campaign against the Galla tribe, now known as the Oromo, a non-Christian people who were constant enemies of the central government.

Immediately attracted to the Galla as a fruitful field for missionary work, Krapf established a mission station. During his stay in Shewa he wrote the first grammar of the Galla language and translated part of the Bible into Galla. He also conceived the erroneous idea that the Galla were spread throughout East Africa.

Goes to Egypt

In 1842 Krapf left his work in Shew and departed for Egypt. Before reaching the port of Mesawa off the Red Sea in Ethiopia, he was attacked and robbed. In May 1842 he sailed from Mesawa to Aden on the south coast of Arabia; from Aden he traveled to Egypt. While serving in Egypt Krapf married a

German woman named Rosine Dietrich, who had been sent by the Basel missionary school. They returned to Aden where Krapf made plans for the future. He thought that if he traveled to the coast of East Africa he could go northward into the interior and once again encounter members of the Galla tribe. The theory was good, but in actuality it proved impossible.

Starts mission in Mombasa

Krapf reached Zanzibar in East Africa in January 1844 after a brief stop at the port of Mombasa, an island off the coast of Kenya in East Africa. Mombasa had impressed him as a good place to conduct his missionary work, so he and his wife returned to settle there the following May. Krapf immediately started to learn the Swahili language. But soon after their arrival the couple became ill with malaria. Then in July Krapf's wife gave birth to a baby girl; both mother and daughter died within a week. Krapf stayed at his post, however, and began translating the Bible into Swahili.

Krapf traveled in the vicinity of Mombasa to try to find a site to build his mission station. He finally decided on the village of Rabbai Mpia, which was only a few miles inland from Mombasa. Situated atop a hill about 1,000 feet high, the village commanded a wide view of the port of Mombasa and the Indian Ocean. When fellow missionary **Johannes Rebmann** (see entry) arrived in June 1846, they began building the mission station at Rabbai Mpia.

Seeks other mission sites

In the following years Krapf traveled throughout East Africa looking for possible mission sites. His plan was to penetrate into the interior by establishing a chain of mission stations that would support each other and provide a link to the coast and the outside world. In July 1848 he left for Usambara, an area south of Mombasa, with a guide and seven porters. In August he met Kmeri, "the only true lion," king of Usambara. Krapf feared a negative reception, but in fact the king welcomed him and expressed pleasure at having Christian missionaries in Usambara.

Sees Mount Kenya

In October 1849 Krapf traveled to Ukambani, the country of the Wakamba. According to Krapf, when he reached the first of the Wakamba villages in November, the people looked at him as though he were a "being from another world." At the village of Kitui, the king, who was named Kivoi, told Krapf he had been to Chagga country and had seen the white mountain of Kilimanjaro, which Rebmann had reported on.

Kivoi mentioned that there was another snow-capped mountain about six days' journey from Kitui. Pointing out a nearby hill, he told the missionary to climb to the top to see the mountain. But once Krapf had ascended the hill he could not see anything because it was too cloudy and rainy. On December 3, 1849, just as Krapf was preparing to leave Kitui, he was able to get a good view of the two white peaks of Mount Kenya, which reached to 17,058 feet. He thus became the first European to see Mount Kenya.

Returns to England

In 1850 Krapf made a voyage down the east coast of Africa in a small Swahili boat. Traveling as far as Cape Delgado in what is now Mozambique, he heard stories of Lake Nyasa (Malawi) in the interior. On his return to England he made a report in person to the Church Missionary Society about his mission efforts in East Africa. Endorsing his work, the society authorized him to found a mission in the Ukambani country. During a later visit to Germany he discussed his explorations, particularly his stories of snow-covered mountains in tropical Africa, with such well-known scientists as **Alexander von Humboldt** (see entry).

Krapf returned to Rabbai Mpia in April 1851. The following July he departed for the interior with the aim of setting up a mission station in the highlands beyond the Athi River. During the voyage he was abandoned by his porters, so he decided to detour to Kitui, where Kivoi had been so helpful. Greeting Krapf, the king said he would give any help he needed, but first Krapf must accompany him on a journey to the

Tana River. They left for the Tana in late August, only to be ambushed by robbers several days later. Kivoi was killed during the assault but Krapf made a miraculous escape from the arrows of their attackers. During his flight into the forest, Krapf turned a corner and came face to face with two rhinoceroses.

Discovers a river and two mountains

Krapf's discovery of the upper reaches of the Tana River came about virtually by accident: he stumbled upon it while looking for water. While taking the opportunity to explore the Tana for a short distance, he saw a tall mountain on the other side of the river. He named it Mount Albert in honor of Queen Victoria's husband, who was a supporter of missionary activities; another mountain he named Mount William in honor of the king of Prussia.

When Krapf returned to Kitui, the Wakamba blamed him for the death of Kivoi. Facing intense hostility, he realized it was not possible to set up a mission in Ukambani. He retreated to Usambara and received permission from Kmeri to establish a mission station there. By this time, however, Krapf's health was failing and he knew he would be unable to lead this mission himself. After a stop at Rabbai Mpia, he left for Germany in September 1853. Traveling by way of Cairo, Krapf met Richard Burton, who was intrigued with his tales of the Tana River, which Burton thought might be the source of the Nile River.

Settles in Germany

Krapf stayed in Germany for a year before going back to Africa. By the time he had reached Ethiopia he realized his health would not allow him to continue. In September 1855 he returned to Germany. He settled in the village of Korntal near Stuttgart and remarried. He and his second wife had a daughter; after his wife died he married for a third time, in 1869. Krapf spent his time writing his notes on his experiences; he also pursued his studies of African languages and published several grammars. In 1862 Krapf returned to East Africa for a few months to found a mission for the United Methodist Free Church; he made another trip in 1867. Ill health prevented him from staying very long either time. Krapf died in Korntal on November 26, 1881.

Jean-François de Galaup, Comte de La Pérouse

Born 1741,
Guo, France

Died c. 1788,
South Pacific

The Count of La Pérouse was a French naval officer who led a major expedition to the Pacific following the explorations of James Cook. He disappeared in the South Pacific.

Jean-François de Galaup, comte de La Pérouse, was born at Guo near Albi in southern France. He entered the navy at 15. In 1759, while serving on board the *Formidable,* he was wounded and captured by the British during a naval battle off the coast of Brittany. After his recovery he served in the Seven Years' War, or the French and Indian War, off the east coast of North America.

Fights in American Revolution

In 1775 La Pérouse was promoted to lieutenant. In 1780 he achieved the rank of captain and served in the American Revolution after France became allied with the newly formed United States. During that war, he distinguished himself by commanding an attack that took British forts in Hudson Bay in August 1782. He demonstrated his humanity by leaving the remaining settlers enough arms and provisions to enable them to survive during the oncoming winter. He also arranged for

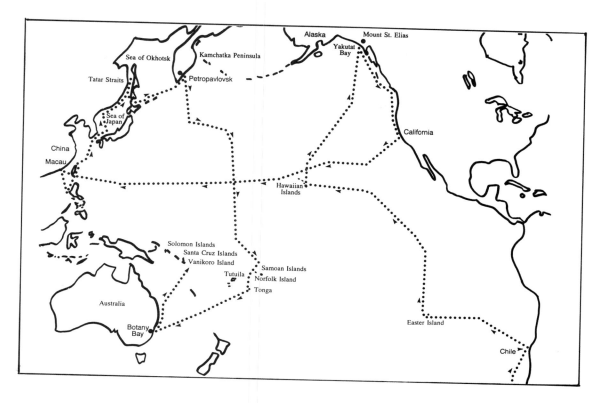

the release of one of his British prisoners, Samuel Hearne, so that Hearne could go back to England to publish an account of the trip he had taken from 1770 to 1772 to the Arctic Ocean.

Leads expedition to the Pacific

In 1783 the French government decided to send an expedition to the Pacific to follow up on the work of **James Cook** (see entry), the pioneering British explorer. In particular the French wanted to search for the Northwest Passage from the Pacific to the Atlantic and explore the coast of North America, the coasts of China and Siberia, and the South Seas. King Louis XVI himself helped to draw up the proposal for this voyage of exploration, and La Pérouse was selected to lead the expedition. The king gave him an audience before his ships sailed for the Pacific.

La Pérouse was placed in command of two ships, *La Boussole* and *L'Astrolabe*; Paul-Antoine de Langle was cap-

Before disappearing in the South Pacific, La Pérouse explored the coast of North America, the coasts of Siberia and China, and previously unknown islands in the South Seas.

509 | Jean-François de Galaup, Comte de La Pérouse

tain of *L'Astrolabe*. The party left Brest harbor on August 1, 1785, bound for Brazil. Passing south of Cape Horn, La Pérouse stopped in Chile for more provisions. From Chile the ships sailed to the Sandwich Islands, as Hawaii was then called, and turned north toward Alaska. After landing at Yakutat Bay near the Saint Elias Mountains in Alaska, La Pérouse took the fleet south along the coast as far as California, proving that there was no northwest passage in that region.

Discovers islands in Pacific

The party stayed for a short time in Monterey, the capital of Spanish California. La Pérouse then sailed across the Pacific, in the process finding several islands unknown to Europeans. The ships reached Macao, a Portuguese colony on the south coast of China, in January 1787. After six weeks of reprovisioning and making repairs, they left Macao and headed for the Sea of Japan and the Sea of Okhotsk in the northwest Pacific.

As La Pérouse sailed up the Tatar Straits, he named several points on both of its shores and speculated, correctly, that Sakhalin must be an island, not a peninsula attached to the Asian mainland. In September he put in at the Russian port of Petropavlovsk-Kamchatski on the Kamchatka Peninsula. During his stay he discovered La Pérouse Strait, then sent one of his officers, Baron Jean de Lesseps, overland across Siberia to report on his discoveries.

Reaches Australia

Next La Pérouse turned south toward Australia. In December 1787 he reached Tutuila, now the chief island in American Samoa, which had been discovered by **Louis Antoine de Bougainville** (see entry) in 1767. When a party from *L'Astrolabe,* including Captain Langle, went ashore to look for water, they were killed by the Samoans. Deciding not to seek reprisal, La Pérouse sailed via Tonga and Norfolk Island to Botany Bay, near present-day Sydney, Australia. He landed there on January 26, 1788, just eight days after the first

British convict ships arrived to found the colony of New South Wales.

Although Captain Arthur Phillip, the new governor, had already gone north to Sydney to look for a more favorable site, most of the British ships were still at Botany Bay, and they helped anchor the French ships. Setting up camp on the northern shore, at a spot that is now called La Pérouse, the French maintained good relations with the English during their six-week stay.

Lost at sea

La Pérouse led the ships out of Botany Bay on March 10, 1788, and headed into the Pacific. He was never heard from again. When the French government realized that La Pérouse's party was missing, it immediately equipped an expedition under the command of Bruni d'Entrecasteaux to look for them. D'Entrecasteaux had no success.

As Franco-British relations deteriorated during the French Revolution, the British were rumored to have killed La Pérouse in order to keep him out of their new colony in Australia. It was not until 1826 that the mystery was solved, when **Jules-Sébastien-César Dumont d'Urville** (see entry) found the remains of *La Boussole* and *L'Astrolabe* on Vanikoro Island in the Santa Cruz group to the south of the Solomon Islands. Fortunately, the records of most of La Pérouse's discoveries were saved because they had been sent back to Paris from Kamchatka.

René-Robert Cavelier de La Salle

Born 1643,
Rouen, France
Died March 19, 1687,
Navosta, Texas

René-Robert Cavelier de La Salle was a French adventurer who was the first European to sail down the Mississippi to its mouth; he later led a disastrous French expedition to Texas.

René-Robert Cavelier de La Salle was born into a well-to-do family in Rouen, the capital of the French province of Normandy. He studied at a Jesuit school in his hometown and then became a novice, or student for the Catholic priesthood, at a Jesuit seminary in Paris. Showing a gift for mathematics, de La Salle taught the subject to secondary school students while pursuing his own studies. La Salle was not a successful seminarian, however—the Jesuits thought he was too adventurous and unstable. He quit the seminary in 1667 after being turned down twice for a chance to be a missionary.

Searches for Ohio River

La Salle had family connections in New France, which is now Canada, so he immigrated there soon after leaving the seminary. After his arrival in Quebec sometime before November 1667 he was granted a gift of land on the island of Montreal. Two years later he sold the land for a profit. With this money La Salle decided to finance an expedition to find the Ohio River, which he thought would lead to the South Seas and eventually to China.

La Salle's expedition attracted the attention of a Catholic order, the Sulpicians, who sent two of their members along to serve as missionaries. The party left Montreal in July 1669. Since none of the explorers had had any traveling experience, the trip turned out to be a disaster. After they had crossed Lake Ontario, they were forced to spend a month in the village of the hostile Seneca tribe. They were finally rescued by an Iroquois who offered to guide them to the Ohio by way of Lake Erie. But before they had gone as far as Lake Erie, La Salle became sick with fever. Then the two missionaries were lured away to visit the Potawotomi tribe, who had never been evangelized.

Because of his illness, La Salle told his companions he was going to return to Montreal; however, he did not reach Montreal until the fall of 1670. No one knows where he went from 1669 to 1670, but many supporters have claimed that he discovered the Ohio River and possibly the Mississippi River during this period. Evidence shows this is almost certainly not true: the Mississippi was not located until 1673, when it was found by **Louis Jolliet** (see entry) and Jacques Marquette.

Explores southwest in North America

La Salle made other unknown trips from 1671 to 1673. In the fall of 1673 he returned to Montreal where he allied himself with Governor Frontenac of New France during a dispute that was going on in the colony. As a result, La Salle was given a title of nobility—this is why he is often called Sieur de La Salle—and command of a French fort at the site of present-day Kingston, Ontario. In 1677 he went back to France. In May 1678 he received permission from King Louis IV to explore the western part of North America between New France, Florida, and Mexico.

The following September La Salle started his explorations by constructing a fort on the Niagara River between what is now Ontario and New York. He was accompanied by Dominique La Motte, Henri de Tonty, Father Louis Hennepin, and Father de La Ribourd; Tonty would later lead expeditions throughout the Mississippi River valley and Father Hennepin would travel to the mouth of the Mississippi. At some point La Salle was forced to spend the winter of 1678-79 at Fort Frontenac at Kingston. When he returned he found his men had built a sailing ship, the *Griffon,* to explore the Great Lakes. They sailed on August 7, 1679.

Explores Great Lakes

The explorers traveled through Lake Erie into Lake Huron and then to the Straits of Mackinac, which separates Lake Huron from Lake Michigan. Leaving the *Griffon* at Mackinac, they traveled south on Lake Michigan in canoes. In the middle of winter they reached a village of the Illinois tribe near the present-day city of Peoria. Discouraged by the Native Americans from continuing, several of La Salle's men deserted. But La Salle built a fort that he called Crèvecoeur in the area to serve as a supply center for future explorations. He then sent Hennepin to lead an advance party to the Mississippi while he headed back to Canada.

Upon his return to Canada in 1680, La Salle met several disappointments: the *Griffon* had been lost, the fort on the Niagara had been burned down, and a supply ship had sunk. At Fort Frontenac he learned that Fort Crèvecoeur had been burned and that, moreover, many of his men had deserted and were returning to Canada, robbing his supply posts along the way. Setting an ambush, La Salle captured them at the beginning of August. He then retraced his steps and went all the way back to Fort Crèvecoeur, hoping to find Tonty, whom he had left in charge. Since Tonty was not among the corpses left behind at the burned fort, he was apparently alive; it was not until May 1681 that the two explorers met again, when Tonty rowed a canoe back to Mackinac.

La Salle led a successful expedition down the Mississippi River to the Gulf of Mexico in 1678-82; a second expedition through the Gulf of Mexico, in 1684-87, had fatal consequences. ▶

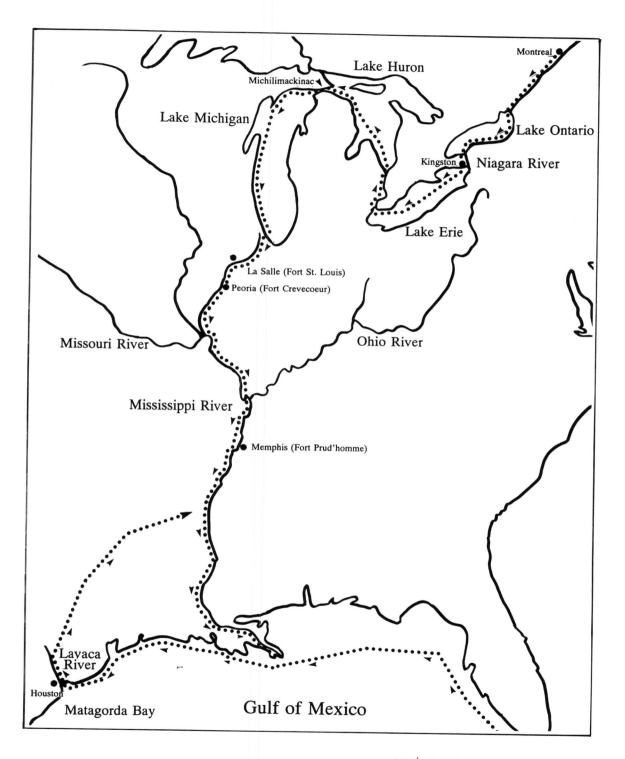

Lake Huron

Michilimackinac

Lake Michigan

Montreal

Lake Ontario

Kingston

Niagara River

Lake Erie

La Salle (Fort St. Louis)

Peoria (Fort Crevecoeur)

Missouri River

Ohio River

Mississippi River

Memphis (Fort Prud'homme)

Lavaca River

Houston

Matagorda Bay

Gulf of Mexico

Travels length of Mississippi River

In the spring and summer of 1681 La Salle returned once again to Montreal, where he tried to calm his creditors as well as enemies who were spreading rumors about his mismanagement. With a party of 40 men he departed for the wilderness in the fall and winter of 1681, reaching Fort Crèvecoeur in January 1682. From Crèvecoeur they descended the Illinois River, reaching the Mississippi in February. They built canoes and headed down the river, passing the mouth of the Missouri River. During the trip they passed the mouth of the Ohio, the river that La Salle had long been seeking. The party stopped at the site where the city of Memphis, Tennessee, now stands, and built a fort called Prud'homme.

In March a party from the Arkansas tribe were threatening to attack La Salle and his men; however, La Salle was able to make peace and in fact took possession of the territory in the name of the king of France. Leaving Prud'homme, La Salle's party continued down the river and passed the farthest point reached by Jolliet and Marquette. They spent time among the Tensas and Natchez tribes before reaching the Gulf of Mexico on April 9, 1682. La Salle erected a great cross and led ceremonies proclaiming his new discoveries to be part of France.

La Salle, Tonty, and their men started back upriver the next day. Along the way they were attacked by Native Americans. When La Salle became seriously ill he stopped to rest at Fort Prud'homme, sending Tonty ahead to report on their discoveries to the governor of New France. Following his recovery, La Salle continued his journey to Michilimackinac, where he arrived in September 1682.

Sent back to France

In the winter of 1682-83 La Salle returned to the Illinois River and built Fort St. Louis, near the present-day town of La Salle, Illinois. In the meantime, a new governor had arrived in New France, and he was quickly influenced by La Salle's enemies. On the governor's orders, La Salle was sent to France in

December 1683 to report on his conduct. La Salle found little support in France for his ideas on developing the Mississippi Valley.

La Salle did find, however, an influential party that was trying to interest the French government in sending an expedition to the mouth of the Rio Grande in the Gulf of Mexico. Their goal was to conquer New Mexico and/or New Spain (Mexico) and take over the valuable mines in the region. In order to find a place for himself in this scheme, La Salle purposely falsified his discoveries by drawing a map that placed the Mississippi River much farther west than it actually is: La Salle's "map" showed the river emptying into the Gulf of Mexico in what is now Texas rather than the actual site in Louisiana.

Heads expedition to Gulf of Mexico

La Salle was able to convince the king and rich French merchants to back an expedition to the Gulf of Mexico. He left France at the end of July 1684, heading a party of four ships and 320 men and women. As a result of poor planning and La Salle's ongoing quarrel with the naval captain, the boats were overloaded and there was a shortage of water. La Salle was forced to dock the fleet at the French colony of Haiti, where he received word that the ship carrying most of the expedition's supplies had been captured by the Spanish.

The three remaining ships left Haiti on November 25, 1684, and headed toward the Mississippi delta. On December 27 and 28 La Salle and his men saw the muddy waters that indicated they were near the mouth of the great river. Since La Salle had made miscalculations in his navigation and chose to believe unreliable old Spanish charts, however, he concluded they were much farther east than they actually were. Instead of investigating the immediate area to confirm their location, he directed the ships to sail west.

Sails off course to Texas

By the time La Salle realized his mistake, the ships were

off Matagorda Bay south of what is now the city of Houston. After one of the ships ran aground while sailing into the bay, local Native Americans tried to ransack the wreckage. The Frenchmen shot at them, and from then on the French and the Native Americans were enemies. In March the naval captain returned to France with one of the ships, leaving La Salle with only one ship. By that time the remaining men had also become discouraged, so La Salle was facing a tense situation.

In May 1685 the Frenchmen began construction of Fort St. Louis at the mouth of the Lavaca River. From there, La Salle and other members of the expedition made exploring trips into the surrounding countryside. In April 1686, when a drunken pilot wrecked the last ship, the little colony was left without any means of escape. La Salle decided the only way was to travel overland to find the Mississippi and then to head up the river to the Great Lakes, where he could find French missions and traders. He left Fort St. Louis at the end of April with 20 men, but through various mishaps the number was reduced to eight by October, and he was forced to return.

Killed by his own men

La Salle departed for the Great Lakes again on January 12, 1687, with a party of 17, leaving 25 people behind at the fort. By this time the men hated La Salle for causing them such misery. On the night of March 18 five of the men killed La Salle's nephew, a servant, and a guide. The next morning, at a spot just north of the modern town of Navasota, Texas, they shot La Salle in cold blood. They left his body for wild animals to eat. A remnant of La Salle's party reached Montreal on July 13, 1688. A group that had been left behind at Matagorda Bay was attacked by the Karankawa tribe; all were killed except for two small boys who were taken by a Spanish raiding party.

Michael J. Leahy

Born 1901,
Toowoomba, Queensland, Australia

Died March 7, 1979,
Zenag, New Guinea

During the late nineteenth and early twentieth century, the great island of New Guinea came under the political control of various European powers. The Dutch claimed the western half and ruled it as part of its vast East Indian empire. The British claimed the southeastern quarter, then turned it over to the Australians when they formed a self-governing dominion. German traders on the islands and mainland of the northeast eventually induced the German kaiser to take over that section. But the territory was quickly conquered by the Australians and British during the early days of World War I.

Following the war, the Australians extended their control over the coastal region of the eastern half up to the mountain spine that runs through the length of the island. By the 1930s, they had established that the island was rather sparsely populated by different tribes along the coast and in the main river valleys. The Australians also concluded that because of the immense and impenetrable mountain range there could be few inhabitants in the interior. This view was entirely wrong.

Michael J. Leahy was an Australian miner who explored wide areas of New Guinea while searching for gold.

In fact, the high mountains hid enormous valleys where agriculture tribes had developed a complex social system and dense populations, much greater than those of the lowlands. It was one of the great shocks to contemporary knowledge of the world when the first Westerners stumbled upon these "Shangri-las" in the years immediately before the outbreak of the World War II. It was also an enormous surprise to the Papuan tribes, who were virtually living in the Stone Age. They were still dependent on stone tools; although they used copper for ornaments, they had no other use for metal. The Papuans were probably the last humans to learn about tobacco, and they had no inkling of the great world outside their valleys.

Leahy traverses island

The lure that led men into the mountainous New Guinea interior was the discovery of gold. In 1922 an important gold find was made on the Bulolo River in the hills southwest of the large coastal town of Lae. Many prospectors rushed to the area and about $75 million worth of gold was exported during the 1930s. One of these miners was Michael J. "Mick" Leahy, who was born in Toowoomba in the Australian state of Queensland in 1901. He was the fourth of nine children of an Irish immigrant. When news of another gold strike, this time at Edie Creek, reached Australia in 1926, Leahy left his "T-model Ford on the side of the road." Quitting his job as a railway clerk, he went to seek his fortune in the New Guinea bush.

In 1930 Leahy and fellow miner Michael Dwyer traveled upstream on one of New Guinea's river systems, the Ramu, and, without knowing it, crossed over the divide and started to follow another stream. This stream eventually became the Purari River, one of the main rivers emptying out into the south coast. By following this route, Leahy and Dwyer were among the first Westerners to traverse the island.

Leads prospecting expedition

During their exploration of the headwaters of the Ramu and Purari, the two Australians had noticed what seemed to be promising mineral deposits. In 1931 they mounted a prospecting expedition to explore this area. It turned out to be a disaster. They had hired an airplane to reconnoiter the area thy were exploring on foot: the plane crashed into a mountain wall and was discovered only because the pilot's severed head rolled down the mountain onto a Papuan hunting trail. When the land expedition was attacked by the hostile Kukukuku tribe, Leahy was clubbed in the head and his brother Patrick ("Paddy") was shot in the arm and shoulder with arrows. Another miner nearby was clubbed to death.

These difficulties did not deter Leahy. In 1932 he returned to an inland area called Bena Bena with his 18-year-old brother Dan. They built an airfield that was to serve as the western base for penetration of the interior by both government officials and gold prospectors. Several gold claims were staked in the area. Using the field as their base for further exploration, in March 1933 the brothers flew into the first of the great mountain valleys, Mount Hagen. Leahy wrote:

> What we saw was a great flat valley, possibly twenty miles wide and no telling how many miles long, between two high mountain ranges, with a very winding river meandering through it. Below us were evidences of a very fertile soil and a teeming population—a continuous patchwork of gardens laid off in neat squares like chessboards, with oblong grass houses in groups of four or five dotted thickly over the landscape. Except for the grass houses, the view below us resembled the patchwork fields of Belgium as seen from the air.

Continues exploration

Ground expeditions followed, usually led by Jim Taylor, the Australian government representative to the area. Through the use of a combination of aerial reconnaissance and land exploration, several other valleys were discovered and opened up—the Goroka, Chimbu, Wabag, and Wahgi. In each case, the explorers were the first white men the Papuans had ever seen. When the planes first flew over the valleys, the inhabitants threw themselves on the ground in terror. In later accounts to anthropologists, they said they had told one another, "If we look at this thing, we shall surely die."

Leahy continued his explorations in 1933 and 1934, eventually coming out of the mountains and meeting Papuans who were already in touch with Europeans from the north coast. As it happened, none of the lands they had opened proved to contain any gold. Even the initial claims at Bena Bena were not commercially worthwhile. In 1934 another expedition led by Tom and Jack Fox went almost to the border of Dutch New Guinea without finding any trace of gold. When they got back to Mount Hagen and told Leahy, he recorded his reaction: "When we had heard it all, Danny and I walked back to the base camp in almost complete silence, both of us feeling that we had been robbed of our principal interest in life."

The Australian government continued its explorations. Taylor reached the last of the great valleys, Telefomin, in 1939, immediately before the outbreak of World War II. On the Dutch side of the border, the mountain valleys were actually discovered during the war. The largest, the Grand Valley of the Baliem River, was accidentally discovered by a U.S. Army Air Force pilot in 1944 when he flew into a gap in the mountains. It was promptly named "Shangri-La" by the war correspondents who were thinking of the mythical valley in the Himalayas described by James Hilton in his novel *Lost Horizon*.

Receives recognition

Leahy continued an adventurous career. In 1935 he traveled to London, England, to claim priority for his discoveries before the Royal Geographical Society. He became the center of an international incident in 1936 when, before the League of Nations, the Italian government justified their invading Ethiopia as being similar to Leahy's "pacifying" Papuan tribes. When World War II broke out Leahy was offered the rank of sergeant by the Australian army, but he turned it down to become a lieutenant for the U.S. Air Force. He was awarded the U.S. Medal of Freedom in 1948.

In 1940 Leahy had married a childhood sweetheart in Queensland, with Taylor as his best man. Leahy and his wife had five children, but Leahy never acknowledged the three illegitimate sons he had with New Guinea women; they lived with his brother Dan. After the war, Leahy acquired an agricultural property at Zenag in the eastern highlands of New Guinea. It prospered, especially after the independence of Papua New Guinea, which he had opposed. In 1971 the Explorers' Club in New York awarded him its highest medal for opening one of the least-known places on Earth; during the same ceremony **Neil Armstrong** (see entry) was similarly honored for his walk on the M\oon. Leahy died in Zenag on March 7, 1979.

Leif Eriksson

Born late 970s,
Iceland

Died 1020,
Greenland

Leif Eriksson was a
Norse explorer who
sailed from Greenland
to North America,
landing at four coastal
locations around the
year 1000.

The most reliable evidence of Leif Eriksson's exploration of North America remains the sagas written almost 200 years after the events they describe. The two sagas chronicling the explorations of Leif Eriksson and other Norsemen are *Erik the Red's Saga,* which credits Eriksson with bringing Christianity to Greenland in 999 at the request of Norway's King Olaf I, and *Greenlanders' Saga,* which credits the discovery of Vinland to Bjarni Herjolfsson and not Eriksson, who was its first explorer and name-giver. Scholars believe the two sagas do not share the same origin, and were written independently of each other, sometime in the thirteenth century and most likely after 1263, using older stories from the oral tradition.

The son of Erik the Red, the founder of Greenland, Leif Eriksson was probably born in Iceland in the late 970s and moved with his family to Greenland in 985 or 986, settling at a place called Brattahlid on the southwest corner of the island along the Eriksfjord. Icelandic sagas describe Eriksson as "tall and strong and very impressive in appearance. He was a shrewd man and always moderate in behavior." Eriksson earned the name Leif the Lucky for his exploits. An expert sailor, he was the first Viking to sail directly from Greenland to Scotland and then to Norway, and back again.

Herjolfsson inspires Eriksson

The Norse explorers used familiar landmarks and the shortest distance between two points as navigational tools. In the summer of 986, Bjarni Herjolfsson sailed from Norway to Iceland to meet his father, who had unexpectedly moved to Greenland; without charts or compass, Herjolfsson turned toward Greenland but strong north winds and then fog threw his ship off course. When the sun broke through, the ship sailed another day before land was sighted: it was not mountainous but full of forests and low hills. For two days Herjolfsson moved along the coast where the land remained lined with trees. He did not go ashore. A southwest wind carried his ship three more days to mountainous land with glaciers. A strong wind then carried the ship for another four days to Greenland.

Herjolfsson's journey fueled the imagination of Norse explorers who believed land existed beyond Greenland. The distance between the present-day Cumberland Peninsula and Greenland is just 200 miles across the narrowest stretch of what is now Davis Strait. From mountains beyond the eastern settlement, land to the west could probably be seen. To the family of Erik the Red, Herjolfsson's story called for action. Leif Eriksson purchased Herjolfsson's ship and asked his father to go with him on a voyage of exploration; however, Erik the Red fell off his horse on his way to the boat, breaking the bones in his foot. Eriksson departed without him.

Sets out on voyage

In 1001 Eriksson left Greenland with a crew of 35, sailing in reverse order of Herjolfsson's course. He landed first at a place he named Helluland ("the Land of Flat Stone") which is thought to be on the southern end of Baffin Island in the Canadian Arctic. From there he went to a place he called

Markland—("Wood" or "Forest Land")—which is thought to be somewhere on the coast of Labrador. He then landed on an unnamed island, which is possibly Belle Isle in the Strait of Belle Isle, which separates Labrador from the island of Newfoundland. According to legend, "There was dew on the grass, and the first thing they did was to get some of it on their hands and put it to their lips, and to them it seemed the sweetest thing they had ever tasted."

Discovers Vinland

Eriksson and his companions reached a part of the New World that he named Vinland ("Land of the Vine" or "Wineland" or, possibly, "Pastureland") in the fall of 1001. Scholars agree that Vinland is on the North American continent, but its exact location is in question. Eriksson's party landed at the mouth of a river on the west of a large peninsula pointing north and followed the river upstream to a lake. This geographical description was the only one given of Vinland, but the astronomical readings show that it was south of Greenland. The site could be L'Anse aux Meadows on the northeastern tip of Newfoundland, where remains of a Norse settlement were found in the 1960s, but no clear-cut archaeological record exists.

No one theory explains the existing evidence of Vinland. In *Greenlanders' Saga,* the explorers found grapes in Vinland and brought a boatload back with them; although grapes cannot grow farther north than 45° N, **Jacques Cartier** (see entry), who discovered the St. Lawrence River, found grapes on both sides of the river in the 1530s. Eriksson's expedition spent the winter in Vinland and built a large house and temporary buildings at a place named Leifrsbudir, or "Leif's Booths"; these were the first structures built by Europeans in North America. Eriksson's expedition returned to Greenland in the spring of 1002.

Eriksson's brother explores region

The year following Eriksson's voyage, his brother Thorvald returned to Leifrsbudir to explore the region more extensively, spending the winter of 1003-04 there. The next spring and summer he explored Vinland, finding it beautiful and well-wooded. After spending the winter of 1004-05 in Leifrs-budir, Thorvald went north to Markland the following spring. There the Norsemen encountered and clashed with the Skrael-ings, who were either Native Americans or Eskimos. When Thorvald was killed by an arrow, his crew returned to Leifrs-budir for the winter and then sailed back to Greenland in 1006. Learning of Thorvald's death, his brother Thorstein tried to sail to Markland to recover his body but ran into storms that drove his boat back into the North Atlantic. Thorstein died on his return to Greenland.

Settlement founded in Uinland

In 1010 Thorfinn Karlsefni, who had married Thorstein's widow, Gudrid, sailed from Greenland with 160 men and some women on board three ships to found a settlement in Vinland. They built houses at Leifrsbudir, and in the summer of 1011 Gudrid gave birth to a son, Snorri. At first the Norse-men traded for furs with the Skraelings but soon warfare broke out in the winter of 1011-12. The Norsemen returned to Greenland in 1013.

Half-sister takes control

Following the return of Thorfinn Karlsefni, Erik the Red's illegitimate daughter Freydis went into partnership with two brothers, Helgi and Finnbogi, to trade for furs and wood in Vinland. Once in Leifrsbudir, Freydis had her supporters murder Helgi and Finnbogi and their followers. According to the saga, when the men in her party refused to kill the women, she did it herself. Freydis then confiscated her enemies' goods and returned home, living off the profits.

In Greenland, Leif Eriksson had inherited his father's estate at Brattahlid along with his position as leader of the colony. When confronted with the news of Freydis's crimes, he could not bring himself to punish his half-sister. Upon Eriksson's death in about 1020 the estate was passed on to his son, Thorkell.

Meriwether Lewis

Born August 18, 1774,
Albemarle County, Virginia

Died October 11, 1809,
Central Tennessee

William Clark

Born August 1, 1770,
Caroline County, Virginia

Died September 1, 1838,
St. Louis, Missouri

Meriwether Lewis

Meriwether Lewis and William Clark led the first official United States expedition across North America to the Pacific Ocean.

Meriwether Lewis grew up on a farm near Charlottesville, Virginia, where his family was friends with Thomas Jefferson, whose famous estate, Monticello, is just outside Charlottesville. Lewis received his education from private tutors. At 18, after his father's death, Lewis managed the family plantation. An officer in the local militia, Lewis was called to active duty in 1794 during the Whiskey Rebellion; he then joined the U.S. Army and served as a captain in the First Infantry under General Anthony Wayne in the wars against the Native Americans in the Northwest Territory. When Jefferson was elected president in 1801 he chose Lewis to be his personal secretary—a position equal to today's White House chief of staff and which Lewis held for two years.

United States makes Louisiana Purchase

President Jefferson and Napoléon Bonaparte signed the Louisiana Purchase, a treaty that doubled the land area of the

United States: for $15 million France turned over its claims to the western basin of the Mississippi River, called the Louisiana Territory, which had recently been reacquired by France from Spain. The Louisiana Purchase was of strategic importance in the western expansion of the United States in the nineteenth century. The land extended from the Mississippi River to the Rocky Mountains and from the Gulf of Mexico to the Canadian border, with the final boundaries not being settled for many years.

The treaty was signed on April 30, 1803, and formal transfer took place the following year. Jefferson had already requested funds from Congress to send an exploring party to the West in search of an overland route to the Pacific Ocean. Following intensive lobbying on the part of Lewis, he was chosen as the expedition's leader.

William Clark

Lewis appoints Clark co-leader of expedition

Jefferson sent Lewis to Philadelphia for several weeks to study botany and astronomy to learn how to conduct the scientific investigations the president desired. With Jefferson's approval, Lewis invited William Clark to be co-leader of the expedition. The Clark family had been Virginia neighbors of the Lewises before joining pioneers traveling across the Appalachian Mountains into Kentucky. The boyhood friends had later served together in the frontier wars. Clark was the younger brother of George Rogers Clark, a Revolutionary War hero.

Jefferson gives instructions

Jefferson prepared orders for the expedition with the advice of eminent scientists at the American Philosophical Society in Philadelphia, the center of the Enlightenment in the United States. The chief instruction was to find "the most

Meriwether Lewis
William Clark

direct and practicable water communication across the continent for the purposes of commerce." This commerce clearly included the fur trade, which Jefferson hoped to divert from the British Hudson's Bay Company into American hands. The expedition was supposed to travel up the Missouri River, cross the Rocky Mountains, and then descend the western slope by the most practicable river, "whether the Columbia, Oregon, or Colorado, or any other river" to the Pacific. The instructions included a list of observations to be made and specimens and mineral samples to bring back.

Make final preparations for expedition

Leaving Philadelphia in early July 1803, Lewis traveled to Pittsburgh and next took a boat down the Ohio River to Louisville, where he was joined by Clark and his African American servant York. Along the way, Lewis and Clark enlisted in the U.S. Army 14 soldiers and nine Kentucky hunters. The party spent the winter of 1803-04 on the east bank of the Mississippi at the mouth of the Dubois River, in American territory. The formal cession of the Louisiana Territory had not yet taken place.

During the winter, several boatmen and hunters and a Native American interpreter were added to the expedition. Clark took charge of training the men in military drill, building boats, and making preparations for the trip. Lewis spent his time in St. Louis, where he gathered information from fur traders who were familiar with the upper reaches of the Missouri River and with Native Americans in the upper country. On March 9, 1804, Lewis was an official witness to the transfer of Upper Louisiana from Spain to France and then, on the following day, of the same territory from France to the United States.

The Voyage of Discovery begins

The expedition, known as the Voyage of Discovery, set out on May 14, 1804, with 45 men in three boats—two large, open canoes and a 55-foot keelboat with 22 oars. Twenty-nine men were picked to travel all the way to the Pacific while the

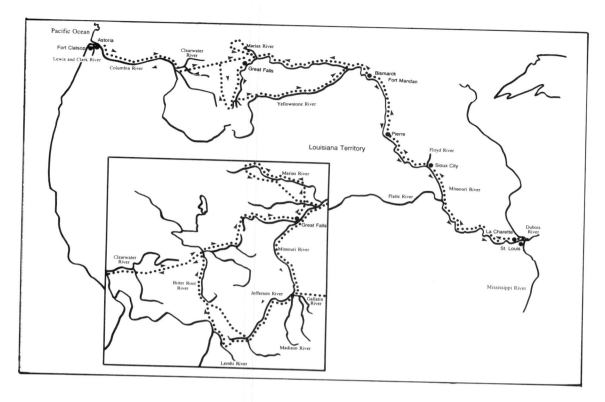

others were to turn around at approximately the halfway point, taking the expedition reports back to St. Louis, Missouri. The first part of the journey up the Missouri River was through well-traveled country. On May 25 they passed Femme Osage, the last European settlement and home of the famous frontiersman **Daniel Boone** (see entry).

In late July, near the mouth of the Platte River in northwest Missouri, the explorers met the Oto and Missouri tribes and informed them that their territory had been taken over by the United States. They also made a present of trinkets, medals, and flags to the chiefs. In August, Sergeant Floyd died suddenly of a "bilious colic." The only member of the expedition to die, he was buried on a bluff near the site of Sioux City, Iowa. The Floyd River was named in his honor.

Meet with Native American tribes

The party met with the Omaha tribe and with bands of

The Lewis and Clark expedition made the first journey through the uncharted West to the Pacific Ocean.

Meriwether Lewis
William Clark

Sioux. A minor incident occurred on September 25 near present-day Pierre, South Dakota, when a group of Teton Sioux made threatening movements. The expedition countered with a show of force followed by conciliation with the Native Americans. Lewis and Clark wrote in their journals that the Americans had broken the Sioux blockade of the Missouri and opened it up for free movement. This turned out to be premature since the United States and the Sioux continued to fight each other until the Battle of Wounded Knee in 1877.

On October 8, Lewis and Clark reached the territory of the Arikara tribe, who had friendly relations with fur traders, several of whom were in the village and available to serve as interpreters. One of the Arikara chiefs agreed to accompany the Americans upstream to the encampments of the Mandan tribe, who lived near the modern city of Bismarck, North Dakota. Their territory was the farthest point west about which the Americans had any definite knowledge. Lewis and Clark had planned to spend the winter there.

Spend winter at Fort Mandan

The expedition reached the small cluster of Mandan villages at the end of October and spent three weeks building a stockade that they named Fort Mandan. They were now 1,600 miles from St. Louis and had traveled an average of nine miles a day. The Americans spent five months at Fort Mandan where they were visited by Native Americans and fur traders. One of the visitors was Toussaint Charbonneau, who had a Native American wife named Sacagawea, a member of the Shoshoni tribe in what is now the state of Idaho. She had been captured in a raid by the Minnetaree tribe and sold to Charbonneau. She was pregnant and gave birth to a baby boy named Pompey on February 11, 1805. Lewis and Clark hired Charbonneau and his wife as interpreters and guides.

The party spent the winter hunting and bartering for supplies. In the spring they made two cottonwood logs into canoes to replace the keelboat, which was returning to St. Louis with 13 men. The expedition set out again on April 7, 1805, into unknown country. Clark wrote in his journal: "I could not but esteem this moment of my departure as among the most happy of my life." They reached the junction with the Yellowstone River in what is now Montana on April 25.

Explore unknown territory in Montana

Clark took charge of the canoes, which were becoming dangerously waterlogged, while Lewis, accompanied by his big Newfoundland dog, Scannon, walked along the shore, exploring, hunting, and gathering specimens. On June 3, 1805, the expedition reached a place where "the river split in two." Lewis followed the northern fork, which he decided was not the main course. He named it the Marias River, in honor of his cousin, Maria Wood. He then turned around and caught up with Clark. They cached a large amount of supplies at the juncture of the two rivers in anticipation of their return.

They followed what they had decided was the main stream and stopped by the major waterfall on the Missouri at Great Falls, Montana. They built crude wagons to haul the boats and supplies around the rapids, taking one month to make the 18-mile portage. On July 25, they reached the place where three smaller streams come together to form the Missouri River, and named the three rivers after Presidents Jefferson and Madison and Albert Gallatin, the secretary of the treasury.

Lewis crosses continental divide

Heeding Sacagawea's advice, they followed the southwest branch, which they had named after Jefferson. The river quickly narrowed and the angle of descent grew steeper. Lewis took three other men and went ahead to see if he could reach a Shoshoni village, where he might be able to get horses and guides to take them across the mountains. On August 12, Lewis reached the source of the Missouri and crossed over the continental divide to the source of the Lemhi River, a tributary of the Columbia.

The next day Lewis stumbled upon a group of Shoshoni, who were initially hostile, but he was able to reassure them

Meriwether Lewis
William Clark

about his peaceful intentions. He took the Native American chief and some of his warriors to meet Clark and the rest of the expedition. When they entered the camp, Sacagawea recognized them as her own people. One of the women was a childhood friend who had been captured with her and then escaped. The chief was her brother. Interpretation between the two groups required Lewis or Clark to speak in English to one of the fur traders, who then spoke in French to Charbonneau, who then spoke in Minnetaree to Sacagawea, who translated into Shoshoni.

Forced to take difficult overland route

Because the Lemhi River was unnavigable the explorers were forced to continue their journey by land. They bought 29 horses from the Shoshoni, and the chief agreed to go with them partway as guide. The ensuing trip proved to be most difficult. The trail was steep, crooked, and dangerous; it took them 50 days to cover 300 miles. They were often hungry and often had to eat horse meat and dog meat.

On September 5, 1805, the explorers reached a village of the Flathead tribe, where they were able to get food and more horses. They passed through the Bitterroot Range by way of Lolo Pass and descended the mountains into the valley of the Clearwater River in northwest Idaho on September 20. They were in the territory of the Nez Percé ("Pierced Nose") tribe and made it to a Nez Percé camp where they were fed so much that they all became sick.

Reach Pacific Ocean

After building five canoes to float down the Clearwater River, they arrived at the Snake River on October 10; they reached the Columbia River on the Oregon border on October 16. Along the way they bartered for food with the Native Americans, but they had very little to trade. They often performed for their supper. One of the men played his violin while York danced, and Lewis showed off his watch, telescope, and compass. After making the portage around Cascade

Falls on November 2, the explorers found the river was subject to tidal flows and knew they must be close to the Pacific. They got their first view of the ocean on November 7, 1805.

Build Fort Clatsop for winter stay

Lewis and Clark joined in the construction of winter headquarters at a place they named Fort Clatsop in honor of the local tribe. It was located on the Lewis and Clark River near the mouth of the Columbia, not far from modern Astoria, Oregon. The fort is now a national monument. Since they were short of supplies and the local Native Americans were not especially cooperative, the party survived on elk meat preserved in sea salt. The Pacific Northwest coast is rainy in winter, and they saw only six days of sunshine from January to the end of March.

Start trip back East

Leaving behind letters for any European traders who might travel along the coast, Lewis and Clark headed east on March 23, 1806. Rowing upstream on the Columbia River, they had difficulty getting food; in exchange for dog meat they sold their services as doctors in the villages they passed along the way. When they reached the Clearwater they recovered horses they had left behind and used them to travel over the mountains.

Lewis and Clark take separate routes to explore

In June the party split up at Bitter Root River. Lewis found a shortcut and was able to make it to Great Falls on the Missouri only six days after crossing the continental divide. He then spent some time exploring the Marias River. Along the way, he had a minor skirmish with the Blackfoot and Gros Ventre tribes. He was shot in the leg by a hunter who was nearsighted and thought Lewis was a bear. Lewis was disabled for a month.

Meriwether Lewis
William Clark

Clark and the rest of the party, including Sacagawea, followed the route they had taken as far as the Three Forks area. From there they went through a pass now known as Bozeman Pass, pointed out by Sacagawea, that led to the Yellowstone River. When they reached the Yellowstone, a Native American raiding party slipped in one night and stole half of their horses. As they followed the river downstream, they passed a gigantic rock, which Clark climbed to carve his name and the date July 25, 1806. He named the rock Pompey's Rock in honor of Sacagawea's little boy; today it is a national historic landmark near Billings, Montana.

Depart St. Louis for Washington

The two parties reunited on the Missouri River. They reached the Mandan villages on August 14, 1806, and persuaded Chief Big White to come with them to Washington, D.C. Sacagawea and Charbonneau stayed behind. Lewis and Clark returned to St. Louis on September 23, 1806. "We were met by all the village," wrote Clark, "and received a hearty welcome from its inhabitants." From St. Louis they traveled to Washington to report personally to President Jefferson.

Lewis and Clark honored

The expedition had been a great success. Both Lewis and Clark were awarded large land grants in the West. In 1806, Lewis was appointed governor of the Louisiana Territory— the part north of the present state of Louisiana, which was called the District of Orleans. In 1809 he was traveling to Washington on official business when he stopped at an isolated cabin in Tennessee to spend the night. He was later found dead with a gunshot wound in his head. It was never clear what happened, but Lewis, who was subject to depressive moods, probably shot himself.

Clark entered the fur-trading business and became a partner in William Henry Ashley's Missouri Fur Company. He was appointed governor of the Missouri Territory and served until it became a state. He was then appointed superintendent of Indian affairs, a position he held until his death in 1838. Clark adopted Pompey, Sacagawea's son, and educated him at the best schools on the East Coast. When Pompey was 18, he met a German prince who was traveling in the United States; he went to Europe with the prince, spending six years touring the continent. He returned to the United States and became an important fur dealer and guide. He moved to California and became the mayor of San Luis Rey. He died in 1866 on his way to Oregon. Sacagawea is thought to have died from fever in December 1812.

Charles A. Lindbergh

Born February 4, 1902,
Detroit, Michigan
Died August 26, 1974,
Maui, Hawaii

Charles A. Lindbergh was the first person to fly across the Atlantic Ocean—an accomplishment that caught the imagination of the world and made him a popular hero.

Charles Augustus Lindbergh was born in Detroit, Michigan, on February 4, 1902, and spent his childhood in Little Falls, Minnesota. His father, a Swedish immigrant, was elected to Congress in 1907 and served five terms representing the sixth district of Minnesota, where he was a leading isolationist.

Becomes aviator

Lindbergh attended public and private schools in Washington, D.C., and Minnesota. He entered the University of Wisconsin in 1920 but dropped out after two years and entered flying school in Lincoln, Nebraska. After fewer than eight hours of instruction, he began flying barnstorming flights with a stunt aviator in Nebraska and made his first parachute jump in June 1922. Lindbergh bought his first plane, a World War I Curtiss Jenny, for $500, making his first solo flight in April 1923. In 1924 he signed up to take flight training at Brooks

Army Base in San Antonio, Texas, and a year later was commissioned in the United States Air Service Reserve. He began flying air mail service flights between Chicago and St. Louis on April 15, 1926.

Enters flying competition

During one of these routine flights, Lindbergh decided he wanted to win the $25,000 Orteig Prize a wealthy financier was offering to the first person flying nonstop from New York to Paris. Trying to scrape together the money to buy a plane and finance the flight, Lindbergh made a presentation to a group of St. Louis businessmen, who agreed to fund Lindbergh's attempt, thinking a successful flight would help promote St. Louis as a future site of aviation. Lindbergh decided to name his plane the *Spirit of St. Louis* in recognition of the financial support.

Makes preparations for flight

Lindbergh traveled to San Diego, California, to the Ryan Air Craft Factory, where he had his airplane constructed according to his specifications. He began making detailed plans for the solo flight, including sleep deprivation training. Lindbergh started by staying awake 24 hours at a stretch, then 30, then 35, and finally 40 hours at a time. When the plane was ready, he took off from San Diego on May 10, 1927, stopped in St. Louis, and then flew on to Curtiss Field on Long Island in New York. He made the flight in 21 hours and 20 minutes, a new record.

Plagued by sleeplessness on flight

After resting and getting his equipment ready, Lindbergh took off from Curtiss Field at 7:52 A.M. on May 20, 1927. He had been so nervous the night before that he had been unable to sleep, thereby prolonging his hours of sleeplessness. Lindbergh's flight plan took him up the coast of New England and Nova Scotia and then over the Gulf of St. Lawrence to the island of Newfoundland. The last land he saw in North America was at Cape Race on the eastern tip of Newfoundland.

As he flew across the North Atlantic, eating only sandwiches, he was constantly assailed by the need to sleep. He dozed off several times and once awoke to find that he was skimming the waves of the North Atlantic. He had no radio aboard the plane, and no one knew if he was alive or dead. He also had to make all of his own navigational calculations with the chance that any error would push him far off course. Lindbergh knew he was safe when he flew over the southern coast of Ireland during the day on May 21, 1927.

Makes first New York to Paris nonstop flight

When Lindbergh reached the coast of Normandy, it was approaching nightfall. He found his way to Paris by following the course of the Seine River upstream. Unknown to him, his progress was reported by telephone and radio by watchers who passed the news to Paris. As he got closer to the city, Parisians began pouring out of the city and heading for Le Bourget Field where he was scheduled to land. More than a million Parisians were at Le Bourget—Lindbergh had caused the greatest traffic jam in French history.

As Lindbergh began to land at the airfield, he could not fathom the reason for the large crowd. When he touched ground and the crowd surged toward his plane, he could not believe the crowd was there for him. He had made the first flight across the North Atlantic from New York to Paris, a distance of 3,610 miles, in 33 hours, 29 minutes, and 30 seconds.

Hailed throughout the world

Lindbergh instantly became a world hero. He was received by royalty and heads of state throughout Europe and was awarded several medals. There were numerous awards in the United States, including the Medal of Honor by a special act of Congress, as well as ticker-tape parades in New York and St. Louis. He made an air tour of the United States, traveling to 75 cities. At the invitation of the president of Mexico, in

December 1927 he made a nonstop flight from New York to Mexico City that took 27 hours and 10 minutes. At a reception at the American Embassy, he met Ann Morrow, the daughter of the American ambassador. They were married on May 27, 1929; his wife soon became his co-pilot and navigator as they flew together to foreign countries.

Son kidnapped in "crime of the century"

Lindbergh was an intensely private person who was put off by his popular fame. After his marriage, he took a job as technical adviser to Transcontinental Air Transport and Pan American Airways, flying many of their new routes. He bought an estate in New Jersey outside New York City and lived there quietly. This peace was shattered in 1932 when Charles Augustus, the Lindbergh's only child, was kidnapped. The kidnapping soon became the world's biggest media event, labeled as the "crime of the century." After several months, the boy's body was found, and an unemployed German immigrant, Bruno Hauptmann, was found guilty of the crime and executed. As a result of the notoriety of the case, federal law was changed to make kidnapping a federal crime.

Moves to Europe for privacy

The Lindberghs had other children, but relentless press attention made the family feel harassed. To maintain their privacy, they left the United States and moved to England in December 1935. Lindbergh later moved to France and worked with a famous botanist, Dr. Alexis Carrel. He designed a perfusion pump used in zoological experiments and published a scientific book in collaboration with Dr. Carrel.

Supports U.S. neutrality in war

In 1938 and 1939 Lindbergh traveled to Germany, where he was decorated by the Nazi government and other countries of Europe; he commented favorably on the state of the German Luftwaffe and the corresponding lack of preparation by the Western democracies. When Lindbergh returned to the United States he spoke out forcefully in favor of American neutrality. The combination of these actions led to much unfavorable comment, including public statements by President Franklin D. Roosevelt. Lindbergh was forced to resign his Air Corps Reserve commission.

Regains public esteem

Henry Ford hired Lindbergh in 1943 to plan aircraft operations in the South Pacific. He also worked for the United Aircraft Corporation. After the war, it was revealed that he had been employed as an unpaid consultant to the air force on secret projects during the last two years of the war. The combination of this news and the popularity of his wife's books about flying and their life together led to Lindbergh's restoration in the public's esteem. He spent the following years speaking out on various topics and writing books, especially about the spiritual aspects of life and environmental concerns.

Has final career as writer

Lindbergh's book *The Spirit of St. Louis* won a Pulitzer Prize in 1953 and was made into a movie starring James Stewart as Lindbergh. Both he and his wife were accomplished writers, which contributed to their influence and popularity. Altogether Ann Morrow Lindbergh wrote eight books and published volumes of her letters and diaries; her husband wrote six books. President Dwight D. Eisenhower appointed Lindbergh a brigadier general in the air force in 1954, thus completing the aviator's public acceptance. He and his wife built a house on a remote part of the Hawaiian island of Maui where he died on August 26, 1974.

David Livingstone

Born March 19, 1813,
Lanarkshire, Scotland

Died April 30, 1873,
Africa

D avid Livingstone was born in Lanarkshire, Scotland, on March 19, 1813, to devout but poor parents. The second son of a traveling tea salesman, Livingstone was apprenticed as a "piecer" at ten years of age to work in a local cotton mill. After working from 6:00 A.M. until 8:00 P.M., he studied for two hours at night school and then read when he got home. After being promoted to cotton-spinner, Livingstone expanded his studies to religion and medicine. When the night school closed, he read at work by "placing the book on a portion of the spinning jenny, so that I could catch sentence after sentence as I went by." By tireless self-application, he taught himself Latin, Greek, and mathematics. He was admitted to the University of Glasgow to study Greek and theology, and then went to the University of London to pursue a medical degree. Next, he became a member of the London Missionary Society and was ordained as a minister in 1840.

David Livingstone was a Scottish missionary who became the first European to cross Africa; he led several expeditions to explore the lake system of central Africa.

Goes to Africa as missionary

Livingstone's original intention was to go to China as a medical missionary but the outbreak of the Opium War between Britain and China in 1839 prevented him, so he chose Africa instead. Livingstone sailed to Cape Town, spending a month there before sailing to Algoa Bay, where he arrived on March 15, 1841. He then made a ten-week, 700-mile journey by oxcart to Kuruman, a mission station among the Tswana people established by Dr. Robert Moffat, who pioneered the route from South Africa to western Zimbabwe.

Livingstone was not satisfied working for someone else and wanted to "preach the gospel beyond every other man's line of things." By August 1843 he had founded his own mission station at Mabotsa, 250 miles north of Kuruman. While there, he was attacked by a lion and his life was saved by a companion who distracted the lion's attention. Livingstone's survival was in doubt; his left shoulder was broken in several places, and he never fully regained the use of his left arm.

Livingstone returned to Kuruman to recuperate and while there married Mary Moffat, Dr. Moffat's daughter, who could use her father's authority to allow Livingstone to move freely about southern Africa. The newlyweds went back to Mabotsa, but Livingstone soon decided to be on his own again and left, first to a place 40 miles to the north, and then in 1847 to Kolobeng on the eastern edge of the Kalahari Desert. Within a couple of years, Livingstone became restless again—exploration of southern Africa was his real desire.

First exploring trip a success

Livingstone wanted to go north of the Kalahari Desert to Lake Ngami, which no European had seen. One possibility was establishing a mission among the Makololo people, a Tswana tribe ruled by the renowned chief Sebituane, who lived north of

Livingstone made several important discoveries during his expeditions in South and central Africa from 1841 to 1873. ▶

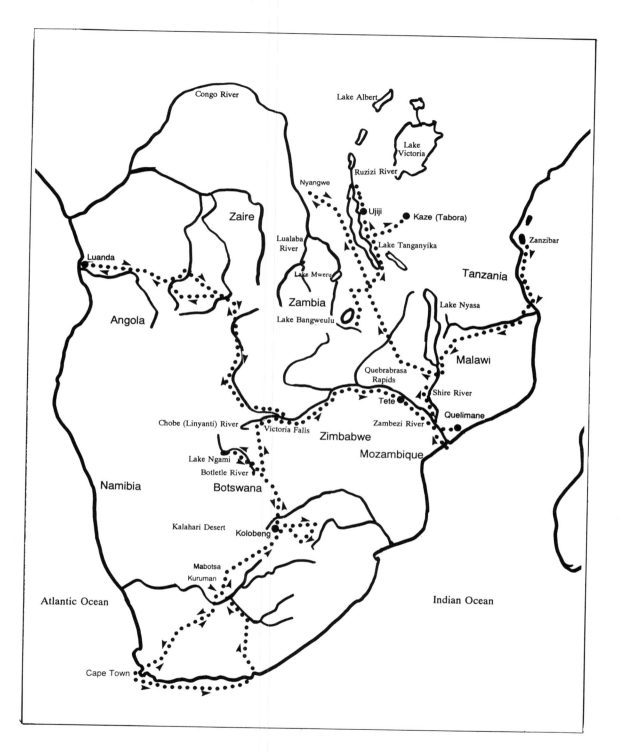

Congo River
Lake Albert
Lake Victoria
Nyangwe
Ruzizi River
Zaire
Lualaba River
Ujiji
Kaze (Tabora)
Luanda
Lake Tanganyika
Zanzibar
Lake Mweru
Tanzania
Angola
Zambia
Lake Bangweulu
Lake Nyasa
Quebrabrasa Rapids
Malawi
Shire River
Tete
Chobe (Linyanti) River
Quelimane
Victoria Falls
Zambezi River
Lake Ngami
Zimbabwe
Botletle River
Mozambique
Namibia
Botswana
Kalahari Desert
Kolobeng
Mabotsa
Kuruman
Atlantic Ocean
Indian Ocean
Cape Town

545 | David Livingstone

the lake. Livingstone enlisted the financial support of a wealthy young big-game hunter named William Colton Oswell and his friend Mungo Murray. Livingstone departed on his first exploration with the two English companions on June 1, 1849, guided by an African named Ramotobi, who knew the Kalahari well. The expedition consisted of 80 oxen, 20 horses, and 30 to 40 porters and drivers. This expedition faced a number of challenges posed by the environment, for example, water often became scarce, and only through the ingenuity of Ramotobi, who knew where to dig for it, was disaster prevented. An even larger problem was the scorpions, whose bites could induce severe pain and even paralysis; the cures, such as searing with a hot iron, were often as bad as the bite.

The frequent sightings of mirages were also disconcerting, as the explorers were duped into thinking they were close to Lake Ngami. At one point, even Ramotobi got lost, but Oswell saw a Bushman woman running away, caught up with her, and persuaded her to lead them to a large pool eight miles away. On July 4, 1849, the explorers reached a previously unknown river, the Zouga—now called the Botletle. The local people confirmed that it led to Lake Ngami; the explorers followed it for 280 miles, reaching the lake on August 1, 1849.

The Makololo lived another 200 miles to the north. The local ruler refused to supply guides for the Europeans, who were forced to return to Kolobeng. On his return, Livingstone sent an account of the expedition, barely mentioning Oswell and Murray, to the Royal Geographical Society in London. As a result, he received his first recognition as an explorer, being awarded one-half of the 1850 royal grant for geographical discovery.

Takes family into bush

In 1850 Livingstone tried to reach the Makololo once again, taking his pregnant wife and three small children with him. The animals were attacked by tsetse flies—carriers of parasites that cause sleeping sickness—and two of the children became ill with malaria. Oswell, who happened to be close by, helped them make it back to Kolobeng. Mary Livingstone then gave birth to a baby girl, who also caught malaria and died six weeks later.

Livingstone refused to give up, writing in his diary: "I mean to follow a useful motto and try again." Mary's mother pleaded with him not to take the family along, but he insisted. He asked Oswell to accompany them and proposed taking a different route from the disastrous trip of the previous year. They departed in April 1851. Oswell shot fresh game, but often there was nothing to shoot. Their guide, Shobo, turned out to be incompetent, getting lost several times before he finally deserted them altogether. After the spare water was lost in an accident south of the Chobe River, the Livingstone party went for four days without water. The Livingstones faced the real prospect of watching their three children die of thirst. Everyone was saved when they found the Mababe River on the fifth day.

Unfortunately the Mababe was infested with tsetse flies, and 43 of the oxen died. When the explorers reached the Chobe, Livingstone and Oswell went ahead in a canoe to meet Sebituane. The chief, who had traveled 400 miles, was waiting on an island in the middle of the river "with all his principal men around him, and engaged in singing when we arrived." Sebituane wanted guns from the Europeans and welcomed the idea of setting up a mission station in his country. He died from an infection in an old wound less than a month after meeting Livingstone.

Discovers Zambezi River

Livingstone and Oswell traveled northeast through the Makololo country looking for a good site for a mission station, which they did not find. However, at the end of June 1851 at the village of Sesheke in what is now Zambia, they saw a great river—the Zambezi—whose course that far in the interior of Africa was unknown to Europeans. Livingstone had made a second major discovery and a means to bring Christianity and trade to Africa. Next, Livingstone decided to continue on to reach the west coast of Africa. Oswell wrote: "He suddenly announced his intention of going down to the west coast. We were about 1,800 miles off it. To my reiterated objections that it would be impossible—'I'm going down. I mean to go down,' was the only answer." Livingstone wrote in his own journal:

> I at once resolved to save my family from exposure to this unhealthy region by sending them home to England, and to return alone, with a view to exploring the country in search of a healthy district that might prove a center of civilization, and to open up by the interior a path to either the east or west coast.

Livingstone and Oswell returned to the Chobe River to get his family and then headed back to Kolobeng; Mary gave birth to another child in the middle of the desert. From there they went to Cape Town where they arrived in April 1852; Livingstone put his family on a ship to England, where he entrusted them to the care of the London Missionary Society.

Goes on without family

When Livingstone returned to Kolobeng, he found that his mission station had been destroyed by Boer raiders, with whom he had been in conflict for years. The Boers disliked the missionaries, who were getting in the way of the Boers' efforts to drive the Africans off the land and to use them as farm laborers. Livingstone continued north and reached the Makololo country on May 23, 1853, where he was greeted by Sebituane's son and successor, Sekelutu. Sekelutu accompanied him on a trip up the Zambezi to look for a site for a mission station. Leaving Sekelutu at his headquarters at Linyanti on November 11, 1853, Livingstone traveled into the land of the Barotse people, accompanied by 27 porters and guides supplied by Sekelutu.

Livingstone and his supporters traveled north around Lake Dilolo and through a swampy plain as far as the Kasai River, a tributary of the Congo, which he reached at the end of February 1854. Livingstone was sick with malaria for most of the time but was well cared for by the men in his caravan. At one point, a local chief demanded that Livingstone sell some of the men as slaves in return for food. Livingstone refused, and the expedition was on the verge of starvation. On March 30, 1854, they looked down on the valley of the Kwango River in what is now northeastern Angola. They were arguing with the people of a nearby village, who refused to give them food, when a Portuguese militiaman appeared and directed them to a nearby military outpost.

Traveling by way of Kassange, they reached the city of Luanda, capital of Angola, on May 31, 1854. In four months they had covered over 1,500 miles of unmapped country. Livingstone was housed in the home of the British consul, and his men found work on the docks of Luanda. But Livingstone had not found what he was looking for—a site free from fever among receptive people where he could start a new mission. So, rather than finding a ship to sail back to England, he turned around and on September 20, 1854, headed back inland.

Discovers falls and crosses continent

The return by a different route proved to be more difficult, and it took a year before they reached Linyanti, arriving there on September 11, 1855. As he crossed the Kasai River on his way back, Livingstone recorded that he suffered his twenty-seventh bout of fever. He also almost died from rheumatic fever. Livingstone stayed in Linyanti for seven weeks before traveling downstream on the Zambezi on November 3, 1855. Sekelutu accompanied him for part of the way and furnished him with a large retinue of porters and guides. Within a couple of weeks, they came upon the great falls that the Africans called Mosi-Ao-Tunya ("Smoke That Thunders") and which Livingstone named Victoria Falls in honor of Queen Victoria. "It had never before been seen by European eyes; but scenes so lovely must have been gazed upon by angels in their flight." This discovery of one of the world's most beautiful waterfalls helped make Livingstone's legendary reputation.

Continuing eastward, on November 30 the expedition crossed the Kalomo River into territory inhabited by enemies of the Makololo; they then often encountered hostility from the tribes they visited. Livingstone cut across a loop of the Zambezi, thereby missing the Quebrabasa Falls. They were saved from starvation by a party of men sent out from the Portuguese outpost of Tete in what is now western Mozambique. The expedition reached the port of Kilimane (Quelimane) on the Indian Ocean on May 20, 1856. Livingstone was the first European known to have traveled across the continent.

Leaves mission work

Livingstone's exploit immediately became widely known and made him famous. A Royal Navy ship was sent to bring him back to England. When he arrived in London in December 1856, he was showered with honors and prizes. The president of the Royal Geographical Society said Livingstone had achieved "the greatest triumph in geographical research ... in our times." Livingstone resigned from the London Missionary Society, which found his explorations to be only remotely related to mission work. The British government, however, appointed Livingstone consul for the East Coast of Africa and provided him with £5,000 and several European assistants, including his brother Charles, to explore new regions. He was also given a steamer, which he named the *Ma-Robert*—the Africans' name for Mary Livingstone.

The *Ma-Robert* arrived at the mouth of the Zambezi in May 1858 and steamed up the Zambezi past Tete. Livingstone's plans for using the Zambezi as a quick way into the interior were stopped, however, by the Quebrabasa Rapids he had missed on his previous journey. The rapids stretched for 40 miles and had waterfalls as high as 30 feet, making the river impassable. Livingstone next tried a northern tributary of the Zambezi—the Shire River—but was once again blocked by impassable rapids. Trying once again, he made it as far as Lake Chilwa and then led a small party that found the much larger Lake Nyasa (Lake Malawi) on September 16, 1859. They also discovered one of the busiest slave routes from the interior to the coast.

The following year Livingstone returned to the Makololo country. Sekelutu was suffering from leprosy and had gone into seclusion. He did not live long after Livingstone left on

September 17, 1860, and his kingdom fell apart. When Livingstone returned to the coast, he found a large contingent of missionaries and helped them get established in two stations; but the missions soon failed. Livingstone explored Lake Malawi during September and October 1861.

Grieves at wife's death

On January 30, 1862, a British ship arrived at Kilimane with Mary Livingstone on board. She had changed since her husband had seen her last, and she was now a heavy drinker. Soon becoming ill with fever, she died at the end of April. Livingstone was despondent after her death, writing "I feel as if I had lost all heart now." He made a trip up the Ruvuma River, which now forms the boundary between Tanzania and Mozambique, and found that it led only 160 miles into the interior before it was blocked by rapids. By that time, all of Livingstone's European assistants had either died or returned to England. In July 1863 he himself was recalled and returned to London the following year, ending his career as an explorer of southern Africa. A public hero, Livingstone ran into difficulty from Prince Albert, who defended Portuguese slave trading, which Livingstone denounced.

Livingstone jumped into the public debate over the source of the Nile River, and the Royal Geographical Society commissioned him to travel back to Africa to continue the search for the Nile's source. **Richard Burton** and **John Hanning Speke** (see separate entries) had sought the Nile's source in East Africa in 1857-58 and had come away with differing opinions. Speke had returned in 1861-63, showing that it almost certainly flowed from Lake Victoria. Not everyone, including Burton, accepted that conclusion. Livingstone thought they were all wrong. He believed one of the sources for Lake Victoria could be found to the south in Lake Tanganyika and that the ultimate source was a river and a lake the local people called Bangweulu. He was wrong: Lake Bangweulu does discharge into Lake Tanganyika, but it ultimately flows into the Congo River system.

Encounters more hardships

In 1865 Livingstone left England for what proved to be the last time, traveling to Bombay, India, where he hired **James Chuma** (see entry), who had been with him at Lake Malawi. Next, he went to Zanzibar, where he hired another freed slave named Susi. He was able to find only 60 porters willing to travel inland with them. Everywhere they went they saw the evil effects of the slave trade: "village after village all deserted and strewn with corpses and skulls." Little food was to be found; Livingstone was left with 11 half-starved men with him when he reached Lake Malawi on August 8, 1866. From Lake Malawi they traveled slowly inland to Lake Tanganyika. The journey became a series of disasters; a porter dropped the chronometer, so Livingstone could not make accurate observations of his position. Another porter deserted, taking Livingstone's medicine chest with him. By January 1867 the whole party became ill, and Livingstone came down with rheumatic fever in February. He wrote in his journal: "I feel as if I had now received sentence of death."

Livingstone was rescued by a party of Arab slave traders, with whom he traveled to Lake Mweru, which he reached on November 8, 1867. He left them to search for Lake Bangweulu. Only four men would accompany him; they reached the lake on July 18, 1868. In his desperate situation, his only choice was to go to Ujiji and catch up with the Arabs. "I am nearly toothless and in my second childhood," Livingstone wrote. Along the way, he came down with pneumonia. When he reached Ujiji on March 4, 1869, he found that all his supplies had been stolen. For the next year Livingstone was sick for most of the time and traveled little. During this period he read the Bible four times.

In March 1871 Livingstone and Susi, Chuma, and another faithful attendant, Garner, reached the Lualaba River at Nyangwe. The Lualaba flows north, eventually becoming the Congo; Livingstone wanted to believe that it was part of the Nile system. Nyangwe was a major slave trading post, and Livingstone witnessed a massacre when some Arab slave traders fired into a crowded market, killing many innocent people. No longer wishing to depend upon the Arabs and wanting to tell the outside world of the horrors of the slave trade, he departed with his three faithful companions for a 350-mile walk to Ujiji, "almost every step in pain."

Has famous encounter with Stanley

When Livingstone reached Ujiji, he had no money and nothing to trade for food. He was destitute and in despair. But help was at hand. "Susi came running at the top of his speed and gasped out: 'An Englishman! I see him!' and off he darted to meet him. The American flag at the head of the caravan told me the nationality of the stranger." He referred to the arrival of **Henry Morton Stanley** (see entry), who was actually a Welshman who had taken the name of a New Orleans plantation owner before jumping ship as a teenager. "Dr. Livingstone, I presume?" were the first words Stanley spoke to Livingstone.

Stanley had brought medicine and food sufficient to restore Livingstone's health. The two men set out together to explore the north end of Lake Tanganyika, going farther up the lake than Burton and Speke. They were able to settle one question about the source of the Nile by finding the Ruzizi River at the north end of the lake, which, contrary to Burton's belief, flowed into and not out of the lake. This led Livingstone to mistakenly believe even more firmly that the Lualaba River had to be the upper course of the Nile.

Livingstone and Stanley traveled together to the major trading center of Tabora (Kazeh) in what is now central Tanzania, 300 miles away. There, Livingstone hired porters to assist him in investigating the Lualaba, and Stanley headed for the coast. He promised to obtain porters and supplies in Zanzibar to send back to Livingstone. Historians have often speculated about Livingstone's reasons for not returning to England with Stanley, but there is no definitive answer. In any case, he waited at Tabora for five months until supplies arrived from the coast.

On August 25, 1872, Livingstone began his last journey around the south shore of Lake Tanganyika. He crossed the Kalongosi River, which flows into Lake Mweru and headed south toward Lake Bangweulu. He got hopelessly lost and became ill again; he suffered from dysentery and started bleeding profusely from hemorrhoids on March 31, 1873. A month before his death, he wrote in his journal: "Nothing earthly will make me give up my work in despair. I encourage myself in the Lord my God, and go forward." By April 22, he could no longer walk and had to be carried in a litter. "It is not all pleasure, this exploration," he wrote in his diary. The sad little expedition stopped at a village called Chitambo in northeast Zambia. He made his last diary entry on April 27, 1873. At midnight on April 30 he said to Susi, "All right, you can go now." During the night, one of his companions looked in and saw him kneeling by his cot in prayer. The next morning he was still in the same position, dead.

Faithful companions carry his body across Africa

Livingstone's companions, led by Susi and Chuma, embalmed his body with raw salt after they had cut out his heart and other internal organs. They buried his heart under a tree and then wrapped the body in cloth and bark and slung it on a pole. For eight months they carried it across East Africa until they reached Tabora on October 20, 1873. There they met an expedition commanded by Verney Lovett Cameron looking for Livingstone. They turned the body over to the Englishmen, but traveled with it to the coast and ultimately to England, where there was a large public funeral preceding his burial at Westminster Abbey on April 18, 1874.

Luna

Launched January 2, 1959,
Decommissioned August 1976

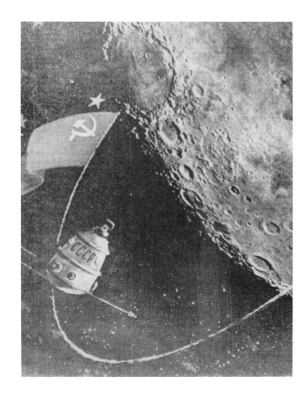

Artists conception of Luna 10 *circling the moon.* ➡

D uring the late 1950s and 1960s the United States and the Soviet Union were engaged in a "space race," which began when the Soviets launched **Sputnik I** (see entry), the first artificial satellite, on October 4, 1957. Space exploration had become possible after World War II when powerful rockets were developed, and the Soviet Union had taken advantage of the new technology with its *Sputnik* program. In response to *Sputnik I,* which had successfully orbited the Moon, the United States launched its first Earth-orbiting satellite, **Explorer I** (see entry), on January 31, 1958. The race was now in high gear: in fact, during the decade following *Sputnik I* the United States and the Soviet Union would collectively launch 50 unmanned space probes to explore the Moon.

In the first stages of experimentation the probes were designed either to fly close to the Moon—to execute a "flyby"—or to crash into the Moon—to make a "hard landing." The next phase of development involved "soft landings," which meant that the instruments on board the spacecraft were

The Soviet Luna
*spacecraft were the
first man-made objects
to travel to the Moon.*

not disturbed upon impact with the Moon's surface. In the last stage the spacecraft were launched into fixed orbits around the Moon.

As each nation attempted to achieve these objectives its scientists needed to develop more powerful rockets and perfect the maneuverability of the spacecraft. The Soviet *Luna* program was the first to accomplish all four stages. Spanning a period of over 17 years, beginning with *Luna 1* in 1959 and ending with *Luna 24* in 1976, this series of unmanned flights advanced scientific knowledge of the Moon with photographs, soil samples, and other significant data. Whereas the United States program would later produce more detailed information, at the time *Luna 1* was launched the Soviets were clearly winning the race.

Experimental spacecraft launched

The Soviet Union sent *Luna 1* into space on January 2, 1959. The name "Luna" was taken from the Latin word for "moon." The first *Luna* was nicknamed Mechta ("Dream"). A small object, only 40 inches in diameter, *Luna 1* was chiefly designed to measure the Moon's magnetic field, which it discovered to be almost nonexistent. The spacecraft flew by the Moon at a closest distance of 4,660 miles, then entered into orbit around the Sun. It broadcast data for a total of about 34 hours.

On September 12, 1959, *Luna 2* entered space. Much larger than its predecessor, *Luna 2* weighed 3,000 pounds and carried 858 pounds of instruments and transmitting equipment. It was the first man-made object to hit the Moon when it crashed between the craters Archimedes and Autolycus in the Mare Imbrium on September 14. Signals stopped at the precise moment when the spacecraft had been predicted to hit the surface.

Significant results produced

Luna 3 embarked on a more significant flight than the other two satellites. It had been designed to fly around the

Moon and give humans their first view of the Moon's "dark" side. The spacecraft weighed 3,300 pounds, of which 614 pounds were composed of the Automatic Interplanetary Station allowed it to operate even when it could not be reached by signals from Earth. *Luna 3* was launched on October 4, 1959, exactly two years after the first flight of *Sputnik 1*. Flying behind the Moon, the craft approached within 4,372 miles of the lunar surface on October 10. Although the photographs *Luna 3* sent back were of poor quality, they nevertheless allowed the first view of several important lunar features, including the Mare Crisium, or Sea of Crises.

The Soviets launched the unsuccessful *Luna 4* on April 2, 1963. The satellite was supposed to make a soft landing at less than 20 miles an hour. The 3,135-pound spacecraft flew within 5,300 miles of the Moon but then entered into orbit around the Sun. The following four *Luna* probes were also unsuccessful.

Soft landing achieved

Success came with the next probe. *Luna 9* made a soft landing on the Moon's surface on February 3, 1966. Touching down in the Oceanus Procellarum, it sent pictures back to Earth within a few minutes of impact. *Luna 9* showed that the Moon's surface was hard, not covered with a heavy layer of dust as some scientists had thought. This confirmed that the surface could support a spacecraft carrying humans. *Luna 9* is still standing on the Moon.

Luna 10 achieved another first by entering into lunar orbit. Launched on April 3, 1966, and weighing 3,500 pounds, the spacecraft maintained contact with Earth for 460 orbits. Its instruments studied micrometeoritic particles and gamma radiations coming from the Moon's surface. *Lunas 11* and *12* both entered lunar orbit successfully during the latter half of 1966. *Luna 12* passed within 62 miles of the Moon's surface. *Luna 13* landed in the Ocean of Storms, while *Zonds 5* and *6*, part of a parallel Soviet program, were the first spacecraft to circle the Moon and return to Earth. *Luna 14* orbited the Moon in April 1968.

These programs were designed to lead to the next accomplishment: landing a craft on the Moon and then returning it safely to Earth. The first attempt, *Luna 15,* launched on July 13, 1969, crash-landed a few days after the arrival of the United States spacecraft **Apollo 11**, which carried **Neil Armstrong** (see separate entries), the first human to walk on the surface of the Moon.

Return to Earth accomplished

Luna 16 was launched on September 12, 1970. The satellite descended from lunar orbit and recovered 101 grams of soil samples by using a hollow drill bit at the end of a boom designed to bend like a human arm. On November 17, 1970, *Luna 17* landed on the Moon and launched a mobile unit called the *Lunokhod 1*. This vehicle traveled around the surface of the Moon for ten months, covering 6.5 miles. It transmitted 20,000 photos back to Earth from two television cameras located in portholes at the front of the vehicle. The instruments eventually froze and the *Lunokhod* ceased to function.

Luna 18 was sent to the Moon on September 2, 1971, but it crash-landed. *Luna 19,* which followed less than a month later, made a total of 1,000 orbits before it lost contact with Earth. *Luna 20* landed successfully in the Mare Fecunditatis, the Sea of Plenty, in February 1972. It drilled for soil samples and returned to Earth on February 25. The Soviets donated slightly more than 2 grams of *Luna 20*'s samples for use by American scientists as part of a United States-Soviet Union scientific exchange program.

Successful returns continued

The last stages of the *Luna* series, spanning a three-year period, successfully continued Earth-to-Moon and Moon-to-Earth flights. *Luna 21* was launched on January 8, 1973, carrying *Lunokhod 2*. The Moon vessel traveled over 23 miles and took 80,000 pictures. *Luna 22,* setting out on May 29, 1974, made over 4,000 orbits of the Moon. *Luna 23* soft-landed on the far side of the Moon and transmitted for about a week in November 1974. Launched on August 9, 1976, the last *Luna* spacecraft—*Luna 24*—landed as planned in the Mare Crisium on the far side of the Moon, taking soil samples and safely returning to Earth.

Although the *Luna* series was terminated, the Soviet Union had been conducting other space programs such as *Voskhod* and *Soyuz*; and within only two years of the launching of *Luna 1,* on April 8, 1961, **Yury Gagarin** (see entry), flying in *Vostok 1,* became the first man to orbit Earth. By the time *Luna 24* returned to Earth, the United States had also made considerable headway in the space race. At that point the two contenders were running neck-and-neck.

Alexander Mackenzie

Born 1764,
Stornoway, Outer Hebrides, Scotland

Died March 12, 1820,
Scotland

Sir Alexander Mackenzie was a Scot who discovered the Mackenzie River in the Canadian Arctic; he was also the first person to cross North America north of Mexico.

When searching for a river route from the Canadian interior to the Pacific Ocean, Sir Alexander Mackenzie canoed through Alberta and British Columbia. He reached the ocean after traversing a complicated series of rivers and portages. Although Mackenzie did not find a route to cross this area exclusively by water, he became the first person to cross North America north of Mexico.

Mackenzie was born in Stornoway in the Outer Hebrides off the northwest coast of Scotland. When he was ten years old, he and his widowed father sailed to New York. Shortly after their arrival the Revolutionary War broke out and Mackenzie's father joined the British forces; he died from illness while in service in 1780. In the meantime, Mackenzie had been sent to school in the city of Montreal in Quebec.

Works in fur trade

At the age of 15 Mackenzie became a clerk in a large

Montreal fur-trading company. Five years later he was entrusted with his first trading mission—the delivery of supplies to the company's post in Detroit, Michigan. He carried out this task so successfully that he was made a partner in the company. He went to work in Grand Portage, the trading post at the end of Lake Superior that served as the company's link with the Canadian interior. When the company's partners held their annual meeting at Grand Portage in 1785, Mackenzie was chosen to oversee the region of the Churchill River, with headquarters at Île-a-la-Crosse in what is now northern Saskatchewan, Canada.

In 1787 Mackenzie's company merged with the much larger North West Company. In 1788 Mackenzie was appointed supervisor of the Athabasca fur district; his headquarters was at Fort Chipewyan on Lake Athabasca in what is now northern Alberta. In his new position Mackenzie became a colleague of Peter Pond, a trader who had explored widely in the interior. Using information from Native Americans with whom he traded, Pond had gained a general idea of the river system of northwest Canada.

Pond had learned of a large river (the Slave) that flowed into Great Slave Lake from the south. He had also heard that a second river flowed out of the western end of the lake and on north to the Arctic. Aware of the discovery by British explorer **James Cook** (see entry) of Cook Inlet on the south coast of Alaska, Pond theorized that the river that branched out of the Great Slave Lake flowed westward to Cook Inlet rather than north. If he was correct, this river would provide the much-sought-after route to the Pacific Ocean. Pond retired in 1788 without testing his theory.

Searches for route to Pacific

Mackenzie decided to test Pond's theory himself. Heading a large party of traders and Native Americans, he started out from Fort Chipewyan on June 3, 1789. The rapids on the Slave River made travel slow and difficult, and the party was delayed by ice on Great Slave Lake. However, once they reached the river flowing out of the lake, which has since been

Mackenzie led two great expeditions, in 1789 and 1792-93, that made a valuable contribution to knowledge of the Canadian northwest.

named the Mackenzie River, they traveled rapidly, averaging 75 miles a day.

Since the river continued westward for the first few days, Mackenzie thought he had found the route to the Pacific. But then the river turned north; and after going several days in this direction, Mackenzie realized that it must flow into the Arctic Ocean. The party followed the river all the way to its outlet in the Arctic, then stayed four days on a nearby island. They started back upstream on July 16, 1789, reaching Fort Chipewyan two months later. Although Mackenzie had found one of the world's great rivers, the discovery was a disappointment to him because it did not offer any practical use for the fur traders who were looking for a way west.

Heads second expedition

Mackenzie decided to make another expedition to see if he could find a better fur-trading route. Before setting out on his journey, he went to London for several months to learn more about navigation and surveying so he could make more accurate measurements of locations. He returned with a supply of basic measuring instruments that he would soon put to good use.

On his second expedition, which began October 10, 1792, Mackenzie and his party initially followed the Peace River to its juncture with the Smoky River. At the point where the two rivers meet, they built a camp and spent the winter. They set out again on May 9, 1793. By the end of May, they reached the point where the Parsnip and Finlay rivers come together in northeastern British Columbia. Mackenzie is credited with the discovery of the Fraser River, which was named for Simon Fraser, the explorer who later followed the river to its mouth. Heeding the advice of local Native Americans, Mackenzie led the canoes up the Parsnip River and made a portage to the McGregor River; from there the explorers canoed to the Fraser River.

At this point, Mackenzie thought he had found the headwaters of the Columbia. The party traveled down the river as far as the site of the present-day town of Alexandria—which was named after Mackenzie—in British Columbia, where the Native Americans advised Mackenzie to go no farther. They said from there on the river was too difficult to navigate because it contained numerous falls and rapids. Mackenzie decided to turn back and went as far as the West Road River. Starting up the West Road on July 4, 1793, they crossed what came to be known as Mackenzie Pass at 6,000 feet and then headed west down the Bella Coola River.

Crosses North American continent

After traveling for some time, the explorers reached the village of the Bella Coola tribe, where Mackenzie made note of the houses, which stood on stilts. He wrote later, "From these houses, I could perceive the termination of the river, and its discharge into a narrow arm of the sea." Mackenzie had reached the Pacific, thus becoming the first person to have crossed North America north of Mexico.

Mackenzie spent a few days exploring the fjords that make up that part of the British Columbia coast. At Dean Channel he learned that Europeans had been there recently: the British navigator George Vancouver had reached the area by sea just six weeks earlier. As a record of his visit, Mackenzie painted an inscription on a large rock in Dean Channel: "Alex Mackenzie from Canada by land 22d July 1793." The inscription has been preserved and can still be seen today in a provincial park.

Becomes fur-trade executive

Mackenzie began his return trip on July 23 and reached Fort Chipewyan a month later. He and his party traveled with unusual speed, given the means of transportation and the obstacles they encountered. Upon his return to Fort Chipewyan, Mackenzie ended his days as an explorer, but he continued to make ambitious plans for the fur trade. Following the winter of 1793-94 Mackenzie went east with the idea of uniting the two largest fur-trading companies, the Hudson's Bay Company and the North West Company. He hoped that together the two companies could cooperate with the East India Company to open a new trade route to China. He advocated these ideas for several years but they were never realized exactly as he imagined. Mackenzie returned to Montreal and served as a director of a trading company until he left Canada for England in November 1799.

While he was in England, Mackenzie wrote an account of his expeditions, *Voyages ... to the Frozen and Pacific Oceans,* which was published in 1801. For his valuable contribution to knowledge of the Canadian northwest, he was knighted and became Sir Alexander Mackenzie in 1802. He returned to Canada that same year; in 1805 he was elected to the Legislative Assembly of Lower Canada. After serving briefly in the legislature he went back to London. In 1808 Mackenzie retired to Scotland, where he spent the rest of his life.

Ferdinand Magellan

Born c. 1480,
Sabrosa or Pôrto, Portugal

Died April 27, 1521,
Mactan, Philippines

Ferdinand Magellan was a Portuguese navigator who led a Spanish expedition around the world. After he was killed in the Philippines, Juan Sebastián de Elcano continued the voyage and became the first person to circle the globe.

A member of the Portuguese nobility, Ferdinand Magellan was born the son of Rui de Magalhaes and Alda de Mesquita in about 1480; his Portuguese name was Fernâo de Magalhaes. He grew up in the royal household. Magellan had been on several Portuguese voyages to the East Indies, the first of which sailed around the Cape of Good Hope in 1505. On these trips he learned about the Eastern spice trade. After his last voyage to the East Indies, Magellan fought with the Portuguese at the town of Azemmour in Morocco; during the battle he suffered a leg wound that left him lame for the rest of his life.

Enters service of Spain

When Magellan returned from Morocco to Portugal, he was falsely accused of corruption. Although he was later acquitted, King Manuel II of Portugal refused to reward him for his services and told him to seek a position from another sovereign. Consequently Magellan traveled to Seville, Spain, with his friend the astronomer Rui Faleiro in 1517. Magellan's plan was to organize an expedition to East Asia for King Charles V of Spain. He insisted that by sailing westward around the southern tip of South America he would reach the Moluccas, also known as the Spice Islands. No Portuguese explorer had yet visited the Moluccas, but Magellan believed they lay in the western half of the New World, which had been granted to Spain in the Treaty of Tordesillas signed by Spain and Portugal in 1494.

Magellan first presented his plan to Spanish officials who were responsible for trade with the new empire opening up in the Americas. They were not impressed, so he lobbied the king's advisors directly; but again he had no success. Finally, accompanied by Faleiro, Magellan approached the king himself; Charles V immediately realized the advantages to Spain if Magellan's theory turned out to be true. Magellan and Faleiro renounced their nationality before the king; it was at this time that Magellan adopted the Spanish name Fernando de Magallanes.

King approves expedition

After long negotiations, during which Magellan had to fight Portuguese intrigues against him, an agreement was signed on March 22, 1518. Magellan and Faleiro were given the titles of governor and captain-general; they were also invested in the Order of Santiago. Any lands they discovered were to be vested in them and their heirs, and they partook in a 1/20th share of the expedition's net profits. King Charles V ordered five ships—the *Trinidad,* the *San Antonio,* the *Concepción,* the *Victoria,* and the *Santiago*—to be equipped for the expedition, which would be under Magellan and Faleiro's command but would be staffed by officials appointed by the king. The ships had a crew of 270 men from nine countries and supplies to last two years.

When Faleiro's health prevented him from making the journey, the king put Juan de Cartagena, the captain of the *San Antonio,* second-in-command to Magellan. Charles V issued instructions about how the expedition should be conducted and what it should achieve. Included were rules on what the commanders and crew should do if the ships were separated at sea, how they should treat the inhabitants of places they visited, and the records they should keep of the voyage. When the fleet sailed out of Seville for the port of Sanlúcar de Barrameda on September 8, 1519, Magellan left behind his wife Beatriz Barbosa, whom he had married in 1517, and their infant son, Rodrigo.

Reaches South America

Leaving Sanlúcar de Barrameda about two weeks later, the ships stopped at the island of Tenerife in the Canary Islands, then crossed the equator on November 5. They sailed into the harbor of Rio de Janeiro on December 13. From there the explorers headed south along the coast of South America to the estuary of the Río de la Plata. Magellan spent some time investigating that great river system to see if it connected with the Pacific, either because he was unaware of or did not believe the findings of the Spanish explorer Juan Díaz de Solís, who discovered the river in 1516.

When he found no outlet for the Río de la Plata, Magellan turned the fleet south; along the way he closely investigated every bay and cove the ships crossed. In March 1520 they arrived at the Bay of San Julián, where they spent four months waiting for spring and repairing the ships. During their stay the Spaniards encountered a group of Native Americans who were dressed in guanaco skins and wore coverings on their feet that led Magellan to call them *patagoes,* which is Portuguese for "big feet." Patagonia, the name of the region, is derived from that nickname.

Discovers Strait of Magellan

The captains of the four other ships soon expressed their unhappiness with Magellan because, throughout the voyage, he had changed the route and made other decisions without consulting them. When Magellan removed the four men from their posts they rebelled; in the ensuing fight three of them were killed, and the expedition continued with a complete change in command. The ships left San Julián in August 1520 and headed south again; the explorers sighted land in the area of the Bay of Santa Cruz. They stayed there until October when they discovered the western passage they had been seeking—the entrance that was to be known as the Strait of Magellan, which starts at the Cape of the Virgins at about 52° south latitude. Magellan sailed into the strait with only four ships, since the *Santiago* had been wrecked on the bluffs of Santa Cruz.

It took Magellan more than a month to traverse the strait. He divided his ships so that each one could inspect the numerous channels of the passage to see if any led to the west. It was not until November 27, 1520, that the explorers reached the western ocean, which they named the Pacific because the waters seemed so much quieter after the stormy passage through the strait. When the fleet reached the ocean there were only three ships left. The captain of the *San Antonio* had decided, without consulting Magellan, that he did not have sufficient supplies to cross the Pacific, so he had turned back and headed for Spain.

Makes difficult crossing of Pacific

The route Magellan took was mainly northward, passing between the coast of Chile and the Juan Fernández Islands. From there he turned to the northwest and passed one of the outlying islands of the Marquesas group; he crossed the equator at 153° west longitude, reaching the island of Guam in the Marianas on March 7, 1521. The crossing had taken five long and difficult months. During this time many of the crew members died and many more became ill from scurvy, which is caused by lack of fresh vegetables and fruits; others died simply from hunger and thirst.

In Guam Magellan and his captains were able to provision the ships and give the sick men some fresh food. They ate meat for the first time in 99 days, having been forced to eat leather off the yardarms while crossing the "Sea of the South."

Magellan was killed near the island of Cebu in the Philippines before he could accomplish his goal of reaching the Molucca Islands.

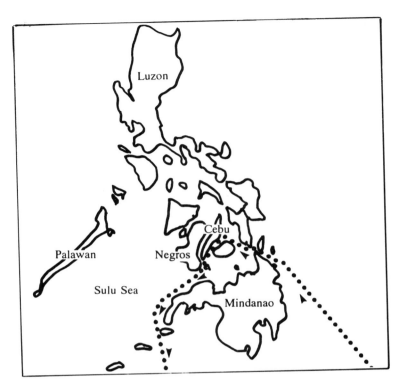

By March 16 they reached the island of Samar in the archipelago that they named after Saint Lazarus and which was later to be called the Philippines in honor of King Philip II of Spain.

Misunderstanding causes death

From Samar Magellan sailed into the Philippine archipelago and reached the island of Cebu. After a voyage of 13,000 miles the crew rested for several days, repairing the ships and stocking provisions. The Spaniards were welcomed by the inhabitants of Cebu; the king of the island even expressed the wish to become a vassal of the king of Spain. But Magellan, ignoring a distinct instruction of Charles V, took a force of 60 men to the nearby island of Mactan to try to persuade the local leader to recognize the chief of Cebu as his ruler. One thousand warriors attacked Magellan's party, killing Magellan and eight of his men and wounding many more. Magellan died on April 27, 1521, having failed to reach the Moluccas.

When the survivors returned to Cebu, Duarte Barbosa was chosen as Magellan's successor and named captain of the fleet. But Barbosa himself violated another of the Spanish king's instructions by accepting an invitation from the leader of Cebu to attend a banquet with 30 of his men. In the middle of the banquet the Cebuanos turned on the Spaniards and killed all of them.

Magellan's goal achieved

Left with fewer men, the survivors decided to burn the *Concepción* and continue with only the *Trinidad* and the *Victoria*. Gonzalo Gómez de Espinosa was chosen as captain-general of the *Trinidad* and Juan Sebastián de Elcano was chosen to command the *Victoria*. From Cebu the two ships sailed through the Philippines, touching at several islands, including Negros, Mindanao, the northeastern corner of Borneo, and several of the smaller islands north of Celebes. They reached the island of Tidore in the Moluccas on November 8, 1521, finally accomplishing Magellan's goal. In Tidore the ruler, Sultan Almanzor, greeted them warmly, swearing to be a vassal of the king of Spain and not to trade with any other European nation. The ships were loaded with cloves, one of the most highly valued spices.

When the expedition left Tidore the *Trinidad* was so weighted down with goods and was in such bad condition that it began to take on water; it was eventually forced to turn back to make repairs. Since the repairs would take some time, Espinosa and Elcano decided to return to Spain using separate routes: Espinosa would remain behind with the *Trinidad* with the intention of sailing back home to the east across the Pacific to Panama, while Elcano would continue westward with the records of the voyage. Elcano and the *Victoria* left Tidore on December 21, 1521.

Elcano circumnavigates globe

Elcano headed first for the island of Timor. Trying to avoid Portuguese ships that protected the Indian route for their

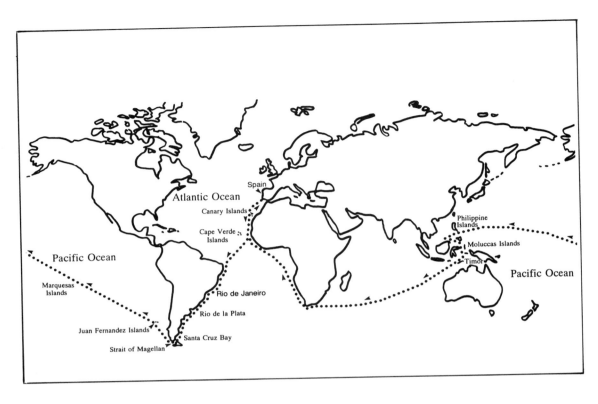

After Magellan's death, Elcano sailed back to Spain aboard the Victoria on a route that made the first circumnavigation of the globe.

exclusive use, he crossed the Indian Ocean as far to the south as possible from the African coast. He did not touch land until he reached Santiago Island in the Cape Verde Islands on July 13, 1522. To deceive the Portuguese who owned the islands, Elcano pretended he was returning from a voyage to the Americas. He needed their help in resupplying his ships, which had traveled for 150 days straight, more than Magellan had taken in going from America to Guam.

On Cape Verde Elcano discovered an amazing fact: the journals of the voyage were off by one day from the actual date. In traveling around the world from east to west, which is opposite to the direction of rotation of the earth, he had "lost" a day. The reason is that when a ship sails "against" the sun, each sunrise to sunrise is a little longer than 24 hours and the difference equals exactly one day after a complete circling of the globe. As the first man to travel around the world, Elcano was obviously also the first man to experience this phenomenon. The variance was later adjusted by establishing the International Date Line along 180° of longitude.

The *Victoria* arrived at Sanlúcar on September 6, 1522, then went on to Seville a few days later. Only 18 men survived the voyage that had lasted 14 days short of three years. The news of its arrival and of the first circumnavigation of the globe traveled quickly across Spain and the rest of Europe. The sale of the cargo brought back from the Moluccas earned a large profit, part of which went to the 18 returning men. King Charles V received Elcano with great honor, and a globe was erected in his home village of Guetaria, with the legend "The First One to Circle Me."

Espinosa captured

Meanwhile, Espinosa spent several months traveling among the islands of the Moluccas. He signed treaties of friendship and commerce with local rulers, guaranteeing Spanish control over the major source of spices in the East. Fearful of carrying the large cargo across the Pacific, he built a warehouse on Tidore and left some of his men to guard it. He then set out with 54 men on April 6, 1522. He sailed to the northeast and discovered the Palau Islands in western Micronesia and some of the Marianas farther north. Espinosa sailed east at around latitude 40° N, which in time was to become the route for Spanish ships coming from the Philippines. However, he ran into so many storms and contrary winds that he was forced to turn back; 32 men had already died of scurvy.

Six months after his departure, Espinosa returned to Tidore, only to find that the Portuguese had seized the island as well as the Spaniards he had left behind. They also captured Espinosa and the *Trinidad,* which served out its remaining days in Portuguese service in the East Indies. Espinosa was held in captivity on different islands for several years until he was finally released on the Indochinese peninsula and forced to make his way, overland and alone, back to Spain.

Thomas Manning

Born November 8, 1772,
Norfolk, England

Died May 2, 1840,
Bath, England

Thomas Manning was the first Englishman to travel to the Forbidden City of Lhasa in Tibet.

Thomas Manning was the fourth Westerner and the first Englishman to visit Lhasa, the capital of Tibet and the center of Lamaism, a Buddhist sect. He became interested in Tibet through his study of the Chinese language. His accounts of his experiences in Lhasa provide valuable information about the city during a period when foreigners were forbidden entry.

Manning was born the son of a clergyman in the English county of Norfolk on November 8, 1772. He enrolled at Cambridge University in 1790 and studied mathematics there until 1795 but never received a degree. He remained in Cambridge as a private tutor until 1800, when he went to Paris to learn Chinese. Manning stayed in Paris for three years, studying the language under a notable scholar of the day. When war broke out between Great Britain and France in 1803, he was given a pass signed by Napoleon I to return home.

Goes to China and India

Manning decided he wanted to travel to China to continue his studies. He acquired a basic knowledge of medicine and, with the support of **Joseph Banks** (see entry), president of the Royal Society, was appointed as a doctor at the British East India Company post in Canton. He traveled to Canton to begin his work in 1807. Three years later he went to Calcutta, the center of the East India Company's operations. While he was in Calcutta, Manning asked the company to sponsor him on an expedition to Tibet. When his request was turned down he set out for Tibet on his own.

Enters Lhasa

Accompanied only by his Chinese servant, Manning traveled to Rangpur in what is now northern Bangladesh. He entered the remote Himalayan kingdom of Bhutan in September 1811 and reached the Tibetan border on October 20. Using his medical knowledge, he was able to cure a Chinese general who was at the border post. Upon his recovery, the general agreed to let Manning travel with him to Lhasa, the capital of Tibet. Since entry into Tibet was forbidden to Westerners, Manning tried to disguise himself with Chinese robes. When his disguise proved to be inadequate for the cold Himalayan winter, he was forced to barter for something warmer. Manning reached Lhasa in December 1811, becoming the first Englishman to enter the city.

Describes Lhasa

Once he was in Lhasa, Manning was impressed by the Potala, the great stone palace, home of the spiritual and political leader of Tibet, the Dalai Lama. Standing nine stories high, the Potala is an immense cluster of whitewashed buildings that house reception rooms, chapels, and living quarters for monks. The central portion of the Potala is painted red and topped with gold-covered roofs and towers.

Manning's impression of Lhasa itself was not quite so positive:

Westerners in Lhasa

Until the Chinese conquered Tibet in 1951, Lhasa was the center of Tibetan Buddhism. Because the lamas, or Tibetan monks, were hostile to foreigners Lhasa was called the Forbidden City. For centuries it was closed to outsiders; as a result travelers and explorers, especially Westerners, were tempted by the challenge of entering the city. Odoric of Pordenone, a Christian missionary from Italy, is considered to have been the first Westerner to see Lhasa and its Buddhist monasteries during his trip through Asia in 1328. Europeans would not visit the city for another 300 years.

In 1661 Johann Grüber, a Jesuit missionary of Austrian descent, became the second Westerner to enter Lhasa. Grüber wrote the first account of the prayer wheel, a small cylinder with a prayer inscribed inside that Tibetans twirled to send their prayers to heaven. He also made drawings of the local scene, including a portrait of the Dalai Lama, the supreme religious leader of the Lamaist sect of Buddhism, and the Potala, the hill in Lhasa where the Dalai Lama's palace is located.

Not quite 50 years later another European came to the city and stayed for several months, during a period when a Mongol king had replaced the Dalai Lama. Ippolito Desideri, a Jesuit missionary from Italy, made the trip in 1716 with a fellow missionary who spent only a few days in Lhasa before returning to India. After his companion's departure Desideri was the only European in Lhasa. He was granted permission to teach about Christianity and he learned the Tibetan language. In less than a year he was able to present the Mongol king with a report on Christianity written in Tibetan. Desideri was the first European to learn Tibetan. The next Westerner and first Englishman to visit Lhasa was Thomas Manning, who followed Desideri nearly a hundred years later.

If the palace exceeded my expectations the town as far fell short of them. The habitations are begrimed with smut and dirt. The avenues are full of dogs, some growling and gnawing bits of hide which lie about in profusion, and emit a charnel-house smell; others limping and looking livid; others ulcerated; others starved and dying, and pecked at by ravens, some dead and preyed upon. In short, everything seems mean and gloomy, and excites the idea of something unreal.

Meets Dalai Lama

Manning was impressed by the ninth Dalai Lama, however, even though at the time the religious leader was only seven years old. Manning was allowed an audience with the ruler and, performing the traditional *kowtow,* presented him with gifts. The Dalai Lama, who was seated on a high throne, blessed Manning's head, which had been shaved for the occasion. Next he offered Manning a cup of buttered tea, the traditional Tibetan drink. Manning commented in his diary: "This day I saluted the Grand Lama! Beautiful youth. Face poetically affecting. Very happy to have seen him and his blessed smile. Hope often to see him again."

Leaves Lhasa

On April 19, 1812, Manning was forced to leave Lhasa because of the ill-will of the Chinese officials who advised the Dalai Lama. Another Englishman was not to visit Lhasa for nearly a century, when in 1904 Sir Francis Younghusband led an expedition to counter the growing influence of Russians in the city. During his stay he negotiated a treaty that gave the British political rights in Tibet.

Manning arrived in Calcutta in the summer of 1813. Having received no official encouragement to make the trip to Tibet, he refused to give the authorities any information about his journey. He returned to Canton and stayed there until 1816, when he traveled to Beijing to serve as the interpreter for a British ambassadorial party that was being sent to the Chinese emperor.

Returns to England

Following his return to England in 1818, Manning became known as the foremost Chinese scholar in Europe. He was also famous for his beard, which reached down to his waist. He lived surrounded by Chinese books in a small country house with no furniture. In 1838, after suffering a stroke that paralyzed his right hand, Manning moved to the town of Bath in order to take advantage of its famous medicinal springs. Before he left for Bath, however, he plucked out the hairs of his beard, one by one. Manning died in Bath on May 2, 1840.

Jean-Baptiste Marchand

Born 1863,
Thoissey, France

Died 1934,
Paris, France

Jean-Baptiste Marchand was a French soldier who led an expedition from the Atlantic coast of Africa to the Nile River in order to expand French territory. He was confronted by the British at the Sudanese town of Fashoda and forced to retreat.

In 1897 France sent Jean-Baptiste Marchand, a major in the French army, to the South Sudan, which is now called Mali, to establish French control of the region; at the same time the British were seeking control of territory from Cape Town, South Africa, to Cairo, Egypt. Shortly after Marchand reached the village of Fashoda on the Nile River, Anglo-Egyptian forces arrived to claim the town for Egypt. This conflict resulted in the "Fashoda Incident," which was one of the major turning points in modern European history. The failure at Fashoda taught the French that they would never be able to achieve their goals without the support of Great Britain. The country's leaders therefore started a conscious policy of befriending the government in London and quickly settled all the major problems it had with the British. The two countries signed a treaty of friendship, the "Entente Cordiale" in 1904. This eventually led to a military alliance that pitted France and Britain against Germany in World War I.

Marchand, the central figure in the Fashoda Incident, was born in the French town of Thoissey in eastern France north of the city of Lyons. Because his family was poor, he was forced to quit school after the first year of high school (*lycée*). At the age of 13 he was apprenticed to a notary, for whom he worked until the death of his mother when he was 20. Marchand then enlisted in the French army; he was promoted to the rank of corporal in 1884, then progressed to sergeant. His superiors thought so highly of him that he was sent to officer training school in 1886; the following year he returned to his former regiment as a second lieutenant.

Earns distinction in battle

In January 1888 Marchand was sent to serve in the French colony of Senegal in West Africa. At that time France was engaged in a colonial war to expand its empire throughout West Africa. When Marchand arrived in Senegal the French were engaged in conflict with the Tukulör in Mali. In early 1889 Marchand was sent to fight the Tukulör; he distinguished himself in his first combat by helping to capture the Tukulör stronghold of Koundian in early 1889. In April 1890, after he took part in the capture of the fortress of Ségou, he was promoted to lieutenant and awarded the Legion of Honor. In February 1891 he was wounded in the assault on the Tukulör capital of Djenné. At some time during this period he traced the Niger River to its source and explored the Ivory Coast.

Following the defeat of the Tukulör, Marchand joined the campaign against another foe of French imperialism, West African ruler Samory Touré, in Guinea. He fought in battles against Touré from April 1891 to the end of 1894. Marchand was wounded in the Battle of Bonua in November 1894, during which Touré's forces defeated the French in spite of Marchand's notable bravery. Marchand returned to France on June 14, 1895.

Proposes expedition to the Nile

Upon Marchand's return to France, he immediately began agitating for a plan he had conceived with his French colleagues in Africa. He proposed to lead an expedition from the French settlement of Brazzaville on the Congo River across Africa to the Nile. The goal was to win French control of the upper Nile and eventually link it with the French outpost on the Red Sea at Djibouti by forming an alliance with Ethiopia.

The Upper Nile had been originally explored by British explorers such as **Richard Burton**, **John Hanning Speke**, and **Samuel White Baker** (see separate entries). An Anglo-Egyptian government had been imposed on Mali, reaching as far south as the sources of the Nile in the country that is now Uganda. The government had been led by Charles "Chinese" Gordon and had used such agents as the American adventurer Charles Chaillé-Long and the German explorer Emin Pasha to control the Upper Nile. But these efforts had been wiped out in 1885 by Muslim forces called the El-Mahdi. Marchand now proposed to step into the confused situation along the Nile by replacing British power with French. In effect, it was a French imperialist design to control the sources of the Nile by taking over a route stretching from the Atlantic Ocean on the west to the Red Sea on the east. This would counter, and derail, British attempts to control Africa from north to south: from "the Cape to Cairo."

Marchand presented his ideas at a meeting with the French foreign minister in July 1895. He then submitted a detailed proposal to the Ministry of Colonies the following September. During this period, governments in France changed frequently because of conflicting political divisions. The colonialist faction contended France should make itself stronger after its defeat by Germany in the Franco-Prussian War of 1870 by expanding outside of Europe into Africa and Asia. The other side argued that France should not weaken itself by using its forces overseas while the main struggle was in Europe. Marchand happened to make his proposals at a time when the colonialists were in control. They were not concerned about offending the British, who they knew were trying to defeat the El-Mahdi so the British could retake control of the Upper Nile. Marchand's proposal was approved by the French prime minister in April 1896.

Leads expedition as far as Congo

In the meantime, Marchand had been making preparations. By the end of April the first of four detachments of officers and supplies had left France. Marchand himself sailed on June 25, arriving at the port of Loango in the French Congo in August. The governor of the French Congo at the time was **Pierre Savorgnan de Brazza** (see entry), a French citizen of Italian descent who had explored the Congo and had founded a French colony along the great river.

Upon reaching Loango, Marchand found it was impossible to move his supplies inland to the Congo River port of Brazzaville because the Basundi and Bakongo tribes were revolting against the French. But Marchand was in a hurry, so on August 18, 1896, he convinced Brazza to declare martial law in the Congo and to place Marchand in control. He then organized his French officers and Senegalese soldiers in a campaign against the rebels. Some of the rebel leaders were captured and executed in October. The last resistance to Marchand ended on December 12, by which time he was in Brazzaville. The rest of his men and supplies reached him by the end of February 1897.

Marchand was now faced with a problem: the French had no transport adequate for carrying the supplies up the Congo. He requested help from the Belgians, who ruled the other side of the river from Léopoldville, which is now Kinshasa. The Belgians initially refused; but new orders came from Brussels approving the use of the steamship *Ville de Bruges*. It made two trips with men and supplies up the Congo as far as it was possible to navigate. Marchand, who was sick with malaria, was on board for the second trip. The *Ville de Bruges* left Marchand and his men at the village of Zinga; from there they proceeded in 72 dugout canoes up the Ubangi River, reaching to Bangui, which is now the capital of the Central African Republic, in early April.

Makes difficult journey to Nile

From Bangui the expedition traveled 450 miles to Ouango, the last outpost before the Mbomu Rapids. At this point,

Marchand seized a small riverboat, the 50-foot long *Faidherbe,* to take down the Nile with the French flag flying. Since they could navigate no farther, however, the *Faidherbe* had to be totally disassembled and hauled overland by the African porters, each carrying a 55-pound load. This considerably slowed down the progress of the expedition. Fortunately, along the way the French discovered two other streams, the Mboku and the Méré, by which the boat could be sailed 160 miles farther. At that point, Marchand ordered a 100-mile-long road built so the pieces of the boat could be carried from Méré to Khojali. Once they reached Khojali in November, they realized they would have to wait until the spring rains before they would be able to proceed any farther. In the meantime Marchand sent part of the force ahead to build a post near the present Sudanese town of Wau on the Jur River.

While they were waiting for the rains to come, Marchand and other members of his force went exploring in different directions throughout the southern Sudan. It was not until June 4 that the boat reached the new French outpost, where it was possible to continue on the Sué River, a tributary of the Nile. After sailing for seven days they reached a vast swamp, the Sudd; it took them three weeks to struggle through the Sudd onto the Bahr-al-Ghazal, a bigger river flowing into the White Nile. In early July they reached the village of Fashoda on the Nile. The French force took possession of a fort outside of the town that had long ago been abandoned by Egyptian troops.

Claims Nile region for France

On July 11, 1898, Marchand held a formal ceremony, raising the French flag over the fort of Fashoda and claiming that part of the Nile Valley for France. Significantly, on their first attempt to raise the flag, the flagpole broke. The Frenchmen were able to celebrate Bastille Day, July 14, at their new outpost. On August 25 El-Mahdi forces attacked the fort, but the French easily drove them away with no loss of life. On September 19 a much more serious challenge confronted them: the British arrived.

A joint Anglo-Egyptian force under the command of Lord Horatio Herbert Kitchener had been fighting the El-Mahdi since 1896. At the Battle of Omdurman on September 2, 1898, they had destroyed the power of the Sudanese in their capital and restored the country to Anglo-Egyptian control. Kitchener had immediately headed up the Nile after his victory to oust the French from Fashoda. At a famous meeting on September 19, 1898, Kitchener demanded that Marchand withdraw. Marchand refused. The matter was then referred to the governments in London and Paris.

Ignited the Fashoda Incident

The news of the confrontation at Fashoda drove the newspapers of both countries into a nationalistic frenzy. The British began threatening the French with recriminations. In the midst of the dispute, the French government sent a message to Marchand by way of a British Nile steamer that reached him on October 9. It announced his promotion to major and ordered him to send an officer to Paris to report on the expedition. When the officer reached Paris on October 27, he found the French government was backtracking. French officials realized they could not confront the British government and they could not afford to finance Marchand's plan for an overland route. Marchand himself took a British steamer down the Nile to Cairo, where he arrived on November 3 to communicate with his government by telegram. The next day, he received instructions from Paris to evacuate Fashoda.

A furious Marchand spent the next several days arguing with his superiors in Paris. He was then ordered to return to Fashoda and carry out his instructions. The only concession the French granted was that he was not required to accept the humiliating offer of the British to evacuate the French soldiers down the Nile on British steamships. They would instead be allowed to continue their march eastward through Ethiopia to the French port of Djibouti at the entrance to the Red Sea. Marchand returned to Fashoda on December 4, 1898. Eight days later his troops played the "Marseillaise," the French national anthem, as they lowered the French flag and marched out of the fort.

Hailed as a hero in France

On May 16, 1899, Marchand and his men arrived at Djibouti, then embarked by steamship for France via the Red Sea. When they returned to Paris at the end of May, they were met by enormous crowds who cheered the French heroes. Popular sentiment was used by French nationalists to try to bring down the government. This attempt failed, and Marchand and his force marched together for the last time in the parade to celebrate Bastille Day. Afterward Marchand was reintegrated into the French army, where he continued to make a name for himself. He served during the Boxer Rebellion in China. Subsequently he was promoted to general and fought with distinction in World War I. He died in Paris in 1934.

Mariner

Launched July 22, 1962
Decommissioned March 16, 1975

Mariner 10 *produced this image of the planet Venus in 1974 from a mosaic of pictures.* ➡

The *Mariner* program consisted of 10 spacecraft launches into outer space over a 13-year period. *Mariner 1* inaugurated the series in 1962; its mission was to reach the planet Venus. However, a computer error—a missing minus sign—caused the spacecraft to plunge into the Atlantic Ocean shortly after takeoff on July 22, 1962.

Mariner 2 was launched on August 27, becoming the first space mission to reach another planet. The 447-pound spacecraft took three and a half months to travel 35 million miles to Venus, passing as close as 22,000 miles to the planet on December 14. *Mariner 2* sent back an enormous amount of information, confirming that the planet suffers from a super greenhouse effect: it is surrounded by dense layers of gases that keep heat from escaping, with temperatures reaching almost 900°F. It also discovered that, unlike Earth, Venus has no detectable magnetic field or radiation belts. The craft lost contact with the Earth on January 3, 1963.

The United States Mariner *program sent space probes to Venus, Mars, and Mercury to collect scientific data.*

Mariners 3, 4, and 5

With Mars—also known as the Red Planet—as its destination, the next *Mariner* was launched on November 5, 1964. The mission had to be canceled, however, because *Mariner 3* was unable to jettison, or release, the cover that protected the spacecraft during launch. *Mariner 4* was launched about three weeks later, on November 28, taking seven and a half months to travel the 325 million miles to Mars. The craft came within 6,118 miles of the Red Planet on July 14-15, 1965. As *Mariner 4* made a loop around Mars, the camera on the spacecraft took 19 printable pictures. The photos showed a pockmarked surface with no unusual features, but later probes found that this was far from the truth.

Mariner 5, the second American probe to Venus, was launched on June 14, 1967, two days after the Soviet Union's *Venera 4,* which was also studying Venus. *Mariner 5* made its closest approach on October 19, 1967, at a distance of 2,480 miles. It transmitted excellent pictures of the planet's upper atmosphere but none of its surface. The previous day, however, the Soviet spacecraft had landed and sent back invaluable data.

Mariner 6 and 7

The next American missions to Mars were the twin probes *Mariner 6* and *Mariner 7.* The two spacecraft each weighed 910 pounds and carried the same instrumentation. Launched on February 24, 1969, *Mariner 6* flew by the planet on July 31. *Mariner 7* was launched on March 27, but it was programmed for a shorter trajectory and made its closest approach on August 5, 1969. *Mariner 6* flew by the equator of Mars, coming within 2,120 miles of the planet's surface. *Mariner 7* flew over the Southern Hemisphere slightly farther out. Since the photographic equipment on these spacecraft was better than that on *Mariner 4,* distinctive features of the planet became apparent: the polar ice, giant craters, and evidence of erosion by wind and water. These data indicated that Mars may once have been more Earthlike, with flowing water and volcanic activity.

Mariners 8 and 9

The United States sent another set of twin probes to Mars in May 1971 to take advantage of the period when Earth and Mars were closest to each other. Although the rocket carrying *Mariner 8* malfunctioned on takeoff and the spacecraft plunged back to earth, *Mariner 9* was one of the most successful of all the *Mariner* flights. Launched on May 31, 1971, *Mariner 9* traveled to Mars in only 167 days, arriving there on November 13. After traveling 248 million miles, the spacecraft reached the planet 4.4 seconds ahead of schedule. Entering Martian orbit, it became the first spacecraft to orbit another planet. The Soviet Union's *Mars 2* followed two weeks later.

Mariner 9 reached Mars in the middle of a giant dust storm. It was not until January 1972 that the storm subsided and the spacecraft's cameras were able to transmit pictures of the surface of the planet. *Mariner 9* orbited Mars for 349 days—much longer than the originally planned 90 days—making 698 orbits and transmitting its last signal on October 27, 1972. During that time, *Mariner 9* took 7,329 photographs and was able to map the entire surface of the planet. It found a giant crater 10 miles high and a 2,500-mile canyon much deeper than the Grand Canyon, which was named Valles Marineris in honor of the spacecraft. *Mariner 9* confirmed that water had once flowed on the planet but found no signs of recent geological activity. The spacecraft also took photos of Mars's two small moons, Deimos and Phobos.

Mariner 10

After the success of *Mariner 9,* the next launch was directed toward the inner planets of the solar system—Venus and Mercury. *Mariner 10* took off from the Kennedy Space Center on November 3, 1973. It weighed 1,108 pounds, 170 pounds of which were measuring devices and instruments. These included two television cameras equipped with ultraviolet filters and instruments to study infrared and ultraviolet radiations and magnetic fields. The cameras took a total of 3,500 photographs of Venus, the first ever made.

Mariner 10 *took this photograph of the planet Mercury as it was leaving orbit.*

En route to Venus, *Mariner 10* had been commanded to make two mid-course corrections, allowing it to pass within 3,600 miles of the planet at its closest approach on February 5, 1974. Photos of the atmosphere of Venus revealed that the clouds that cover the planet are layered and have an unusual circulation pattern. Unlike the *Mariner 2* spacecraft, *Mariner 10* was able to detect a slight magnetic field around Venus. A previous Soviet discovery—that the atmosphere of Venus consists largely of carbon dioxide—was confirmed.

Mariner 10, as it flew by Venus, increased its speed by the planet's gravitational field. The flight was designed to send the spacecraft around the Sun at the exact speed needed to meet Mercury in the same spot every time the planet completed one revolution. This required exact precision because at their nearest approaches, the Earth and Mercury are 57.5 million miles apart. Theoretically, these rendezvous may last forever, but *Mariner 10* stopped transmitting signals after meeting Mercury on March 29, 1972, on September 21, 1974, and on March 16, 1975. The fate of the spacecraft is unknown.

Mariner 10 began taking photographs of Mercury when it was still three million miles away. It took a photo every 42 seconds during the time it approached and then sped away from the planet, eventually taking almost 2,000 pictures. *Mariner 10* revealed that the surface of Mercury is riddled with craters of all sizes, which were created by collisions with meteors. No evidence of any volcanic activity or atmosphere was detected, although there are a few helium atoms. The most obvious feature was a gigantic basin surrounded by tall mountains. The basin was named Caloris, from the Latin word for "heat," because it is in the hottest part of the planet. *Mariner 10* ended the *Mariner* program with spectacular photos of a small planet so distant that it is hard to find with a telescope on Earth.

Beryl Markham

Born October 26, 1902,
Leicester, England

Died August 3, 1986,
Nairobi, Kenya

Beryl Markham spent most of her life in Kenya, a country in eastern Africa, where she was well known for her career as a bush pilot and for her success as a breeder and trainer of racehorses. She was also famous for her record-breaking, though near fatal, solo flight from London to Nova Scotia in 1936. Markham wrote a book about her adventurous life that became a best-seller.

Born in 1902 in Leicester, England, Markham (then Beryl Clutterbuck) was just three years old when her parents moved to Kenya. Kenya had come under British control in the late 1800s, and after the turn of the century many Englishmen established farms there. The highlands offered a pleasant climate and productive soil for growing such tropical crops as coffee. The European farmers prospered over the years and, as more and more settlers arrived, they were able to establish a comfortable life-style in Kenya.

Beryl Markham, a pioneer aviator, was the first person to fly solo across the Atlantic Ocean from London to North America.

Early interest in horses

Markham's father cleared land and started a farm at Njoro, about 70 miles from Nairobi, the new capital of Kenya. After trying to raise various crops, he discovered his true talent as a horse breeder and trainer. Horse racing was a popular sport and social activity among the colonists, and Markham's father began to supply horses for the Nairobi racetracks. Markham spent her childhood on the horse farm, learning to speak several African languages from the families her father employed. She also learned to hunt wild game with a spear, and her father taught her how to ride a horse. In the course of her adventurous childhood, she was attacked by a "pet" lion and once killed a deadly black mamba snake.

As a young woman, Markham started a career of her own as a horse trainer. She was so successful that one of her horses won the most prestigious racing prizes in Kenya when she was only 24. This success helped her to become one of the most socially prominent young women in Nairobi. She met a wealthy young Englishman named Mansfield Markham, whom she married in 1927. The Markhams then moved to England, where Beryl gave birth to a son, but within a short time the marriage ended, and Markham returned to Kenya alone.

First female commercial pilot

Back in the colony Denys Finch Hatton, a well-known big-game hunter, took Markham flying in his airplane. Thrilled by the experience, she decided to learn how to fly a plane herself. Shortly after she began taking lessons, Finch Hatton was killed in a crash, an event that seems to have increased Markham's determination to become an aviator. Within just a few months Markham received her pilot's license, and she then became the first woman in Kenya to receive a commercial pilot's license. Embarking on a career as a bush pilot, she flew alone delivering supplies, passengers, and mail to the remote, or "bush," regions of the country. Since there were no airfields in Kenya, Markham landed her plane in forest clearings or fields.

Daring solo flight

When Markham had been licensed for less than a year, she undertook a daring solo flight to England. She left Nairobi in a single-engine, 120-horsepower airplane that had no radio, no direction-finding equipment, and no speedometer. On the first day she flew northeast to Juba, a town in the Sudan, but was forced down a short distance from the airport by a storm and engine trouble. The next day she flew to Malakal on the Nile River. She tried to reach Khartoum, the capital city of the Sudan, on the following day but made it only halfway before the plane's engine failed. Landing in the desert, she repaired the engine as best she could. Local people helped her push the plane to harder sand, where she took off again and made it to a nearby airfield. The next morning Markham flew on to Khartoum, but the engine died twice along the way. In Khartoum it was discovered that the engine had a cracked piston ring. She was unable to get spare parts there, so she flew on to Atbara, where she replaced the piston.

When the engine continued to malfunction, Markham was forced to land outside Cairo, Egypt, in the middle of a dust storm that was so severe she could not see the ground as she was landing. After the British Royal Air Force repaired the engine for her, she flew on across the Mediterranean Sea, wearing an inner tube around her neck as a lifesaving device. Although bad weather plagued her flight across Europe, she finally landed safely in London. Her flight from Kenya had taken 23 days.

Return to England

After years of bush flying in Kenya and locating big game by air for safaris, Markham returned to England, where she hoped to win one of the big prizes that were being offered for record-breaking achievements in aviation. She had originally thought of competing in a race to South Africa with a former flying instructor, Tom Campbell Black, but decided instead to try for the prize of flying solo from London to New York. Such a flight had never been accomplished because it meant flying against the prevailing winds. In the Northern Hemisphere the jet stream travels from west to east.

When **Charles Lindbergh** (see entry) made his solo flight across the Atlantic, he had the wind pushing him on. Other aviators had attempted to make the flight from east to west but had fallen short of the mark. In 1932 Jim Mollison had flown from Ireland to eastern Canada; in 1934 John Grierson had flown the whole distance, but his trip took six weeks because he made four stops along the way.

Markham's aim was to fly nonstop from London to New York in order to show that commercial air service between the two cities was possible. For the trip she borrowed an airplane—a single-engine Vega Gull with a 200-horsepower engine—that could fly up to 163 miles per hour and that was fitted with extra tanks so it could travel 3,800 miles without refueling. The plane had no radio equipment, however, so contact with Markham would be impossible once she took off. Markham left London at 8:00 P.M. on September 4, 1936, facing a strong head wind, low clouds, and blustery weather. She was seen over Ireland at 10:25 P.M.; at 2:00 the next afternoon she was spotted by a ship in the Atlantic; and at 4:35 P.M. she was reported to be flying over the tip of Newfoundland, the easternmost part of North America. Then she disappeared.

First transatlantic solo flight

A telephone call from a small town in Nova Scotia finally brought news of the aviator. She had survived her trip, but the plane had crash-landed in a peat bog. With the nose of the plane stuck in the mud, she had climbed out and greeted two fishermen by saying, "I'm Mrs. Markham. I've just flown from England."

Her flight across the Atlantic had almost ended in tragedy when the fuel line to one of the plane's tanks froze, causing the engine to fail and the plane to fall toward the ocean. Just before Markham reached the sea, the line warmed up and the gasoline started to flow again, allowing her to pull the plane up to safety. It was another frozen fuel line that caused her to crash in Nova Scotia.

Disappointed that she had not managed to fly all the way to New York City, Markham was afraid the flight would be considered a failure. In fact, news services carried the report

Did Markham actually write *West with the Night?*

According to *The Lives of Beryl Markham,* a biography by Errol Trzebinski (Norton, 1993), Markham did not write *West with the Night.* The real author was her third husband, Raoul Schumacher, who was a writer and journalist. Trzebinski interviewed friends of Markham who said that when the book was published they assumed she had not written it. She never showed any interest in writing, they say, and she did not even like to read; in fact, she began writing the book only after she met Schumacher.

Markham's friends recall Schumacher and Markham saying they were writing the book together; much of the manuscript, which Markham kept all her life, was in her husband's handwriting. Further proof is the book itself. It contains literary references that only Schumacher could have made and inaccurate descriptions of flying that Markham would not have put in her narrative.

Why, then, did Markham not tell the truth? Her friends think she may have intended to reveal Schumacher as the actual author, and that might explain why she kept the manuscript. Moreover, she may have been so caught up in the book's success when it was published that she could find no graceful way to say she had not written it. As many people have commented, however, the question of who actually wrote *West with the Night* may be irrelevant, since the book continues to be a classic account of growing up in Kenya.

throughout the world, and she was hailed as a heroine. In Nova Scotia a U.S. Coast Guard plane met her, and she co-piloted it to New York, where she met Mayor Fiorello LaGuardia and rode in a motorcade through the city. Markham returned to England to find she had become a celebrity. She lived there for the next few years but did not take up flying again. Although she talked about entering another of the great air races, her interest seems to have faded after her friend Campbell Black was killed in the race to South Africa.

Best-selling book

In 1939 Markham moved to the United States. For some time there were plans to make a movie about her famous flight across the Atlantic. While the film was never made, she received an offer to write about her experiences. Her book, *West with the Night,* was published in 1942 and was favorably received. After reading it, the American writer Ernest Hemingway said, "She can write rings around all of us who consider ourselves writers." Appearing on 13 best-seller lists after it was published, *West with the Night* tells the story of Markham's childhood in Kenya, her unconventional career as a bush pilot, and her pioneering transatlantic flight. Eventually sales began to decline, and the book was forgotten.

For a number of years Markham lived in California, where she remarried and ran an avocado ranch. In 1952 she returned to Kenya and took up the career she had started thirty years before—raising and training horses. From 1958 to 1972 she was the most successful trainer in Kenya, winning all of the major racing prizes and becoming a local legend. During Markham's final years she once again become a well-known personality. *West with the Night* was republished, becoming a best-seller, and she was the subject of a television documentary. She died in Kenya in 1986 at the age of 84.

Abu al-Hasan 'Ali al-Mas'udi

Born c. 895,
Baghdad, present-day Iraq

Died 957,
Egypt

Al-Mas'udi's accounts of his travels provide valuable information about the geography, history, and local customs of the places he visited. A man of many interests, he also wrote about science, literature, philosophy, and religion. His book *Muruj adh-Dhahab* ("Meadows of Gold") presents a history of the world from creation to 947 A.D; his 30-volume "History of Time" has been lost.

Travels in Persia

Abu al-Hasan 'Ali al-Mas'udi, a descendant of the prophet Mohammed, was born in Baghdad. Indirect evidence suggests that he was born around 895; the earliest date appearing in his own writings is 912, which he mentions when relating an anecdote about meeting an official of the Abbasid dynasty in Baghdad. By the year 915 he was traveling east in Persia, where he passed through the provinces of Khuzestan, Ahvaz, and Fars; he visited Persepolis, the ancient Persian capital,

Al-Mas'udi was an Arab scholar who traveled extensively in the Muslim world and gave one of the first accounts of the Caspian Sea, the Aral Sea, and the lands north of the Caucasus.

Qumis, Khurasan, and Seistan. Unlike most Muslim travelers of this period, al-Mas'udi showed his intellectual curiosity by visiting the temples of the Zoroastrians, the ancient religion of Persia before it was conquered by the Muslims.

Goes to India

Later in 915 al-Mas'udi went to India where he stayed until the following year. Although his exact route is not known, evidence indicates that he took the caravan route from Khurasan to the Indus Valley. Now part of Pakistan, the Indus Valley was already settled by Muslims; however, al-Mas'udi journeyed beyond that area to the western Deccan, the central plateau of India, in what is now the region of Bombay. He visited the ports of Chaul and Kanbaya and discussed the effect of the monsoon on that part of the subcontinent. He also wrote about plants, including oranges and coconuts, and animals such as elephants, peacocks, and parrots. In writing about his visit to India, al-Mas'udi mentions China and Sri Lanka ("Sarandib"), yet it is obvious he did not visit those places, having only reported what he heard from others.

Visits island near Africa coast

After al-Mas'udi returned to Baghdad from India in late 916 or early 917, he went from Oman on the east coast of Arabia to an island off the east coast of Africa. Trade relations between Oman and East Africa dated from ancient times, but al-Mas'udi writes about the difficulty of travel between the two places, giving a long list of shipwrecks and drowned persons. On his return from Oman, al-Mas'udi went back to Baghdad where he seems to have stayed for several years. There is no record of his activities until 918; however, according to accounts of the following ten years he traveled in Iraq, Syria, and the Arabian Peninsula. He was in the Syrian city of Aleppo in 921 and from there went to the Mediterranean. In 925 he was in northern Iraq in Tikrit (the hometown of Saddam Hussein).

Observes several religions

In 926 al-Mas'udi traveled to the southern part of Syria, or Palestine as it is known today. He states that he was in Nazareth, where Jesus Christ grew up, and also went to Jerusalem and Nablus as well as the Jordan Valley and the Dead Sea. While in Palestine al-Mas'udi visited Christian churches and talked with Jewish and Christian scholars. He also learned about the Samaritans, a small Jewish sect who had remained in Palestine through the centuries while rejecting much of contemporary Jewish tradition, including the Torah.

While visiting Damascus in Syria in 927, al-Mas'udi saw the ruins of the great cities of Palmyra and Baalbek. He also met the Sabians, another ancient Middle Eastern sect bypassed by Judaism and Islam. On his return to Iraq in 928, al-Mas'udi sailed down the Euphrates River from Syria. During his trip he witnessed the siege of the western Iraqi city of Hit by the Carmathians. In 930 he paid another visit to Ahvaz and Fars in Iran.

Writes about inhabitants of Caucasus

At about this time—after 932 and before 941—al-Mas'udi traveled to the Caspian Sea and Armenia. He was the first person to give a written description of the Aral Sea. When he sailed across the Caspian, he observed that contrary to current belief this body of water was not part of the Black Sea. He also collected extensive information about the non-Muslim peoples who lived in the Caucasus Mountains and to the north, passing on some of the earliest knowledge about the Khazars, Bulgars, and Russians.

Writes his great work

In about 941 al-Mas'udi went back to Arabia, probably as part of the pilgrimage to Mecca that Muslims try to perform during their lifetime. He visited both Medina and Mecca, journeying as far south as San'a in Yemen. In January 942 he was in Egypt, where he observed the Christian festival of the

Epiphany celebrated by the Coptic Christians of Egypt. Later that year he was in Antioch in northern Syria; in 946 he traveled to Damascus. Starting from the time he was in Egypt, he began drafting his great work of travel and geography, *Meadows of Gold*. He also drafted a highly accurate map of the world: it shows the Atlantic and Indian oceans connected to the south of Africa, the Nile Valley is in its correct position, the Indus and Ganges rivers in India are also properly located, Sri Lanka is off the southeast coast of India, and the two great inland seas, the Caspian and the Aral, are correctly positioned. In his final years, al-Mas'udi traveled back and forth between Syria and Egypt. He died in Egypt in 957.

Robert McClure

Born 1807,
Wexford, Ireland

Died 1873,
London, England

S ir Robert McClure was the first man to confirm the existence of the Northwest Passage, a route between the Atlantic and Pacific oceans that had eluded explorers for centuries. McClure made his discovery while in the process of searching for the party of **John Franklin** (see entry), which had disappeared in the Canadian Arctic during Franklin's own quest for the Northwest Passage. McClure's ship was frozen in the ice for three winters and he had to abandon it when a rescue team finally arrived. Although he was later censured for not returning with his ship, he received a knighthood for his discovery of the Northwest Passage.

Robert John Le Mesurier McClure was born in Wexford, Ireland, and educated at Eton, an English private school, and at Sandhurst, the British military academy. He entered the Royal Navy in 1824. He first traveled to the Arctic in 1836-37 as mate on the *Terror* under the command of Sir George Back on an expedition to Hudson Bay and the Melville Peninsula. On his return to England in 1837 McClure was promoted to

Sir Robert McClure was a British naval officer who was sent on the search for Sir John Franklin and discovered the Northwest Passage north of the American continent.

the rank of lieutenant. He then served on British ships in the Great Lakes and in the Caribbean for the next ten years.

Conducts Franklin search missions

In 1848 McClure was chosen to be an officer on the first ship sent out to look for the missing Franklin expedition, serving under Sir James Clark Ross, who discovered the North Magnetic Pole in 1829. After finding no trace of Franklin they returned to England in the fall of 1849. On a second attempt to find Franklin, McClure was appointed to command the *Investigator* under the general command of Captain Richard Collinson, who sailed on the *Enterprise*. This time they proposed to solve the mystery of Franklin's disappearance by attacking the problem from the opposite side—from the Pacific Ocean and Alaska.

The *Investigator* and the *Enterprise* left England together on January 10, 1850, but were separated by a storm in the Pacific Ocean soon after they had passed through the Strait of Magellan. As McClure's ship headed through the Pacific, it was hit by a sudden storm that knocked down all three masts. When McClure brought the *Investigator* into the harbor at Honolulu, Hawaii, on July 1, 1850, he learned that Collinson had sailed from there only the day before.

Does not follow orders

By cutting through the Aleutian Islands rather than following his instructions and sailing west of them, McClure reached Bering Strait between Alaska and Siberia before Collinson. For reasons that have since caused much speculation, he had not waited for his superior but had set out on his own. McClure's goal was to reach Melville Island in the northwestern Arctic, which had been visited by the British explorer William Edward Parry as early as 1819.

After ramming the *Investigator* through one patch of pack ice, McClure's party had to use five rowboats to tow the ship past Point Barrow. Forced by the pack ice of the Beaufort Sea to travel eastward along the coast of Alaska to the

Mackenzie delta, they turned northward east of the Mackenzie. They reached the south shore of Banks Island, which had been spotted from the north by Parry, who named it in honor of **Joseph Banks** (see entry), president of the Royal Society.

Investigator iced in

Off the east coast of Banks Island, McClure saw a channel, later named Prince of Wales Strait, which offered a clear stretch of water leading to the northeast. As he sailed up the strait he realized that if this body of water connected with Melville Sound, which had already been sailed by Parry, he would have found the long-sought-after Northwest Passage.

By then, however, it was getting late in the year. On September 17, 1850, at a point about 30 miles from Melville Sound, McClure was forced to stop by the increasing ice and rising winds. Strong gales pushed the *Investigator* 30 miles farther back down the channel. The expanding ice finally toppled the ship on its side, threatening to crush it against the rocky coast. Convinced they were doomed, the crew broke out the store of alcohol. On September 28, however, the storm died and the ship righted itself. It then remained iced in for the winter.

Finds Northwest Passage

The following October, McClure took seven companions and headed north over the ice in sledges. On the fifth day, they reached the north end of Banks Island. About a week later they climbed a small mountain and looked out on Melville Sound—McClure and his men had found the Northwest Passage. On the return trip, McClure ran ahead of the rest of his crew. He got lost and arrived at the ship barely alive after a sleepless night of fighting his way through a storm.

The *Investigator* stayed locked in the ice during the winter of 1850-51. During that time, McClure sent out three land parties to try to find traces of the Franklin expedition, but without any success. In the summer of 1851 he tried once again to sail through Prince of Wales Strait into Melville

Sound; this time he was stopped by ice 25 miles short of his goal. Next he decided to sail south and try to get around Banks Island from the west side. Initially he made very good time—300 miles in three days. Then, on August 20, 1851, the ship became stuck in the ice once again. It was wedged in a small channel of open water too narrow for turning around, so McClure continued north for another week. Once the ship sailed around the northern end of Banks Island into Melville Sound it was again stopped by ice.

Situation becomes critical

McClure found a small harbor on the north coast of Banks Island, which he named Mercy Bay, and stayed there during the winter of 1851-52. While his men spent their time hunting, McClure took a small party north to Melville Island, hoping to find another of the ships sent out to search for Franklin. He did find a note from Francis McClintock, the leader of the other search party, who had been on the island the previous June.

During the summer of 1852, McClure tried to free the *Investigator* from the ice that blocked Mercy Bay, but to no avail. By September it became obvious that they were going to have to spend another winter in the Arctic; food supplies, unfortunately, were beginning to run dangerously low. Two of the junior officers showed signs of insanity, and 20 men were ill with scurvy, a disease caused by lack of vitamin C in the diet. The following spring, McClure proposed to split his crew into different groups to try to get help overland.

Help arrives

In the meantime, the British government had sent out ships to look for McClure and Collinson, who had also disappeared. In September 1852 Captain Henry Kellett found a note on Melville Island that McClure had left five months previously, indicating his location. Since his ship was also iced in by the winter, Kellett could not go look for McClure until the following spring. On April 6, 1853, shortly before he was to send out his land parties, McClure and his first officer were walking on the beach discussing the burial of a crew member who had died of scurvy. They looked up to see a strange man running down the beach toward them. It was Lieutenant Bedford Pim, an officer from Kellett's ship who had been sent to fetch them.

Finally goes home

At first, McClure refused to abandon the *Investigator,* and three more men died while waiting for supplies. When only four men volunteered to stay with him, McClure was forced to give up and leave the ship in Mercy Bay. Once his men reached Kellett's ship and crowded on board, it was too late in the year to depart. The following year, on the orders of Sir Edward Belcher, they abandoned Kellett's two ships and used supply ships to sail back to England via Baffin Bay. They arrived home in September 1854, more than four years after they had left.

McClure was given credit for discovering the Northwest Passage, even though he had not been able to navigate it. Although he was censured for not returning with his ship, he was promoted to captain, knighted, and awarded £10,000. The journal of his voyage was edited and published in 1856. McClure served in the Pacific Ocean from 1856 to 1861; after that tour of duty he returned to the Admiralty Office in London. He was promoted to rear admiral in 1857; he became a vice admiral in 1873 shortly before his death.

Fridtjof Nansen

Born 1861,
Oslo, Norway

Died 1930,
Oslo, Norway

Fridtjof Nansen was a Norwegian explorer who led the first expedition across Greenland and made a famous voyage to the Arctic that came closer than any previous attempt to reaching the North Pole.

Fridtjof Nansen was born in the Norwegian capital of Oslo, then known as Christiania. His mother, Adelaide, was a baron's daughter who eloped with a baker's son and had five children. When he died, she married a lawyer, Baldur Nansen, and had two more sons, of whom Fridtjof was the older. Nansen grew up on the couple's farm outside of Oslo and loved the outdoors, spending much of his free time camping and skiing. He attended the University of Christiania and majored in zoology. One of his professors there suggested that a trip to the Arctic on a sealing ship would be a worthwhile experience. Nansen sailed aboard the *Viking* for six months in 1882. While the ship was caught in the ice pack off the east coast of Greenland for 24 days, Nansen developed the desire to explore the great island.

Plans trip to Greenland

When he returned to Oslo, Nansen became the curator of

natural history at the Bergen Museum in Norway's second-largest city. He took some time off to study marine zoology in Naples, Italy, in 1886. On his return from Italy, he worked on a plan to cross Greenland from east to west. He traveled to Stockholm to consult with the Swedish explorer A. E. Nordenskiöld, who had attempted a Greenland crossing in the opposite direction in 1883. After receiving financial backing from a Danish financier, Nansen recruited a small crew made up of two Lapps and three young Norwegians, including Otto Sverdrup. They trained during the winter of 1887-88 in the mountains outside of Bergen. A few days before departing, Nansen defended his doctoral thesis at the university; the expedition then set out for Greenland in May 1888. Since they traveled on a sealing schooner that spent most of its time hunting seals, they did not reach the east coast of Greenland until July 17.

Leads first crossing of Greenland

The sealing ship let Nansen and his colleagues off at sea two miles from Cape Dan. As they rowed their small boats ashore, they were hit by storms; over the next two weeks ice floes forced them 300 miles south. Once they reached the shore they rowed 200 miles back north, a trip that took them another two weeks. Arriving at Umivik Fjord on August 12, 1888, they set out overland three days later. The first part of the trip was the worst—they had to climb up the rocky mountains that ring the east coast of Greenland to an altitude of 7,930 feet before they reached the interior plateau.

By the time Nansen and his men crossed over the coast ranges, they had used up all of their water. They were able to obtain water by melting snow in tin flasks they had put under their clothing to warm with their own body heat. The going was easier when they came to an inland plain on September 2 and could use their skis. By the middle of September they had reached the highest point at 8,920 feet; a few days later they sighted the peaks of the west coast of Greenland.

As the men ran down the mountain in their excitement, they almost fell into a giant snow crevasse; their progress was slowed by a large field of such crevasses. They arrived at the edge of the ice field on September 25. Nansen and Sverdrup built a small boat to float down the Ameralik Fjord 60 miles to the Danish settlement of Godthåb. The remainder of the party walked along the shoreline. When Nansen reached Godthåb on October 3, 1888, the Danish official in charge greeted him by saying, "Allow me to congratulate you on taking your doctorate." Nansen and the members of his expedition were the first Europeans—and perhaps even the first humans—to cross Greenland.

Devises unique plan

During the course of the expedition Nansen invented the Nansen sledge, a kind of sled on narrow runners that was used in many later polar explorations; he also designed the Nansen cooker, an efficient alcohol-fueled stove. Nansen was able to send word of his accomplishment back to Europe, but it was too late in the year for the party to travel back themselves. They spent the winter in Godthåb, where Nansen used the occasion to study the local Inuit. When the explorers finally returned to Oslo, they were welcomed as national heroes. Soon thereafter Nansen married Eva Sars, an opera singer and the daughter of one of his zoology professors; they were happily married for many years.

While he was in Greenland, Nansen had noted that the native Inuit made tools from driftwood that came from Siberia and Alaska. This observation led him to think about the forces of the currents in the Arctic Ocean, especially in regard to the American ship *Jeannette,* commanded by George Washington De Long, which had broken up in the ice north of Siberia in 1881. Three years later wreckage from the ship came ashore in southwestern Greenland on the Arctic Ocean. Nansen used this as evidence for his idea that the currents in the Arctic would be strong enough to carry a ship to the North Pole simply by drifting.

Tests plan

Nansen's plan was well received in Norway and he was able to get money to test his theory from many supporters, including the king of Norway. With this money Nansen built a ship called the *Fram* ("Forward"), which he designed to resist the pressure from the ice that covered the northern ocean. The *Fram* left Norway on June 24, 1893, rounding North Cape at the northernmost tip of Europe and heading east along the Siberian coast. The ship stopped briefly to take 34 Siberian dogs on board, then continued north.

The *Fram* ran into the ice pack on September 20; by September 27 it was completely frozen in and remained there for the next 35 months. By December the pressure of the ice threatened to crush the little ship, but Nansen's ingenious design allowed it to lift itself out of danger. Later a large chunk of ice raised above the surface threatened to override the *Fram* and force it down below the surface, but once again it escaped. During this long period the men on board occupied themselves making scientific observations, but life was inevitably very boring.

Sets farthest-north record

In the spring of 1895 the ship, which was still about 350 miles away from the North Pole, broke free of the ice and started heading west. Realizing he would never reach his goal by depending on the currents alone, Nansen set off overland by sled on March 14 with dog teams and one companion, Hjalmar Johansen. Nansen's plan was to reach the North Pole in 50 days. They traveled until April 8 when long ridges of ice prevented them from going any farther; however, they had gone 160 miles farther north than any previous explorer and were only 240 miles from the Pole.

When Nansen and Johansen turned back they headed for the group of islands known as Franz Josef Land, but a navigational error took them off course. As they went farther south the weather became warmer with the onset of summer and the ice began to break up, making travel increasingly difficult. As the two men became progressively weaker they were forced to kill their dogs for food. On July 24 they saw the north coast of Franz Josef Land and on August 7 they reached the edge of the ice. They were able to build a boat with which they sailed into the open seas.

Rescued by British party

At the end of August Nansen and Johansen made a camp on an island, where they spent the entire winter in a small hut. They survived on bear meat. As it happened, an English expedition under the command of Frederick Jackson had also been camped on the same island during the winter. On June 17, 1896, Nansen heard dogs barking. As he reports in his book, *Farthest North*, he started following the sound then heard a shout:

> Soon I heard another shout and saw a man.... We approached one another quickly. I waved my hat; he did the same. I heard him speak to the dog, and I listened. It was English.... It was sometime before the English explorer, Frederick Jackson, said: "Aren't you Nansen? ... By Jove! I am glad to see you!"

On August 7, 1896, Nansen and Johansen sailed in one of the English ships back to Norway. A week later the *Fram* arrived; the ship had continued to float west and was finally freed from its ice trap north of Spitsbergen. Nansen and his party returned to Oslo to a tumultuous welcome. Among the well-wishers was Nansen's three-year-old daughter Liv, whom he had never seen. The explorers were honored at a state banquet by King Oscar of Sweden and Norway.

Becomes great humanitarian

Neither Nansen nor the *Fram* had reached the North Pole, yet the expedition provided important information about the Arctic Ocean and the Arctic regions. For instance, Nansen discovered that a frozen lake surrounds the North Pole; his research on oceanography, meteorology, diet, and nutrition also prepared the way for future Arctic explorers. He published *Farthest North,* an account of his adventures, in 1897; six volumes of scientific reports appeared from 1900 to 1906. Nansen started the Nansen Fund, a foundation that would enable him to continue his scientific research; he was also appointed professor of zoology and then oceanography at the university in Oslo.

He continued to study oceanography and made several important scientific expeditions to the North Atlantic.

When Norway separated from Sweden in 1905 Nansen became his country's first ambassador to Great Britain. After World War I he worked with famine victims in Russia and he helped prisoners of war return to their home countries. In 1921 he was appointed the United Nations high commissioner of refugees; the following year he received the Nobel Peace Prize.

U.S.S. *Nautilus*

Launched January 21, 1954
Decommissioned 1980

The U.S.S. Nautilus was the first nuclear-powered submarine and made the first trip under the Arctic Ocean and the North Pole.

As the first nuclear-powered submarine (also called an atomic submarine), the U.S.S. *Nautilus,* unlike conventional submarines, could sustain submersion for prolonged periods. The *Nautilus* was also larger than any submarine up to that time, measuring 319 feet in length and weighing 3,180 tons. With propulsion turbines driven with steam produced by an atomic reactor, the vessel was capable of speeds exceeding 20 knots (20 nautical miles per hour), which could be sustained almost indefinitely. When the *Nautilus*—which shares the name of Captain Nemo's submarine in Jules Verne's science-fiction novel *Twenty Thousand Leagues under the Sea*—made the historic voyage under the North Pole, it set standards for future nuclear submarine performance. The voyage was also an important event in the history of the nuclear navy, producing public relations benefits as well as scientific results.

First endurance test fails

The U.S.S. *Nautilus* was launched on January 21, 1954.

From a defense point of view, the advantage of nuclear-powered submarines was their ability to remain submerged much longer than conventional diesel-powered submarines. Thus they were much more difficult to detect. In order to test the *Nautilus*, the navy gave it a mission of traveling all the way under the polar ice of the Arctic Ocean.

The first attempt was made in August 1957 when the ship entered the Greenland Sea between Greenland and Spitsbergen and made three probes toward the North Pole. It reached within 180 miles of the Pole before being forced to turn back because an electrical power failure closed down the master gyroscope, which was needed for navigation.

Second attempt made

The *Nautilus* again went to sea in June 1958. Under the command of William R. Anderson the submarine approached the Pole from the Pacific side, which is more difficult because

The U.S.S. Nautilus is towed past the San Francisco skyline on May 28, 1985, while a navy helicopter hovers overhead. The vessel is on its final voyage to the navy museum in Connecticut.

there are thick ice jams in the bottleneck between Alaska and Siberia. The *Nautilus* had to submerge in fairly shallow water at a depth of only 160 feet because ice had formed in the Chukchi Sea. Since the average depth of the ice was only 10 feet, there was plenty of room for the ship to maneuver. However, it unexpectedly encountered a tongue of ice reaching 62 feet deep, which it cleared by only 8 feet.

Anderson had lowered the submarine to a depth of 140 feet, only 20 feet above the ocean floor, when suddenly they encountered another ice tongue that was 85 feet deep. It cleared the top of the ship by a mere 5 feet. Since there were 300 miles of shallow seas ahead, the captain decided to turn the submarine back rather than risk disaster. The *Nautilus* returned to its base at Pearl Harbor in Hawaii.

Secret mission undertaken

On July 22, when ice conditions were more favorable, the submarine embarked once again. Its mission was secret: the families of crew members thought the *Nautilus* was headed on a routine training run to Panama. After pulling out of Pearl Harbor, the ship went underwater and headed north. Traveling at more than 20 knots, it reached the Aleutian Islands on July 26. When the ship entered the Bering Sea the water became much more shallow, as little as 80 feet, requiring Anderson to reduce the speed to 10 knots. Crossing the Arctic Circle at 6:25 A.M. on July 29, the submarine passed the point where it had run into ice the month before; it came up to periscope depth so that the officer in charge of the watch could search for ice. Encountering the first ice in the early morning of July 30, the ship surfaced so crew members could get a better look; they went up on deck and took a chunk of the ice as a souvenir.

Searches for passage under ice

Still on the surface of the ocean, the *Nautilus* began a 24-hour search for a passage under the ice, where water was at least 300 feet deep and therefore safe. When no passage could be found the submarine turned east along the northern coast of

Alaska as far as Point Barrow. Soon Anderson located a tongue of the Barrow Submarine Canyon, where the water reached depths of 420 feet. This was the ship's passageway to the north.

Reaches the North Pole

At 5:00 A.M. on August 1, the *Nautilus* submerged and headed north. The next day it crossed a 9,000-foot underwater mountain range that had never before been recorded. At 10:00 A.M. on August 3 the submarine passed 87°N, the farthest point ever reached by a ship. The *Nautilus* arrived at the North Pole at 11:15 P.M. on August 3, 1958. In celebration the crew deposited mail in the shipboard post office to be stamped "North Pole."

Receives national recognition

From the North Pole, the *Nautilus* headed south toward the channel between Greenland and Spitsbergen, where the Gulf Stream pushes the ice much farther north. Reaching the edge of the ice at 5:12 A.M. on August 5, Anderson sent radio messages back to the United States to report that the mission had been successfully completed. Near Iceland a helicopter escorted Anderson from the ship back to Washington. The *Nautilus* sailed on to England, where the crew was greeted with much fanfare. The trip had been one of the major experiments in proving the value of the nuclear submarine. Since the *Nautilus* voyage, atomic submarines have achieved submerged speeds of over 30 knots and have circumnavigated the globe without surfacing.

The *Nautilus* was decommissioned in 1980; five years later it was put on exhibit at the U.S.S. *Nautilus* Museum and Submarine Force Museum in New London, Connecticut.

Vasco Núñez de Balboa

Born 1475,
Jerez de los Caballeros, Spain

Died January 1519,
Santa Maria la Antigua del Darién, Panama

Vasco Núñez de Balboa, a Spanish explorer, crossed the Isthmus of Panama and became the first European to see the Pacific Ocean from its eastern shore.

L ike most explorers of his time, Vasco Núñez de Balboa came to the New World in search of riches. He was successful, though he soon fell into poverty and eventually met a violent end. When Balboa climbed a mountain to view the Pacific Ocean for the first time, he was reportedly accompanied by only his dog, Leoncico.

Expedition to the New World

Balboa was born at Jerez de los Caballeros, a town in the Spanish province of Extremadura. Coming from a family of impoverished gentry, he served as a page to a Spanish nobleman, Don Pedro Puertocarrero. In 1501 he left Spain with the expedition of Rodrigo de Bastidas, who had been inspired by reports from **Christopher Columbus** (see entry) that pearls could be found on the northern coast of Venezuela.

The expedition was a success. Bastidas and Balboa were able to trade their European goods for a large quantity of pearls and gold. They then sailed west from the Gulf of Mara-caibo to the mouth of the Magdalena River in what is now Colombia. Farther west they found a harbor they named Carta-gena, which was later to become the main Spanish port in northern South America. They continued to follow the shore-line until it turned southward to the Gulf of Urabá, located on the northwestern coast of present-day Colombia. When their ship began to take on water, they headed north to the island of Hispaniola. They were forced to abandon the ship on its south-ern coast, however, and their goods were confiscated by the governor of the island. Balboa was left penniless.

Balboa tried to make a living as a farmer in the new Spanish colony of Santo Domingo, which is now the Domini-can Republic, but he was unable to pay his creditors. In 1510, in an attempt to escape his situation, he stowed away with his dog, Leoncico, on board a ship in Santo Domingo harbor. The ship turned out to be one of two commanded by Martín Fer-nandez de Enciso, who was taking relief supplies to the settle-ment of San Sebastián on the Isthmus of Darien, now called the Isthmus of Panama. San Sebastián had been founded by **Alonso de Ojeda,** a Spanish adventurer, who had relinquished command of the garrison to **Francisco Pizarro** (see separate entries), another Spanish explorer. Once he had been discov-ered on the ship, Balboa proved to be a great help to Enciso, who turned out himself to be an ineffective leader.

Balboa's leadership of the expedition

Upon reaching San Sebastián, the Enciso party found that it had been burned down by native people. Balboa then con-vinced the group to follow him to the Gulf of Urabá, which he had seen on his earlier expedition. Near a native village they founded the town of Santa Maria de la Antigua del Darién. After a quarrel with Enciso, Balboa arrested Enciso and sent him back to Spain. Balboa himself then assumed the offices of captain-general and governor.

Balboa ventured into the neighboring region of Coiba. He befriended a local chief, Careta, and married the chief's daughter. Balboa arranged an alliance between the Spaniards and Comogre, another powerful chief. Comogre's oldest son saw how avid the Spanish were to find gold, and he offered to lead them to the other side of the peninsula if they would help defeat one of his tribe's enemies. The Spanish agreed and, under Balboa's command, set out with 190 Spanish soldiers and 810 Native Americans. On September 1, 1513, they sailed across the gulf to the Isthmus of Darien.

Part of Balboa's expedition remained behind while he led a group through some of the roughest terrain and densest rain forest in the world; even today there is no road that traverses this region. Unlike other Spanish *conquistadors,* Balboa had befriended the native people and treated them well. Several of the natives therefore went with him on his journey across the isthmus. On the way Balboa's party fought enemy tribesmen in the Sierra de Quareca; they massacred 600 of the tribesmen and destroyed their village.

First sighting of the Pacific Ocean

Many of the Spanish soldiers were ill, so Balboa set out from the village with a small party of 67 to cross the mountains in the center of the peninsula. Legend has it that on the morning of Sunday, September 25, 1513, accompanied by only his dog, Balboa climbed a peak and became the first European to look out on the Pacific Ocean from its eastern shore. The other Spaniards, including Pizarro, then joined him. Erecting a pile of stones and a cross, they knelt and sang a Catholic hymn of thanksgiving. They marched to the ocean shore and formally took possession of it in the name of King Ferdinand and Queen Isabella of Spain. Twenty-six of the men witnessed this act on September 29, St. Michael's Day, and Balboa named the place Bahía San Miguel (St. Michael's Bay).

The Spanish spent a month on the Pacific shore collecting gold and pearls and visiting the Islas de las Perlas, or the Pearl Islands, in the Caribbean Sea. Crossing the isthmus by another route, they conquered more native chiefs and took even more gold. They reached the settlement of Darién on January 19, 1514, without the loss of any Spanish lives.

Balboa's violent end

Upon his return, however, Balboa learned that back in Spain Enciso had made unfavorable reports of his actions and that King Ferdinand was sending out a new governor, Pedro Arias de Avila. When Arias de Avila arrived, he developed an intense hatred toward Balboa and spent several years spinning plots against him. In the meantime, Balboa had crossed the Isthmus of Panama. He had also built a fleet of four ships, with which he intended to sail south to Peru. Finally able to make up convincing charges against Balboa, Arias de Avila sent Pizarro to arrest him. In January 1519 Balboa was tried and convicted of treason and publicly beheaded.

Peter Skene Ogden

Born 1794,
Quebec, Canada

Died September 27, 1854,
Oregon City, Oregon

Peter Skene Ogden was a Canadian fur trapper and trader who made five extensive expeditions throughout the American West; he was the first to cross the West from north to south.

Peter Skene Ogden became an explorer as a result of his work as a fur trader for the Hudson's Bay Company. Known for his ruthless and brutal dealings with Native Americans, he could speak several native languages. Since he could also speak French fluently, he was known among the trappers as "Monsieur Pete." He was married to two Native American women and had children with both of them. In 1853, the year before his death, he anonymously published a book about his experiences called *Traits of American-Indian Life and Character.*

Ogden was born in Quebec City in Canada. Ogden's parents were natives of the United States who went to Canada during the American Revolution because they supported Britain. When Peter was four years old, his family moved to Montreal, where his father was appointed a judge. Montreal at that time was the center of the fur trade in North America. There was bitter competition between the Hudson's Bay Company, controlled from London, and the Montreal-based North

West Company. Unlike his brothers, who followed their father into the legal profession, Peter entered the fur trade as an employee of the North West Company in 1809; he was stationed at Ile-a-la-Crosse.

Gains reputation for violence

Ogden quickly gained a reputation for being one of the most violent and ruthless of all the traders engaged in a notoriously cutthroat business. He was accused of a number of crimes that culminated in March 1818 when he was indicted for the murder of a Native American who traded with Ogden's rival, the Hudson's Bay Company. In order to put him out of the reach of the law, the North West Company sent Ogden to its most remote posts in what is now the Pacific Northwest of the United States.

Unfortunately for Ogden, the two rival fur companies decided that their competition was only helping their American rivals and in 1821 they decided to unite under the name of the Hudson's Bay Company. Ogden was so hated by the directors of the Hudson's Bay Company that one of the provisions of the agreement was that he was not to be employed by the joint company. Having no means of support, Ogden traveled to Montreal and then to London to try to convince the company to rehire him.

Sent to Spanish territory

At about this time, the Hudson's Bay Company sent out George Simpson to take charge of its posts in territory that is now Oregon, Washington, Idaho, and British Columbia. This area had been claimed by both Great Britain and the United States; the dispute was not to be settled until 1846. Directly south was Spanish territory that was just then coming under the control of the new Republic of Mexico. Simpson felt that if Britain was to prevail it would have to make use of its most ruthless men, including Ogden; under Simpson's influence, the company agreed to reemploy Ogden. In 1824 Ogden was instructed to travel to the Snake River country in present-day Idaho.

On December 20, 1824, Ogden left Flathead House at Flathead Lake in northern Montana with a party of 58 people. Near present-day Missoula, Montana, he met the famous American trapper **Jedediah Smith** (see entry); they joined forces for the next two months, trapping as far south as the Bear River in southeastern Idaho. When they parted Ogden journeyed farther south, where one of his men sighted the Great Salt Lake from a mountain peak, probably the second time it had been seen by Westerners. Ogden's party camped at Mountain Green east of the Great Salt Lake. In May 1825 a larger party of American trappers arrived at the camp. They attacked Ogden and took all the furs he had collected and persuaded most of his trappers to leave with them. After this misfortune Ogden returned to the British post near Walla Walla in Washington the following November.

Makes important discoveries

During the winter and spring of 1825-26 Ogden trapped in the Snake River country as far east as the Portneuf River in eastern Idaho near present-day Pocatello. He then returned to Walla Walla. In 1826, after only two months of rest, he returned to eastern Oregon to the Malheur River. He then traveled to the Klamath River in northern California, where he saw and named Mount Shasta, the tallest peak in the Cascade Range, before turning back north. In the region around Goose Lake on the California-Oregon border, the only thing that was available to drink was liquid mud. Ogden wrote, "This is certainly a most horrid life."

Sometime during 1827, while he was in the territory that is now Utah, Ogden discovered the river that was later named for him. In 1828-29 he went south into Nevada, becoming the first Westerner to see the Humboldt River, which rises on the western slope of the Rockies and disappears in the Humboldt Sink east of Reno. This was later to be one of the main routes west for American pioneers headed to California. In his diary at this point Ogden made the cryptic but disturbing notation: "280 Indians camp attacked."

Leads final expedition

Ogden's widest-ranging expedition was his last. Leaving the Columbia River in October 1829, he went south to the Humboldt Sink where he had been the previous year. After he and his men had a clash with the local Native Americans, they moved out of that area to the southwest. Along the route they discovered Carson Lake in western Nevada. As they continued southwest they came to the Sierra Nevadas, the great range that extends through eastern California. Ogden and his men are credited with having been the first to explore the eastern face of the Sierras Nevadas.

Ogden led his party south until they reached the Colorado River. They were very likely the first Westerners to have approached the river from the north. They visited the Mojave tribe near present-day Needles, California, where Jedediah Smith had been in 1827. Ogden then ordered an exhausting march across the desert. At one point they had to eat their dying horses for food and drink the horses' blood to keep from dying of thirst. In a clash with the Mojave, Ogden and his men killed 26 Mojave warriors.

Makes first crossing of West

Leaving the desert, Ogden and his party followed the Colorado south all the way to the Gulf of California; they became the first Westerners to cross the American West from north to south. Heading back north, Ogden led his men through Cajon Pass near San Bernardino, California, into the San Joaquin Valley. Avoiding the Mexican mission stations, he reached northern California, then took his previous trail north from Klamath Lake. As they were crossing the Columbia River near The Dalles, Oregon, one of the boats capsized, drowning nine men; all of Ogden's records of his monumental last trip were lost.

Goes to British Columbia

On his return to Walla Walla in July 1830, Ogden was ordered to head north to what is now British Columbia. He established a Hudson's Bay Company post at the mouth of the Nass River, near the present-day border of southern Alaska. In 1834, after successfully fending off competition from Americans and Russians, he was made director of all of mainland British Columbia for the Hudson's Bay Company. It was about this time that Simpson wrote of him that he was "one of the most unprincipled Men in the Indian Country ... madness to which he has a predisposition will follow as a matter of course." However, Ogden's "unprincipled" behavior seemed to suit the fur-trading frontier because he continued to prosper and the company continued to promote him.

Spends final years in American territory

After spending a year's furlough in England in 1844, Ogden returned with a secret British surveying team that was tracing a route from eastern Canada to the Columbia River as part of the negotiations between Britain and the United States over the Oregon Country. The team's work was discontinued in 1846, however, when a British-United States settlement extended the 49th parallel boundary all the way to the Pacific, thereby giving Washington and Oregon to the United States.

Ogden and the Hudson's Bay Company remained in the newly created American territory pending the arrival of an effective American government. In December 1847 Ogden became a hero when he led a team that negotiated the release of American prisoners taken by members of the Cayuse tribe after they had attacked a mission station near Walla Walla. Known as the Whitman Massacre, it had been a brutal attack in which the missionary Marcus Whitman, his wife, and 12 other mission workers were slain by the Cayuse. Ogden spent his last years at Fort Vancouver, Washington. In August 1854, after becoming ill, he traveled to the American settlement of Oregon City to seek medical help. He died there at the age of 64.

Alonso de Ojeda

Born 1465,
Cuenca, Spain

Died 1515,
Santo Domingo

Alonso de Ojeda was born in the Spanish city of Cuenca in the province of Castile. He came from an aristocratic family and served in the household of an important nobleman, the Duke of Medina Celi. He fought with the Duke in the last campaign to drive the Muslims out of Granada in southern Spain. In 1493 Ojeda commanded one of the ships in the second expedition **Christopher Columbus** (see entry) led to America. During this voyage Ojeda took part in campaigns against the Native Americans and he went on exploring expeditions into the interior of the island of Hispaniola.

Alonso de Ojeda was a Spanish adventurer who explored along the northern coast of South America and founded a colony in Colombia.

Leads expedition to South America

Upon his return to Spain, Ojeda became associated with **Amerigo Vespucci** (see entry), for whom the Americas were later named, and Juan de la Cosa, who produced one of the first maps of the Americas. Ojeda was able to obtain financing for a fleet of four ships to sail to South America. Cosa served as pilot and Vespucci commanded two of the vessels. The party left Cadiz sometime between May 16 and 20, 1499. The voyage violated the monopoly that King Ferdinand had granted to Columbus; the expedition even used a copy of Columbus's map. It is thought that Ojeda's fleet reached land in modern Suriname. Vespucci then headed to the southwest toward Brazil while Ojeda traveled north and westward.

Visits Caribbean and South America

Ojeda made his first landing on Trinidad, where the Spaniards clashed with the Caribs, who inhabited many of the islands of the Caribbean. Leaving Trinidad, Ojeda sailed through the Gulf of Paria and landed on the mainland of the continent. When he visited Margarita Island he recognized the potential for a commercial pearl fishery in the area. After his ships touched at the island of Curaçao, Ojeda sailed to Lake Maracaibo on the mainland. Finding Native American villages on stilts, which reminded him of Venice, he named the area "Venezuela," or little Venice. Ojeda then proceeded as far as La Guajira in the country that today is Colombia; his ships arrived in Hispaniola on September 5, 1499. The party stayed in Hispaniola for nearly a year before returning to Spain with a cargo of pearls, brazilwood (used for making dyes), and Native American captives to be sold as slaves.

Founds first Spanish colony on mainland

In 1501 Ojeda requested permission to make another voyage to the Western Hemisphere. The king gave his assent, naming Ojeda governor of Coquivacoa, the local name for the area around Lake Maracaibo. He was authorized to take as many as ten ships to America to cut brazilwood. In the end, he was able to raise enough money to outfit only four. Ojeda's party sailed from Cadiz in early January 1502, reaching the Gulf of Paria in early March. One of the ships was wrecked; another went to Jamaica for supplies. When the Spaniards were reunited, they decided to make a base camp by attacking and capturing a Native American village.

Arrested and sent back to Spain

Ojeda and his men thus established the first Spanish colony on the mainland of America on the Guajira Peninsula. The colony was immediately a failure. In May or June 1502 Ojeda's partners arrested him on charges of cheating them and brutalizing the Native Americans. The Spaniards abandoned their settlement and went to Santo Domingo, where Ojeda was tried and found guilty. The sentence was overturned, however, on November 8, 1503, after he had returned to Spain.

Commissioned to found colony

In 1504 Ferdinand authorized Ojeda to establish a colony in the Gulf of Urabá in northwestern Colombia near the Darien Peninsula, although it is unclear whether he made a voyage there. In 1508 he was named governor of the province of Nueva Andalucía, the coastline that stretched from La Guajira to the Gulf of Urabá. Stopping in Santo Domingo, Ojeda recruited 220 Spaniards, including **Francisco Pizarro** (see entry), the Spanish explorer who later conquered Peru. The ships sailed from Santo Domingo in November 1509.

Ojeda initially tried to establish his colony on the site of the modern city of Cartagena, the main port of Colombia. However, he once again became involved in a struggle with Native Americans; de la Cosa, among others, was killed on February 28, 1510. Ojeda moved on to the Gulf of Urabá, where his ship was attacked by Native Americans and he was wounded with poisoned arrows. Ojeda saved his own life by applying hot irons to his wounds. When the colony was faced with starvation, Ojeda went back to Santo Domingo to get supplies. In his absence, the colony was taken over and rescued by the Spanish explorer **Vasco Núñez de Balboa** (see entry), who relocated it to Panama during his expedition to the Pacific Ocean.

Dies in poverty

Meanwhile, Ojeda was shipwrecked on the island of Cuba while trying to get back to Santo Domingo. He undertook an epic journey along the southern coast of Cuba and over the sea to Jamaica. By the time he reached Santo Domingo, he was penniless. It is said that he lived in Santo Domingo in extreme poverty until his death in 1515; however, others claim that he joined a monastery.

Francisco de Orellana

Born c. 1490,
Trujillo, Spain
Died November 1546,
Amazon delta, Peru

Francisco de Orellana's story is an example of how an important discovery or achievement can be made as the result of an accident. Orellana was on an expedition in South America with **Francisco Pizarro** (see entry) when he became separated from the main party. Stranded on the Napo River, he drifted to the Amazon River, then floated down the Amazon to its mouth, thus becoming the first European to travel the length of the world's largest river.

Orellana was born in the town of Trujillo in the Spanish province of Extremadura; he was a relative of Pizarro. Orellana may have gone to America in about the year 1527, possibly traveling to Panama and then to Nicaragua. Accompanying Pizarro when he set out to conquer Peru, Orellana participated in battles at Lima, Trujillo, and Cuzco. He lost an eye when he was injured in a skirmish with the Incas. After the conquest of Peru, he was awarded an estate at Puerto Viejo in what is now Ecuador.

Francisco de Orellana, a Spanish conquistador, was the first European to travel down the Amazon River.

Appointed official in Peru

While he was stationed in Peru Orellana heard that Pizarro was being besieged in Lima by a force of Native Americans. He recruited a group of 80 men and rode to help defeat them. In 1538, when civil war broke out between Pizarro and Cuzco governor Diego de Almagro, Orellana took part in Pizarro's victory. As a reward for his services, he was made lieutenant governor of Guayaquil; he refounded the city of Puerto Viejo on the site of the present-day city of Guayaquil.

In 1540 Pizarro's brother Gonzalo left Quito with a large force of Spaniards and Native Americans in search of cinnamon, a valuable spice that was rumored to grow on the eastern slopes of the Andes. When Orellana heard about the expedition, he resigned his office in Guayaquil and gathered a group of 23 men to join Pizarro. By the time they reached Quito, Pizarro had already left. When Orellana and his men caught up with the larger force in Zumaco in March 1541, Orellana was named second-in-command of the expedition.

By the time the expedition reached eastern Ecuador and discovered the Napo River, one of the headwaters of the Amazon River, the men were lost, exhausted, and hungry. As an eyewitness put it, the difficulties were "such that anyone but Gonzalles Pizarre would have abandon'd such an Enterprize as seem'd to be opposed by both Heaven and Earth."

Becomes stranded on Napo

Pizarro decided to build a boat to carry the weaker members of the party and to look for food farther downstream. The work took two months. When the boat was completed, it was launched on the Napo River, with Orellana in charge. According to the accounts left by both parties, this arrangement was made by mutual consent, and when Orellana took leave of Pizarro on January 1, 1542, he clearly planned to return. However, the fast-flowing rivers quickly carried Orellana's boat downstream through an area where they saw no signs of human habitation; finally he and his men realized they would

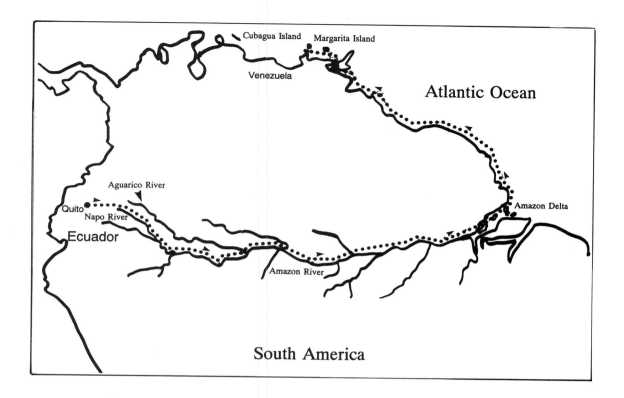

never be able to row back up the river. When the remainder of Pizarro's expedition concluded Orellana's party was missing, they had no choice but to return overland to Quito. Pizarro then wrote a letter to King Charles I of Spain, bitterly accusing Orellana of desertion.

Reaches Amazon

Meanwhile, Orellana had sailed down the Napo to where it met the Aguarico River, which he reached on February 2, 1542. Along the way he and his companions had stopped in Native American villages where they were well received and were given food. Continuing on, they reached the main stream of the Amazon River on February 11. They stayed for awhile in a village called Aparia where they had plenty to eat and started work on a new, bigger boat.

The records of Orellana's journey were kept by Gaspar de Carvajal, a Dominican friar. He recorded that one day while

During his journey down the Amazon River, Orellana reportedly saw native female warriors, whom he called "Amazons"; within a few years the world's greatest river was known as the "River of the Amazons."

they were in Aparia four very tall and light-skinned men, dressed in gold, arrived in the village. The men stayed for a short while and then left. It was the first mention in European literature of "White Indians," about whom there were to be persistent rumors over the centuries but of whom no trace has ever been found.

Leaving Aparia on April 24, the Spaniards entered the domain of the Machiparo. These people were not friendly, and from that point on Orellana and his men had to fight many battles as they made their way down the river. On June 3, they passed the point where another large river joined the Amazon, and its dark waters did not mingle with the brown Amazon for many miles. They named it the Rio Negro, which is the name it still has today.

Sees "Amazons"

Shortly after passing the junction of the Madeira River, the Spaniards were once again attacked. This time the Native American warriors included women. Carvajal immediately labeled them "Amazons," the name given by the ancient Greeks to the mythical women warriors of Scythia. Carvajal described the Amazons as being light-skinned and very tall and robust and armed with bows and arrows. This story created quite a stir when it was published in Europe, and within a few years the world's greatest river became known as the "River of the Amazons."

Orellana reached the mouth of the Amazon on the Atlantic Ocean on August 26, 1542. From there, the Spaniards in their two boats headed northwestward along the coast of Guiana and eventually reached the island of Cubagua near Margarita off the coast of Venezuela. Many of the men returned to Peru, but Orellana went back to Spain, where he arrived in May 1543.

Returns to Amazon

Orellana made a personal report of his expedition to King Charles I. He asked to be named governor of the territories that he had found; his request was granted in February 1544. The king authorized Orellana to lead a colonizing expedition to the Amazon, but he was required to finance the venture himself. During his stay in Spain, Orellana married Doña Ana de Ayala, who came from a good family but had no money. Her lack of a dowry did not help Orellana, who was having difficulty finding the money he needed to finance his expedition.

Having finally raised sufficient funds, Orellana left Spain for the Amazon on May 11, 1545, with a fleet of four vessels and about 300 to 350 men. The ships were in poor condition and there were fewer men than he had wanted. Stopping in the Canary Islands and the Cape Verde Islands along the way, Orellana and his party did not reach the Amazon until the end of December. During the voyage half of the men had either died or deserted, and one of the ships had disappeared in the mid-Atlantic.

Once they had reached the Amazon, Orellana went upstream with one of the ships and a boat. After the ship was wrecked the survivors divided into small groups; some of the men were able to reach Cubagua. Orellana did not return safely, however; sometime during the month of November 1846 he died from fever while traveling in the complicated waterways of the Amazon delta.

Mungo Park

Born September 10, 1771,
Foulshiels, Scotland

Died March or April 1806,
Bussa, Africa

Mungo Park, a Scottish doctor, was the first European to see the Niger River and return to tell about it. He died on a second expedition.

In 1788 the Association for Promoting the Discovery of the Interior Parts of Africa, or the African Association, was founded in London by the famous scientist **Joseph Banks** (see entry). The immediate goal of the organization was to reach the Niger River and determine which way it flowed. The African Association sent out two explorers in its first year, Simon Lucas and John Ledyard, but they both died within a short time of their arrival in North Africa. In 1791 a third explorer, Daniel Houghton, was killed in the country that is now eastern Senegal. Following Banks's recommendation, the association selected a Scottish doctor, Mungo Park, to make the next attempt.

Park was born in the village of Foulshiels near the town of Selkirk in Scotland on September 10, 1771. He was the seventh of 13 children of a tenant farmer, known in Scotland as a crofter. Park took courses in anatomy and surgery at the University of Edinburgh but never graduated. When he left school he went to London where he stayed with a sister and her husband, James Dickson, an amateur botanist who was acquainted with Banks. Through that contact, Park got a job in 1792 as a ship's doctor on a trading vessel bound for Sumatra in the East Indies. Park was very interested in natural history and brought back a collection of botanical specimens that he presented to Banks. Impressed, Banks nominated Park to be the next explorer sent out to find the Niger.

Goes to Africa

Park was interviewed and accepted by the selection committee, which consisted of Banks and one other member, on July 23, 1794. He intended to leave immediately for the Gambia River on the west coast of Africa in the company of the new British consul. But that official kept delaying his departure so long that Park finally set out on his own in May 1795. A month later he reached a trading post at Pisania on the Gambia, where he spent the rest of the year learning Mandingo, the local language. In December, at the beginning of the dry season, Park left Pisania accompanied by a guide, a servant, and four porters.

His initial route generally followed that of Houghton. He journeyed northeast to Medina, the capital of the Kingdom of Woolli, where he was well received by the king. However, the king of neighboring Bondou was more suspicious, and Park appeased him by presenting him with his umbrella. When Park entered lands that were Islamic he began to experience outright hostility because he was a Christian. He passed through the town of Simbing, where Houghton had written his last letter. At the nearby town of Jarra, he learned about the circumstances of his predecessor's death. Also at this point, all of his attendants except for a young slave named Demba deserted him. On his way through the town of Deena, where he arrived on March 11, 1796, he was spit at on the streets.

Park continued on alone, heading north. At the town of Benown he was imprisoned by the local king, Ali, for a month in a mud hut. Attacked by neighbors, Ali and his men left the town, taking Park with them. Along the way, he was subjected to more mistreatment. His captors would not even give him water, and he was forced to drink out of the cattle trough. At the end of June 1796 Park was able to escape with his horse in a crowd of refugees fleeing the fighting. Robbed of his cloak by a gang of robbers, he had to beg to survive. He almost perished of thirst on several occasions. Once he was saved by a rain squall: he drank the water that he wrung out of his clothes.

Eventually Park reached the Bambara country, where the people were friendlier. As he approached the capital of Segou, he saw "with infinite pleasure the great object of my mission—the long-sought-for, majestic Niger, glittering to the morning sun, as broad as the Thames at Westminster, and flowing slowly *to the eastward*." Park had found one of the great missing links in European knowledge of Africa.

Park visited and was impressed with the magnificence of the city of Segou, which had 30,000 inhabitants. The king of Segou refused to receive him but gave him 5,000 cowrie shells, the local medium of exchange, to help him on his way. Park wanted to continue down the Niger to the fabled city of Timbuktu. But he was only able to cover a short distance—to Sansanding and Silla. There, sick and with no resources, on July 29, 1796, he decided he would have to turn back. Returning via Bamako, the present-day capital of Mali, which he passed on August 25, Park was attacked by robbers who left him with nothing but a shirt, a pair of trousers, and the hat where he had stuffed his notes. At that point, he almost gave up. However, his strong religious faith kept him from despair: "I started up, and disregarding both hunger and fatigue, travelled forwards, assured that relief was at hand: and I was not disappointed."

In the next town, Park was treated with kindness and recovered part of his clothes. On September 16 he met a slave trader named Kafra who agreed (for a price to be paid on arrival) to take Park with him along with the column of slaves he was leading to the coast. They waited for the end of the rainy season, leaving the town of Kamalia on April 19, 1797. There were 35 slaves in the column, bound together by ropes around their necks and fetters on their feet. During the march, two of the women committed suicide by eating clay. They reached Pisania on June 11, 1797, and Park paid Kafra with cloth he got from Dr. Laidley. He then found passage to the Caribbean as the ship's doctor on an American slave ship. During the crossing of the Atlantic, 11 of the 130 slaves died.

Returns to England

In Antigua, Park was able to get a ship back to England, arriving in London on December 25, 1797. No one in England even knew that he was still alive. Since he did not want to disturb anyone on Christmas morning, he wandered the empty streets. He came to the gardens of the British Museum and found one gate open. Going inside, he stumbled upon Dickson, his brother-in-law, who was out tending to some gardening chores.

Park was warmly received in London and wrote a book about his African experiences that became a best-seller. On May 25, 1799, he attended a meeting of the African Association at which Banks proposed that Great Britain should take advantage of Parks's journey to send an army to conquer the Niger. It was the first public call for British imperialism in Africa. In the summer of 1799 Park returned to Scotland and took up residence in the small town of Peebles, where he started a medical practice and married the daughter of one of his college professors. He became the neighbor and friend of the famous writer Sir Walter Scott. He was troubled by recurring illnesses from his trip to the Niger and nightmares about being captured and tortured.

Park grew bored with his medical practice, telling Scott that "he would rather brave Africa and all its horrors, than wear out his life in long and toilsome rides over the hills of Scotland, for which the remuneration was hardly enough to keep body and soul together." The British government wanted to send out an expedition to show the flag as a counter to the French in Senegal and to further explore the Niger. When offered the chance to lead this expedition, Park accepted and was given the temporary rank of lieutenant in the British army.

Back to Africa

Park arrived on the Gambia on April 6, 1805, with a force of about 40 Europeans, including 30 soldiers from a British garrison at Goree, an island off the coast of Senegal that had been taken from the French. Park hired an English-speaking Mandingo named Isaaco to serve as guide. The expedition set out from Pisania on May 4, just before the start of the rainy season. By the time the rains started on June 10, two men had already died, and half of the others were sick. When they reached the Niger at Bamako on August 19, only seven Europeans were still alive. The rest had died from malaria and dysentery.

In spite of this disaster, Park insisted on continuing. He hired canoes at Bamako to take the rest of the expedition downstream. On August 26 he came down with dysentery himself. At Sansanding he was met by emissaries of the king of Segou. Park told them that he planned to sail all the way down the Niger to the sea. If he found the way, then he would open up direct trade relations with the Africans, bypassing the Arab middlemen. With this news, the king sent two (broken) canoes for the Europeans. After working 18 days to repair them and join them together, Park launched the vessel as His Majesty's Schooner *Joliba* (an African name for the Niger). While he was doing this, his wife's brother, Alexander Anderson, died, leaving Park with four soldiers, three slaves, and a new guide, Ahmadi Fatouma. Park wrote a letter home from Sansanding on November 19, 1805, and sent it back to the coast with Isaaco.

That was the last word that was ever heard from Park. Five years later, the British government hired Isaaco to go into the interior to try to find out what had happened to him. In Sansanding, Isaaco met Fatouma and got the story. Park and his men had proceeded on their way by using their firearms to force their way down the river, rather than negotiating passage with the local rulers. They passed Kabara, the river port five miles from Timbuktu, but were not allowed to proceed up the canal to the famed trading center. Park sailed around the great 300-mile bend of the Niger past the city of Goa.

In March or April 1806, Park and his remaining men reached the small Hausa state of Yauri, about 600 miles from the Gulf of Guinea and 1,500 miles from Bamako, his starting point. Park sent Fatouma to the local king with a number of gifts. According to Fatouma, the king found the gifts inadequate, and the next morning he ordered his men to attack the *Joliba* at the Bussa rapids. When they were fired upon and realized they could not prevail, Park and the remaining soldiers jumped into the river and were drowned. Only one slave survived and made it to Yauri to tell the story to Fatouma.

Although there are discrepancies in Fatouma's story, it is the most complete account anyone has ever been able to get. Isaaco brought this story back to the coast, and it made its way to England. Park's wife refused to believe it, however, and died in 1840 thinking her husband might still be alive in Africa. One of their three sons, Thomas, a midshipman in the Royal Navy, was given three years' leave in 1827 to search for his father. He died of fever on his way into the interior from the port of Accra. Two Niger explorers, Hugh Clapperton and Richard Lander, traveled to Bussa and Yauri in 1825 and heard stories about Park's death. Lander returned in 1830 and recovered a gun and a robe that had belonged to Park. He lost them during his own adventurous journey. He also saw a nautical almanac that contained Park's writing. This was recovered in 1857 by Lieutenant John Glover and is now in the museum of the Royal Geographical Society in London.

Edward Parry

Born 1790,
Bath, England

Died 1855,
London, England

Sir Edward Parry, a British Arctic explorer, was the first person to find the entrance to the Northwest Passage and then set a record for traveling farthest north.

William Edward Parry was born the son of a doctor in Bath, England. After an education in a private grammar school, he joined the Royal Navy in June 1803 as a volunteer on the *Ville de Paris*. He served on several ships that saw active duty during the Napoleonic Wars, including the protection of British whaling ships north of Norway. In 1810 he was promoted to the rank of lieutenant; three years later he was assigned to *La Hogue,* which was stationed at Halifax, Nova Scotia. He remained in North America, serving on various ships until 1817.

Joins Arctic expedition

On his return to England, Parry, who came from an influential family, arranged to meet **Joseph Banks** (see entry), the president of the Royal Society, Britain's major scientific association. He also met an official in the British admiralty, John Barrow, who was the leading supporter of Arctic exploration at the time. Parry presented Barrow with a volume on navigational astronomy he had written. As a result of these contacts, in 1818 he was given command of the *Alexander* on an expedition led by John Ross to the Arctic in search of the Northwest Passage.

The expedition was not a success. Ross and Parry quarreled because Parry had wanted to explore farther into Lancaster Sound, which he thought might lead to the Northwest Passage, and Ross wanted to turn back. After the party returned to England the matter was presented to the British admiralty, which decided in Parry's favor and asked him to lead another expedition to Lancaster Sound. Parry left England on May 4, 1819, with two ships, the *Hecla* and the *Griper,* under his command. At the same time **John Franklin** (see entry) was sent overland through northern Canada to try to find the Northwest Passage from the landward side.

Heads own expedition

The *Hecla* and the *Griper* arrived at the entrance to Lancaster Sound the following July. Parry's party was very lucky—weather conditions were unusually warm and the ice was abnormally thin. As the ships passed through Lancaster Sound, Parry was able to prove that it did in fact lead westward. During his explorations Parry discovered and named Melville Island—for the First Lord of the Admiralty—as well as the Parry Islands; he also named Barrow Strait for his patron. At Viscount Melville Sound the party encountered pack ice, but a lookout on the *Hecla* was able to spot an area of thinner ice that the ships could break through. In September of 1819 the *Hecla* reached 110°W longitude, an accomplishment that made the crew eligible for a £5,000 bounty established by the British Parliament.

By now the Arctic winter had set in. Parry sighted a small harbor on the south coast of Melville Island; however, it took the crew three days to saw a channel through the ice so the two ships could enter the haven, which Parry named Winter Harbour. As a result of Parry's foresight the crew stayed relatively well disciplined and healthy in spite of the bitter cold, which they were not well equipped to handle. Parry had brought a supply of lime juice and tinned vegetables so his men would not suffer from scurvy; he also organized work projects as well as amateur theatricals, sporting events, and a ship newspaper to keep them occupied.

Sets record

As the weather began to improve, in June 1820 Parry led an overland expedition to the north coast of Melville Island to a place that he named Hecla and Griper Bay. When the ships were able to leave Winter Harbour in August, Parry sailed westward, hoping to travel all the way through the Northwest Passage. However, ice conditions were much less favorable than they had been the previous year, so he was forced to turn back.

It was not until 30 years later that **Robert McClure** (see entry) would find the way out of Melville Sound via a southwest route, thereby completing the journey through the Northwest Passage. In any case Parry had sailed 600 miles farther west than any previous navigator, setting a distance record for a sailing vessel entering the passage from the east; the record has never been equaled. The *Hecla* and the *Griper* returned to England at the end of October 1820 with the loss of only one life. Parry became a national hero.

Returns to explore passage

Encouraged by his success, Parry set out for the Arctic again the following year. This time he wanted to test his theory that the Northwest Passage could be found farther south, on the northwest corner of Hudson Bay. He left England in May of 1821 with two ships, this time with the *Hecla* and a new ship, the *Fury*. He sailed to Foxe Basin, west of Baffin Island, which had been found 200 years earlier by the English navigator Luke Fox. Parry sailed to the west side of the basin to investigate Frozen Strait and Repulse Bay, which were first seen by Europeans in 1742 and which seemed to offer the most likely route west. Finding a dead end, Parry moved up the east coast of a peninsula that he named for Melville until he was forced to stop to put in at Winter Island in October.

During the winter the Englishmen became friendly with a band of Inuit, and Parry learned some of their survival techniques. He also looked carefully at their maps to see if he could find a way west. In May he began sending out land expeditions, but they had no success in locating a route. After spending three weeks cutting a passage through the ice, the *Hecla* and the *Fury* left Winter Island in July 1822. They sailed north of the Melville Peninsula to a small island named Igloolik. Discovering a narrow passageway between Baffin Island and the mainland, Parry named it Fury and Hecla Strait. The party waited all summer for the ice to melt, but when it remained frozen they were forced to anchor for the winter at Igloolik.

During an 11-month stay at Igloolik Parry and his crew learned more about the Inuit; in fact, Parry wrote some of the first anthropological descriptions of his hosts. When summer came the ice still had not broken. By then the crew was sick and provisions were low, so Parry decided to abandon his efforts to push farther west. They left Igloolik for England in August 1823.

Makes second unsuccessful mission

Parry was ill for several weeks after arriving in London; he also became depressed when he learned that during his absence his fiancée had left him for someone else. But he continued to be highly favored by the navy and was given the post of chief hydrographer. He discussed the results of the expeditions made by Franklin, who had traveled down the Coppermine River all the way to the Arctic Ocean. Realizing the narrow Fury and Hecla Strait was always likely to be blocked by ice, Parry concluded that the only way to approach the Northwest Passage was to sail around the north end of Baffin Island through Prince Regent Inlet on the west side of the Melville Peninsula. This is in fact the only navigable route for a small ship, and it was the route followed by the Norwegian explorer **Roald Amundsen** (see entry) from 1903 to 1905 when he became the first person to navigate the Northwest Passage successfully.

The British admiralty sponsored Parry on an expedition to test his new theory. Sailing again with the *Hecla* and the *Fury,* he left England on May 8, 1824. Ice was very heavy that year, so his party made slow progress. By the second week in September they had gone only as far as Lancaster Sound. They forced their way into Prince Regent Inlet and anchored in a small harbor on the northwest coast of Baffin Island; the ships did not leave the harbor until July of the following year. As they sailed north around Baffin Island it looked as though the warm weather would finally break up the ice. But on July 30 they were hit by a storm that grounded the *Fury* on a beach; the ship was severely damaged. After being hit by further storms and traveling ice floes, which also damaged the *Hecla,* the *Fury* had to be abandoned on August 23. Parry's expedition was therefore forced to return to England; they reached London in October 1825.

Goes to North Pole

Once he was back home Parry went through another period of depression. His condition improved, however, when he married Isabella Stanley, the daughter of a wealthy and socially prominent family in October 1826. In the meantime, to compensate for the failure of his last two expeditions, Parry had proposed another voyage, this time to the North Pole. Accompanied by James Clark Ross, who would later discover the North Magnetic Pole, Parry took the *Hecla* to the Spitsbergen Islands north of Norway. The two men left Spitsbergen on June 21, 1827, riding north on a boat with runners that was pulled by 12 crew members. This turned out not to be a good way to travel, however, because they were able to cover only 178 miles in two months. Yet Parry's brief trip still set a polar record of 82°45' that was not beaten for another 50 years. During this and other Arctic voyages Parry was responsible for inventing and devising several pieces of equipment and techniques that benefited future generations of explorers.

Honored for achievements

As a result of his expeditions, Parry received many awards and medals. He had been promoted to the rank of commander in 1820 and to captain the next year. In 1829, following his return from Spitsbergen, he was knighted. That same year he resigned his naval commission to become head of a company that was promoting British emigration to the Australian colony of New South Wales, where he stayed for five years. In 1837 he returned to work with the British admiralty, becoming comptroller of steam machinery. In 1847 he was appointed superintendent of a hospital in London, and in 1852 he was given the honorary title of rear admiral. Shortly before his death in 1855 Parry was appointed lieutenant governor of Greenwich Hospital.

Robert Edwin Peary

Born May 6, 1856,
Cresson, Pennsylvania

Died February 20, 1920,
Washington, D.C.

Robert Peary was an American naval officer who led the first successful expedition to reach the North Pole.

Robert Edwin Peary was one of the most controversial of all explorers. His quest for fame motivated him to overcome severe weather and geographical obstacles to become the first human to reach the North Pole. Peary was born in Cresson, Pennsylvania, on May 6, 1856, and grew up in Maine. He graduated from Bowdoin College in 1877. Four years later he entered the U.S. Navy as a civil engineer; from 1884 to 1885 he worked as assistant to the chief engineer on a canal survey for a proposed route through Nicaragua from the Caribbean to the Pacific. The experience seems to have whetted his enthusiasm for exploration. When he left Nicaragua, he decided to explore the Arctic, perhaps inspired by the exploits of his boyhood hero, explorer Elisha Kent Kane.

Goes to Greenland

Crossing the Greenland Ice Cap was a major goal of Arctic exploration in the 1880s. Norwegian explorer A. E. Nordenskiöld attempted the feat in 1883, then his fellow country-man **Fridtjof Nansen** (see entry) successfully completed the difficult journey in 1888. Peary made his first Arctic expedi-tion in 1886 with Danish Lieutenant Christian Maigaard. They left the west coast of Greenland on June 8, 1886, but were able to travel only 125 miles in 24 days before being forced to turn back.

Following his return from Greenland, Peary was again assigned to Central America to work on the proposed canal. As he prepared to leave Washington, he went to a store to buy a tropical pith helmet to wear on his new assignment. The clerk who waited on him was **Matthew A. Henson** (see entry), a young African American whom Peary hired to be his personal valet; the two became inseparable companions for the next 20 years. On his return from Nicaragua in 1888, Peary married Josephine Diebetsch, whom he had met at a dance in Washington six years earlier.

Proves Greenland to be an island

When news of Nansen's crossing of Greenland reached Peary, he immediately began to make preparations to cross the north end of the island. In 1891 he returned to Greenland, accompanied by Josephine, Henson, and four others, includ-ing Frederick Cook, an American physician who would become Peary's rival. The party landed at Baffin Bay on the western Greenland coast on July 27, 1891. They spent the fol-lowing 13 months in a makeshift shelter, taking measurements and studying the survival techniques of the Greenland Inuit. In April 1892 Peary traveled with a Norwegian hunter overland to the northeast coast of Greenland. They reached a peak from which they could see the ocean on July 4, 1892, thereby prov-ing that Greenland was an island and did not extend farther north toward the Pole. In addition Peary claimed to have seen a channel he called Peary Channel separating the mainland from another island, which he named Peary Land; it was many years before other explorers proved no such channel existed.

Upon his return to the United States, Peary received the acclaim he wanted, and he became convinced his destiny was

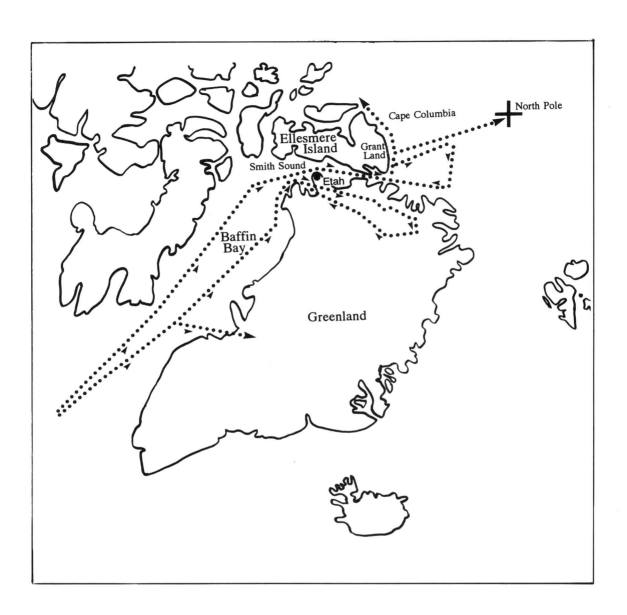

Labels on map: North Pole, Cape Columbia, Ellesmere Island, Grant Land, Smith Sound, Etah, Baffin Bay, Greenland

in the Arctic. In 1893 he returned to the same place in Greenland, where Josephine Peary gave birth to their daughter, Marie, in September of that year. The following spring Peary left the base with a party of eight on dogsleds to try to cross Greenland once again. To his frustration, a series of blizzards forced the explorers to turn back. Peary tried again, starting out in April 1895. This time he and Henson made it back to

Independence Bay on the northeast coast of Greenland, although they nearly killed themselves in their efforts.

During his summer voyages of 1896 and 1897, Peary discovered a group of meteorites in the Cape York area of Greenland. He brought them back to the United States, including one that weighed 37.5 tons, which he sold to the American Museum of Natural History for $40,000. He also brought back six Inuit people to put on display with the meteor. They all caught pneumonia and four died. One of the Inuit, who was named Minik, stayed in New York to reclaim his father's body to take back home. The story received extensive coverage in the New York newspapers.

Tries to reach North Pole

Peary now set his sights on a new goal—being the first human to reach the North Pole. He returned to the United States to raise funds. Several businessmen, most notably Morris K. Jessup, who had made a fortune in banking and railroads, formed the Peary Arctic Club in New York City to provide financial support. Peary used the money to build a base camp at Fort Conger on the northern end of Ellesmere Island in the Canadian Arctic.

Peary traveled to Fort Conger for the first time in January 1899. The rashness of making a trip in midwinter became apparent when Henson helped Peary take off his boots and a few of his toes snapped off. "My God, Lieutenant! Why didn't you tell me your feet were frozen?" asked Henson. Peary replied, "There's no time to pamper sick men on the trail. Besides, a few toes aren't much to give to achieve the Pole." Eventually, parts of seven toes had to be amputated. Peary was in pain for weeks and was lame the rest of his life. According to one story, which was possibly false, while recuperating Peary carved the Latin motto "Find a way or make one" on the walls of the cabin at Fort Conger. The following summer Peary and his men carried 14 tons of supplies to the camp; they returned with more provisions and equipment in 1900. Peary made his first trip north in April 1901 but managed to cover only about 40 miles in eight days.

Continues efforts

Peary made his first serious attempt to reach the Pole in 1902 accompanied by Henson and several Inuit. They left from Cape Hecla at the northern tip of Ellesmere Island on April 6, 1902; after traveling only 82 miles they were forced to turn back on April 21. They were faced by heavy blizzards and shifting ice, and two wide channels or "leads" opened up along the route. Peary returned discouraged, feeling that he was too old to make the trip again and that he would have to give up. "The game is off," he wrote. But when he learned later that an Italian team had bested the previous "farthest north" record, his competitive resolve returned.

Peary learned from failure, adapting equipment to the Arctic conditions, building lighter and broader sledges that could travel better over rough ice fields. He also developed what was later called the "Peary system": sending advance parties ahead to lay down supply depots and to open up a trail and allowing the main party to spend its energy in covering distance. In 1904 Peary commissioned the building of the ship *Theodore Roosevelt* to his specifications and hired Newfound-land-born Bob Bartlett as captain.

Claims to set new record

Peary's next expedition set sail from New York on July 16, 1905, with the *Theodore Roosevelt* headed first for Greenland to pick up a party of Inuit men and women and a team of Siberian huskies. The Inuit were crucial to the success of the expedition: the men constructed the igloos to live in and the women sewed fur and hide garments to wear. Once the race for the Pole began, it was the Inuit men who bore the brunt of the "Peary system," traveling ahead to break the trail.

The *Theodore Roosevelt* fought its way through the ice of Smith Sound to Cape Sheridan on the northeast coast of Ellesmere Island, 90 miles from the base camp at Cape Hecla. The first Inuit advance parties departed on February 9, 1906, with Peary leaving on March 5. The expedition faced increasingly difficult conditions; temperatures reached the record low of -60°F, and both the rugged ice surface and the speed and direction of drift were worse than expected. On March 26, they arrived at the Big Lead, a patch of open water, where they waited a week until the weather turned cold enough to allow ice to form. Peary continued on with Henson and six Inuit. Three days later a blizzard kept them in camp for another week.

By then Peary realized he would not be able to reach the Pole and resolved to set a new farthest-north record. By his own calculations, he achieved this on April 21, reaching a new high latitude of 87°6', 36 miles farther than the Italian record yet 174 miles away from the Pole. The Peary party returned to the coast of Greenland on May 9. Peary's records of this trip and the supporting evidence are so sketchy that doubt surrounds his claim about setting the record. Since Henson had no knowledge of celestial navigation he could not confirm Peary's readings.

Competes with Cook

Peary traveled along the north coast of Ellesmere Island in the *Theodore Roosevelt,* making the first trip to its western point and along the way naming geographical features after his financial backers. He claimed to have spotted a distant land to the northwest, which he named Crocker Land after George Crocker, a director of the Southern Pacific Railroad. No such land exists.

Although Peary was well received upon his return to the United States, financing for another polar attempt was not forthcoming. His supporters apparently felt Peary's last effort had failed, and his book about the 1906 expedition sold only 2,230 copies. When Peary learned that Cook was going to make an attempt on the Pole, however, he redoubled his efforts and over the next few years was able to scrape together the needed funds.

The *Theodore Roosevelt,* once again captained by Bartlett, sailed out of New York harbor one more time on July 6, 1908, stopping at Etah, Greenland, to take on the usual complement of Inuit and dogs. While in Etah Peary heard that Cook had already headed north in March. In what later became a great source of controversy, he possibly confiscated some of Cook's supplies. The ship sailed once again to Cape Sheridan on the coast of Ellesmere Island in early September. The supply base was set up at Cape Columbia, 40 miles west of Cape Hecla, to compensate for the eastward drift of the polar ice.

Bartlett led the first advance party out of the base on February 28, 1909. Henson and three other advance teams left the next morning. Peary set out last. In total, there were 24 men, 19 sledges, and 133 dogs on the ice. The advance teams were scheduled to cover 11 miles a day, which they had great difficulty accomplishing. On the second day, they were stopped by an open channel one-quarter mile wide. The next morning the break closed enough for the men to get across by moving from one floating ice floe to the next. An even wider lead stopped them on March 5 when they were about 45 miles north of Cape Columbia. Peary was forced to wait six days for it to close up.

Sends Bartlett back to base camp

On March 31, Peary, Henson, Bartlett and some of the Inuit reached the farthest advance camp, 133 miles from the Pole. That night Peary told Bartlett he was sending him back to the base camp with some of the Inuit. Peary had decided he would continue on with Henson. Bartlett was furious, thinking he had a prior arrangement with Peary to go to the North Pole. Peary's decision is highly controversial: did he send Bartlett back because he did not want him around to verify his positions? Was he unwilling to share credit with another white man? Was it because Henson really was the better dog team driver? In any case, Bartlett turned back on April 1, and on the morning of April 2, 1909, Peary left for the final assault, accompanied by Henson, Egingwah, Seeglo, Ootah, and Ooqueah.

Reaches North Pole

Peary and his companions had five sledges and 40 dogs. They traveled the remaining distance in the amazing time of five days, averaging 29 miles a day, three times faster than any previous speed. Peary credited the unusually smooth ice for the fast time. Explorers have since found that Peary's claims were false. Further discrepancies occur in Peary's claim that he was the first person to reach the North Pole.

On the morning of April 6, 1909, Henson arrived at a spot that he calculated to be the site of the North Pole. He was alone because of the daily travel routine: Peary would leave camp two hours early to break a trail; the others would pack the camping gear, then catch up with Peary. Then Peary, who was already suffering from the leukemia that eventually caused his death, would ride in one of the dogsleds while Henson went ahead and broke a trail. Consequently Peary and Henson would not see one another until much later.

When Peary reached the site where Henson was standing on April 6, Henson announced, "I think I'm the first man to sit on top of the world." Peary was furious. He attached an American flag to a staff, then the party went to sleep. At 12:50 P.M., when there was a break in the clouds, Peary took a reading that showed they were three miles short of the Pole. After another nap Peary took a second reading; without telling Henson he set out with Egingwah and Seegloo to the spot where he thought the Pole must be.

They spent 30 hours in the vicinity of the Pole, and Henson officially raised a flag on the site Peary had identified. Whether or not it really was the Pole has since been a source of controversy. Peary took a picture of Henson and the Inuit standing in front of a large mound of ice with an American flag planted triumphantly on top. Since he was the only photographer, there is no picture of Peary at the Pole.

Sets travel record

Leaving the Pole on the afternoon of April 7, the six men had an easy return, covering the distance back to the base camp in three forced marches of about 45 miles per march, 48 hours of sledging at an average speed of about 2.8 miles per hour. This is a record that no other Arctic or Antarctic explorer has ever come close to reaching. Peary reached Cape

Columbia on April 23, only five days after Bartlett. Wasting no time, they returned to the *Theodore Roosevelt* two days later, but frozen ice kept the ship from departing south until July 17. It reached the first telegraph station on the coast of Labrador on September 6, 1909, and Peary let the world know that the Pole had been reached.

Claims doubted and confirmed

Peary's triumph was mired in controversy. Five days earlier, on September 1, Cook had announced he had reached the Pole days before Peary in April. Peary immediately challenged Cook, and a furious war of words erupted between them and their supporters. Peary's claim was accepted by the National Geographic Society, the Explorers' Club, and the Royal Geographical Society. In 1911 the Naval Affairs Committee of the U.S. House of Representatives also endorsed him and retired him with the honorary rank of rear admiral.

This dispute has never fully died out, but Cook's claim is dubious; Cook had claimed to have climbed Mount McKinley in 1906, which was proved untrue, and he had no proof to verify his journey to the North Pole. In recent years there have been two major efforts to discredit Peary's claim to being the first to reach the Pole. In September 1988 the British explorer Wally Herbert examined Peary's records and decided that wind-driven ice had pushed him to the west of the Pole. In 1989 a Baltimore astronomer made headlines by claiming that Peary, knowing he was not at the Pole, had falsified his evidence. The National Geographic Society then commissioned a study in 1990 that used photographic and other evidence to show that, within the limits of his instruments, Peary actually was at the North Pole.

Peary spent most of the following years publishing his records and defending his claims. His books about his polar journeys are *Northward over the "Great Ice," Nearest the Pole: A Narrative of the Polar Expedition of the Peary Arctic Club,* and *The North Pole: Its Discovery Under the Auspices of the Peary Arctic Club*. Peary died of leukemia in Washington, D.C., on February 20, 1920.

Annie Smith Peck

Born October 19, 1850,
Providence, Rhode Island

Died July 18, 1935,
New York, New York

Annie Smith Peck's 40-year career as a traveler and record-setting mountain climber began as a hobby and continued to within a year of her death at the age of 85. She climbed mountains throughout the world, and a peak in Peru was even named after her. Born in Providence, Rhode Island, on October 19, 1850, Peck came from a prominent New England family; her father was a successful lawyer. After working for a time as a teacher she attended the University of Michigan. In 1885 she became the first woman to be admitted to the American School of Classical Studies in Athens.

Climbs South American peak

Following her studies in Europe, Peck tried to earn her living by giving lectures on Greek archaeology. When this occupation proved unrewarding financially, she decided to switch to giving lectures on her hobby—mountain-climbing. In 1895 she became the third woman to climb the Matterhorn

Annie Smith Peck, an American traveler and mountain climber, was the first person to climb Mount Huascarán in Peru; she also set a record for reaching the highest altitude in the Americas.

in the Alps, then she went on to climb other mountains in the Alps as well as Mount Shasta in California and Mount Orizaba, at 18,700 feet the highest mountain in Mexico. Buoyed by her success, Peck resolved to climb a mountain that had never been scaled and that was higher than any man had ever climbed.

For this feat Peck chose Mount Illampu, which rises to 21,276 feet north of La Paz in Bolivia and which at that time was thought to be the highest mountain in South America. Traveling to La Paz in July 1903, Peck hired two professional guides and arranged for an American professor of geology to accompany her. The guides proved unreliable and the professor, who was not interested in the climb, became ill along the way. They were able to reach only 15,350 feet before turning back. Peck then went to Peru to climb El Misti, a 19,199-foot peak.

Attempts Illampu again

Depressed by her failure, Peck returned to New York. Yet she was determined to try again, and within a year she had obtained financial support for another expedition to Illampu. She departed on June 21, 1904, taking with her a snowsuit made out of animal skins that **Robert Edwin Peary** (see entry) brought back from the Arctic and that was donated to her by the American Museum of Natural History. Her male companion was an Austrian who had volunteered for the trip—Peck always thought she needed to be accompanied by a man, although they invariably turned out to be unsuited for the task. Climbing Illampu for the second time, she reached 18,000 feet before the pleas of the Austrian and her local guides forced her to turn back.

Not one to give up, Peck traveled to Mount Huascarán in the Andes north of Lima in Peru. She had heard that Huascarán might be even taller than Illampu, although at 22,205 feet it is actually the second-tallest mountain in South America, only 440 feet lower than Mount Aconcagua. Journeying to the city of Yungay at the foot of the mountain, she was accompanied by a young American miner she had met in Yungay as well as some men from Yungay. Almost at the outset she and the miner quarreled about the best way to make the climb, so they ended up taking separate routes. Peck was able to make it to a narrow ledge at 19,000 feet overlooking the glacier that divided the mountain into two peaks, only to descend just in time to miss being buried by an avalanche. After dismissing the miner, she tried climbing up another face of the mountain with the local guides but she was forced to turn back.

Makes two trips back to Huascarán

Peck was broke when she returned to New York. She was able to go back to Huascarán only because a magazine had given her a $600 advance to write a story about her climbing experiences. Traveling to Peru in 1906, she tried twice more—unsuccessfully—to conquer Huascarán with a local companion she called "E-," who turned out to be more useless than her previous partners. When she arrived in New York after her failed attempts, she found that the magazine loved her stories and was willing to sponsor another expedition.

Peck went back to Yungay in 1908, meeting two Swiss guides, Rudolf and Gabriel, whom she had hired for the trip. On this attempt Peck managed to climb to the top of Huascarán, but only with great difficulty. She and her guides lost most of their equipment, including the Peary snowsuit, and they were frequently in danger of sliding down the mountain. At the last minute, just as they were about to surmount the top, Rudolf ran ahead of Peck and reached the peak before her. On the trip back down the mountain Rudolf lost his mittens and suffered frostbite; he would later have part of one hand, including a finger, and half of one foot amputated.

Sets Western Hemisphere record

At the age of 58 Peck had finally conquered Huascarán. Once she had reached the top she tried to determine the mountain's height, but that was impossible under prevailing conditions. Estimates indicated that it reached 24,000 feet. If so, then Peck had set a world's record. However, her great rival,

Fanny Bullock Workman (see entry), refused to concede that Peck had beaten her because Workman had climbed to 23,300 feet in the Himalayas.

Workman went so far as to hire a team of American engineers to travel to Peru and measure Huascarán. They found that the peak Peck had climbed was the lower of the two, measuring "only" 21,812 feet. Peck had therefore set a record for the highest climb in the Western Hemisphere but not in the world. The record was to last for 26 years. Peck was given a medal by the Peruvian government, and the peak she had climbed was named Cumbre Aña Peck.

Writes and travels in last years

When Peck returned to the United States she wrote about her experiences in a book, *A Search for the Apex of America,* which was published in 1911. She went on to climb Mount Coropuna in Peru (21,079 feet); on the peak she hung a banner that read "Votes for Women." Continuing to travel extensively in South America, Peck wrote a guidebook and a statistical handbook on the continent. During 1929 and 1930 she made a tour of the whole continent, using all the commercial airlines that were then in operation and writing a book about her trip.

In January 1935 Peck started out on a trip around the world. She got only as far as Athens where, in February, she became tired while climbing the Acropolis (she was 84 years old). She returned to New York and died there on July 18, 1935.

Auguste Piccard

Born January 28, 1884,
Basel, Switzerland
Died March 24, 1962,
Lausanne, Switzerland

Jacques Piccard

Born July 28, 1922,
Brussels, Belgium

Auguste and Jacques Piccard

Auguste Piccard was born into a prominent academic family in the Swiss city of Basel. He had a twin brother, Jean, who later became an important chemist. The brothers enrolled at the Swiss Federal Institute of Technology in Zürich; Auguste studied physics and Jean chemistry. During this time Auguste, who had become interested in using balloons in experiments, participated in several research studies involving balloons. In 1919 Auguste married the daughter of a professor of history at the Sorbonne in Paris. In 1922 he was appointed to the chair of applied physics at the University of Brussels in Belgium, where his son Jacques was born the same year.

Jacques Piccard graduated from the École Nouvelle de Suisse Romande in Lausanne, Switzerland, in 1943, then continued his studies in economics at the University of Geneva. After serving in the French army from 1944 to 1945 he received his degree in 1946; he taught for two years at the university, then entered private teaching.

Auguste Piccard conducted experiments in achieving the highest and lowest altitudes reached by man. After Piccard's death his underwater research was continued by his son Jacques.

657

Auguste Piccard
Jacques Piccard

Designs special balloon

Having read the works of science-fiction writer Jules Verne as a child, Auguste Piccard was inspired to carry out some of Verne's predictions. The first was to reach the highest altitude achieved by man. He was also interested in studying cosmic rays, so he began planning an experiment that would enable him to observe the rays at an altitude above 16,000 meters.

In order to conduct his experiment Piccard would need to design a low-pressure balloon that could penetrate the potentially fatal, low-pressure isothermal layer of the stratosphere. In 1930 Piccard received funding to build the balloon, which had an airtight cabin that was equipped with pressurized air. The airtight cabin has since become a standard feature in airplanes. The balloon was also very large so it would not have to be completely filled when it ascended.

Piccard tested his balloon on May 27, 1931. Accompanied by Paul Kipfer, he reached an altitude of 51,762 feet (15,781 meters); they were the first people to reach the stratosphere. Upon their return to Earth the scientists were honored in Zürich and Brussels. Piccard was able to exceed his altitude goal of 16,000 meters a year later when, with a cabin equipped with a radio, his balloon rose to 55,563 feet (16,940 meters).

Invents bathyscaphe

Following this achievement Piccard set the goal of reaching the lowest depth. In order to accomplish this he needed to construct a vessel that would penetrate the sea. Using the same basic idea as his stratospheric balloon, he built a free-floating "deep-sea ship" that he called a bathyscaphe. The pressurized cabin of the bathyscaphe was attached to a float that contained lighter-than-water gasoline while another compartment was filled with lead shot to give it stability. When the vessel went below water, gasoline was emptied from the float; when it came up to the surface, the lead shot was released.

Construction of the bathyscaphe was interrupted by World War II. In 1948 Piccard was able to test his first experimental vessel, which he named the *F.N.R.S. 2* for the Belgian scientific foundation that had supported the project. The unmanned *F.N.R.S. 2* descended 4,600 feet (1,400 meters), then carried out other experiments with Piccard on board. There were problems with this first bathyscaphe, chiefly that it could not be towed and had to be carried in the hull of a ship. When the *F.F.R.S. 2* was damaged in heavy seas, Piccard set about building a better vessel. In 1953 he constructed the *F.N.R.S. 3,* which was later acquired by the French navy. At that point Jacques Piccard joined his father in designing bathyscaphes.

Piccards set depth records

While Jacques was in Trieste, Italy, to study the city's port, local citizens commissioned him to build a bathyscaphe named the *Trieste*. In August 1953 the *Trieste* competed with the *F.N.R.S. 3* in the Mediterranean—the Italian vessel, with the Piccards aboard, descended into the water off the coast of Naples and the French went into the sea at Toulon. The *F.N.R.S. 3* reached 6,900 feet (2,100 meters) while the *Trieste* went to a depth of 10,300 feet (2,150 meters). Auguste had achieved his goal. Jacques left teaching to work full-time on bathyscaphes. In 1954 Auguste retired and moved to Lausanne, Switzerland.

Four years later the *Trieste* was bought by the U.S. Navy, which retained Jacques as a consultant. On January 23, 1960, Jacques and naval lieutenant Donald Walsh piloted the *Trieste* to a record depth of 35,800 feet (10,912 meters) in the Mariana Trench in the Pacific Ocean. They reported that even at that depth they saw signs of life.

Jacques wrote about his experience in the August 1960 edition of the *National Geographic* magazine:

Like a free balloon on a windless day, indifferent to the almost 200,000 tons of water pressing on the cabin from all sides, balanced to within an ounce or so on its wire guide ropes, slowly, surely, in the name of science and humanity, the *Trieste* took possession of the abyss, the last extreme on our earth that remained to be conquered.

Piccards design mesoscaphe

Following the success of the bathyscaphe, the Piccards developed the concept of the mesoscaphe—a "middle-depth ship" that would operate at depths down to 20,000 feet. If the bathyscaphe could be compared to an underwater balloon, then the mesoscaphe was designed to be an underwater helicopter. In 1969 the Woods Hole Oceanographic Institution in Massachusetts carried out the Gulf Stream Mission using the Piccards' mesoscaphe to conduct a series of experiments under the Atlantic Ocean.

During the mission Jacques Piccard made a month long journey, from July 14 to August 14, 1969, traveling with the Gulf Stream from West Palm Beach, Florida, to a point 360 miles southeast of Nova Scotia. The six-man crew on the mesoscaphe measured and recorded the physical characteristics of the Gulf Stream and made observations of the rich animal life around them. The project also served the experimental needs of the American National Aeronautics and Space Administration (NASA), which wanted to find out how men would react to confinement in a small space over a fairly long period of time.

Zebulon Pike

Born January 5, 1779,
Lamberton, New Jersey

Died April 27, 1813,
York, Ontario

Zebulon Montgomery Pike was born in Lamberton, New Jersey, on January 5, 1779. His father, who had the same name, was a major in the American army during the American Revolution; after the United States gained its independence from Britain he continued as a regular officer in the United States Army. At the age of 14 the younger Pike became a cadet in his father's company; six years later he was commissioned a lieutenant and assigned to various frontier posts.

Zebulon Pike, an American soldier who led several expeditions to the American West, was one of the first Americans to visit New Mexico.

Searches for Mississippi source and explores rivers in the West

In 1805 Pike was instructed by General James Wilkinson to lead an expedition to locate the source of the Mississippi River. Wilkinson was the governor of the newly acquired Louisiana territory, but he was also in the pay of the Spanish government, which still controlled Florida, Texas, New Mexico, and California. In August 1805 Pike embarked north on the Mississippi River from St. Louis along with 20 men and enough supplies to last four months.

When winter set in the party built a camp below the Falls of St. Anthony at the site of present-day St. Paul, Minnesota. In December Pike departed overland by sledge with a small party to continue his mission. When they reached Leech Lake in northern Minnesota, Pike concluded he had found the source of the Mississippi; actually the farthest reaches of the river are at Lake Itasca to the west of Leech Lake. Finding several British fur-trading posts in northern Minnesota, Pike informed the trappers there that they were trespassing on American territory.

Sent on puzzling mission

Pike returned to St. Louis in April 1806, but he had been there for only a short time when Wilkinson sent him on another mission. In addition to returning members of the powerful Osage tribe who had been taken captive and mediating peace between the Osage and Kansas tribes, Pike was instructed to explore the upper reaches of the Arkansas and Red rivers. There is strong evidence that he also received a secret directive to investigate a route to Spanish settlements in Santa Fe, New Mexico.

Historians have been unable to determine why Wilkinson wanted Pike to travel to Spanish territory. At that time the general was involved in a conspiracy with former U.S. vice-president Aaron Burr to separate the West from the rest of the United States. Whether Pike was supposed to have a role in this conspiracy is not clear. Even more mysterious, there is reason to believe Wilkinson betrayed Pike by warning the Spanish authorities that he was traveling in their territory.

Pike left St. Louis in July 1806 with 23 men, including Wilkinson's son, who was an army lieutenant, and one of Wilkinson's agents, Dr. John Robinson. They followed a route up the Missouri and Osage rivers in central Missouri to the Arkansas River. Along the way the Osages were returned to their homes in eastern Kansas. When Pike's party reached the

Arkansas River, Lieutenant Wilkinson returned to St. Louis with six of the men to report on the progress of the expedition.

Finds Pikes Peak

Pike and the remainder of the party crossed the Rocky Mountains in mid-November. A week later they arrived at the site of present-day Pueblo, Colorado; from there Pike and three of his companions set out to climb the tall mountain that was later named Pikes Peak. Although they were unsuccessful in reaching the top they did climb Cheyenne Peak, a smaller mountain about 15 miles away. After they rejoined the other men, Pike led the party up the Arkansas River to Royal Gorge, which is known as the "Grand Canyon" of Arkansas.

By now some of the men were ill, so Pike built a small fort near the gorge for those who were too sick to continue on the journey. Pike left the fort in January 1807 with Dr. Robinson and 12 others and, in the middle of winter, they crossed the Sangre de Cristo Mountains in southern Colorado. Six men got gangrene from walking through the snow, two so badly that their feet had to be amputated. Pike finally decided to stop on the Rio Conejos to build a small fort; a tributary of the Rio Grande, the Rio Conejos ran through the heart of Spanish New Mexico.

Arrested by Spanish

A few days later, in February 1897, Dr. Robinson left alone for Santa Fe, where he claimed to have business. Within three weeks of his departure a party of Spanish cavalry arrived at the fort to arrest Pike and his men for illegal entry into New Mexico. Pike resisted, saying he thought he was on a branch of the Red River that formed a boundary between American and Spanish territories. There is general agreement among scholars, however, that he knew exactly where he was and he was simply putting on a show for Spanish authorities.

Pike was taken to Santa Fe and then to Chihauhau in the area that is now northern Mexico to meet the Spanish governor. Interestingly, Dr. Robinson was also in Chihauhau when

Pike arrived. Pike was well treated by the Spanish; although his papers were taken away from him, he carefully memorized his trip so he could supply important geographical and military information to Wilkinson when he returned to the United States. He also hid notes in the barrel of his gun.

Starts expansionist movement

In July 1807 Pike was released on the American side of the border at Natchitoches, Louisiana. By then the Wilkinson-Burr conspiracy had been discovered and Pike was suspected of collaborating in the plot. When he protested his innocence to the secretary of war his defense was accepted. In the two-volume report on the expedition that he published in 1807, Pike said that the Great Plains would never be suitable for settlement by Americans; however, he proposed several possible routes through the Southwest to the Pacific Ocean. In his report on Santa Fe he noted the military weakness of the Spanish and the potentially profitable overland trade with Mexico. These comments helped to fuel American expansionism into the Southwest, especially Texas, in the following years.

After the outbreak of the War of 1812 between the United States and Great Britain, Pike was promoted to the rank of brigadier general. He was put in charge of the assault on York, which is now the city of Toronto, in Canada. The attack was successful, but Pike was killed in an explosion on April 27, 1813.

Fernão Mendes Pinto

Born c. 1510,
Monte-mor-o-Velho, Portugal

Died July 8, 1583,
Near Lisbon, Portugal

Fernão Mendes Pinto's action-packed life of adventure in the Far East is stranger and more interesting than fiction. The first European to visit Japan, he claimed to have been shipwrecked, captured, and sold into slavery at least 16 times. He was called the "Prince of Liars" because his account of his travels, *Peregrinação* ("Wanderings"), was so widely disbelieved by his contemporaries. Yet scholars have concluded that the book is factual, and it gives modern readers a glimpse of what sixteenth-century Asia looked like to a European. This daring man, who barely escaped death on many occasions, lived to the age of 74.

Pinto was born in the Portuguese town of Monte-mor-o-Velho not far from the ancient university city of Coimbra. At the age of 10 or 12 he was taken to Lisbon by an uncle and placed in the household of a rich noblewoman. He stayed there a year and a half until "something happened that placed me in such great jeopardy that I was forced to leave the house at a moment's notice and flee for my life." While it is not known

Fernão Mendes Pinto was a Portuguese adventurer who was the first European to visit Japan.

what happened, this incident seemed to have set the tone of his entire life. Pinto fled to the Alfama section of Lisbon where he caught a ship bound for southern Portugal. Fifteen miles from its destination the ship was captured by French pirates. After Pinto was eventually put ashore on the coast of Spain, he made his way to the Portuguese city of Setúbal. Employed by a nobleman, he stayed there for a year and a half.

Sold into slavery

Determined to seek his fortune elsewhere, Mendes Pinto sailed from Portugal on March 11, 1537, bound for India. He sailed around the Cape of Good Hope and arrived at the Portuguese fortress of Diu on the northwestern coast of India in September. He then joined an expedition to the Red Sea and delivered a message to the Portuguese soldiers who were fighting on the side of the Christian king of Ethiopia. Leaving Ethiopia, his ship was captured by Turks and the crew was taken to the port of Mocha in Yemen and sold into slavery. Eventually bought by a Jewish merchant, Pinto was taken to the port of Hormuz on the south coast of Persia, where he boarded a Portuguese trading ship.

Starts trading business

Reaching the Portuguese headquarters of Goa, Pinto entered the service of the newly appointed captain of Malacca on the coast of Malay. He arrived in 1539 and served as an emissary to the kingdoms of Sumatra and Malaya. An astute and avid trader, he then went to Patani on the east side of the Malay Peninsula and started a thriving business with the Thais in Bangkok. After being robbed by pirates, he and his partners got revenge by becoming pirates themselves. He continued to trade along the coast of Indochina. After being shipwrecked on the coast of China, Pinto was reputedly convicted of plundering royal tombs. As punishment his thumbs were severed and he was sentenced to a year of hard labor on the Great Wall. When he was freed by Tatar invaders, Pinto returned overland to Indochina.

Becomes first to see Japan

Sometime in 1542 or 1543, Pinto attempted to reach India by traveling with pirates on a Chinese junk. Driven off course during a storm, he ended up on the Japanese island of Tanegashima, south of Kyushu, to become the first European to reach that country. He was so impressed by the wealth of Japan that when he returned to Canton, China, he urged the Portuguese to take advantage of this new market. He set off with a group of merchants, but they were shipwrecked in the Ryukyu Islands. According to Pinto's account of the event, they were saved by the pleas of the women of the island. He then returned to Malacca.

Taken prisoner by Burmese

From Malacca he was sent on a mission to the Burmese, who had just captured the Kingdom of Pegu. Taken prisoner by the Burmese, he traveled as far as Luang Prabang in what is now Laos before escaping to Goa. His next mission was to establish trade with Java; instead, he became involved in a local war. Again he was saved by his good fortune and left just in time. On the way to China, Pinto's ship was attacked by Japanese pirates and shipwrecked on the coast of Thailand. He and his men built a raft that ended up once again in Java, where they were reduced to cannibalism. In order to survive they sold themselves into slavery.

When he was freed again, Pinto borrowed money to start a second trading operation with Thailand. He became involved in Burmese-Thai wars and wrote the first European account of Burmese politics and history. From Thailand, Mendes Pinto turned his attention once again to Japan, and he soon sailed into the port of Kagoshima. Upon his departure, he brought a Japanese stowaway to Malacca and presented him to Saint Francis Xavier, the Roman Catholic missionary. This incident inspired Xavier to travel to Japan and Christianize the inhabitants.

Devotes life to Christianity

In spite of disastrous reversals during his years in Asia,

Pinto had accumulated a large fortune. He was a wealthy merchant when he made his third voyage to Japan in 1551, when Francis Xavier was installed at the court of one of the feudal lords of southern Japan. He gave Xavier the money to build the first Christian church in Japan.

In 1554 Pinto decided to return with his fortune to Portugal. While waiting in Goa for a ship back to Europe, he underwent a sudden conversion and turned over half of his fortune to the Jesuit missionaries. He was accepted by the order as a lay brother, and he traveled back to Japan with a group of missionaries. At the request of the Portuguese governor, Pinto financed a mission in Goa to establish diplomatic relations between Portugal and Japan. At some point following his final departure from Japan in 1557, he voluntarily separated himself from the Jesuits, although he remained on good terms with the Church.

Retires to Portugal

Pinto returned to Portugal on September 22, 1558. He stayed at court for four years, hoping for some reward or recognition for his years of service in the Far East. When the honor was not forthcoming, he retired to a small estate on the Tagus River opposite Lisbon where he married and raised a family. Sometime between the years 1569 and 1578 he wrote an account of his travels, which was not published until 1614, over 20 years after his death. Translated into most Western languages, it is known in English as *The Voyages and Adventures of Fernão Mendes Pinto*. The book became a best-seller throughout Europe, but contained so many fantastic stories that it was considered to be a work of fiction. As more information about the exotic lands he visited became available the account was recognized to be largely factual. Pinto died on his estate on July 8, 1583, shortly after being awarded a small pension by the Portuguese government.

Francisco Pizarro

*Born c. 1475,
Extremadura, Spain
Died June 26, 1541,
Lima, Peru*

Francisco Pizarro was one of several Spanish soldiers of fortune called *conquistadors* who came to the New World to seize an empire for Spain. Pizarro's field of conquest was Peru; his relative, **Hernán Cortés** (see entry), added Mexico to Spain's possessions. In subduing the Incas, Pizarro took wealth so vast that it is difficult to imagine, even by today's standards. Spain instantly became the most powerful country in the world, and Peru, its residents inspired by religious zeal, was quickly converted to Catholicism.

Pizarro was born sometime around the year 1475 in the town of Trujillo in the Spanish province of Extremadura. He was the illegitimate son of Colonel Gonzalo Pizarro and a peasant woman. Having no formal education, Pizarro was illiterate and worked as a swineherd during his youth. There were only two careers open to a person with his background: either the military or the priesthood. Pizarro chose to become a soldier and took part in campaigns in Italy and Navarre. He drifted to Seville, which was the center of Spanish expeditions to

Francisco Pizarro, a Spanish conquistador who led the first Europeans to Peru, conquered the Inca Empire.

the Americas. He sailed to Santo Domingo in 1502. From there, he went with **Alonso de Ojeda** (see entry) on his expedition to the Gulf of Urabá in Colombia in 1509.

Joins expedition to Panama

When Ojeda left the struggling colony he had founded on the northern coast of South America to get supplies, he left Pizarro in charge of the garrison. Pizarro then went to Panama when **Vasco Núñez de Balboa** (see entry) moved the settlement there. He accompanied Balboa on his trip across the Darien Peninsula to the Pacific in 1513; he is listed in the chronicle of the expedition as being the second European to see the Pacific Ocean. It was Pizarro who later arrested Balboa when he was charged with treason in 1518. Pizarro served as mayor of Panama from 1519 until 1523.

Ever since their arrival in Panama, the Spanish had heard rumors of a rich land to the south called Birú, which is known today as Peru. Pizarro set up a partnership with two other men, Diego de Almagro and Hernando de Luque, to search out these lands. Luque, a priest, put up the money while the other two led the expedition. Almagro and Pizarro had similar backgrounds: they both escaped poverty to become rough-and-ready soldiers of fortune. It was an association that ended with the violent deaths of both men. Leaving Panama in November 1524, Pizarro and Almagro went as far south as the San Juan River, which is now on the border between Ecuador and Colombia. The climate, terrain, and Native Americans they met were all inhospitable. Suffering greatly from hunger, the men barely survived their first voyage. A positive result of their trip was that they collected some gold and heard tales of richer kingdoms to the south. They returned to Panama in 1525.

Sails for Peru

In 1526 Pizarro and Almagro signed another agreement with Luque, in which they agreed to divide any conquered lands among the three of them. Pizarro and Almagro then sailed from Panama with 160 men, who had been difficult to recruit after the hardships of the previous voyage. They retraced their previous voyage to the San Juan, which empties into the bay at Buenaventura. The pilot, Bartolomé Ruiz, was sent ahead to see what he could find. He crossed the equator and came back with stories about a heavily populated, highly civilized land that was rich with gold and silver. He was the first European to see Peru.

The entire expedition sailed southward to the city of Tumbes on the southern shore of the Bay of Guayaquil in Ecuador. They found Tumbes to be a large and beautiful seaport; the friendly inhabitants came out to greet them in large, oceangoing boats made of balsa wood with fine cotton sails. The Spaniards sampled a wide variety of foods and saw llamas for the first time. To the Incas, the Spanish were the exotics, strange and terrifying. Not yet ready for conquest, Pizarro cordially greeted an Inca nobleman on his ship. He also sent two of his men ashore with instructions to travel 200 miles south, where they heard about a great city in the interior that was the capital of a rich and powerful king. Upon their return the men told about a sophisticated and ancient civilization that had developed in total isolation from their world in Europe.

Appointed governor of Panama

In 1528 Pizarro's partners sent him to Spain to seek backing from Emperor Charles V for an expedition to Peru. Pizarro obtained support from the emperor, but he was appointed governor and captain-general of a new province stretching 200 leagues south of Panama. He also struck a deal with Charles that would guarantee him the majority of future profits. Pizarro returned to Panama accompanied by his four half-brothers, Almagro, 180 men, and 27 horses. The groundwork had been laid; this voyage in 1531 was to be one of conquest, not of exploration.

Pizarro and his men traveled once again to Tumbes hoping to find treasure, but they found the city destroyed. He learned about a civil war among the Incas that had resulted in the capture and death of one rival for the throne, Huascar, by his brother Atahualpa. Atahualpa was camped at the city of

Cajamarca, much closer to Tumbes than the distant Inca capital of Cuzco. Pizarro immediately sensed that he could use the civil war to his advantage by manipulating rival groups, just as Cortés had done in Mexico 12 years earlier.

Executes Inca leader

Before leaving Tumbes, Pizarro received reinforcements, and he established a base and supply camp at San Miguel on the Chira River. In September of 1532, five months after landing in Tumbes, he set off from San Miguel. They had to travel through the cold and mountainous country of the Andes but reached Cajamarca on November 15, 1532. The following day Atahualpa visited Pizarro with a large retinue of brilliantly uniformed warriors. While Atahualpa was distracted by a Spanish priest, Pizarro gave a signal for his men to massacre the Inca guards. He then took Atahualpa prisoner.

In order to obtain his release, Atahualpa offered to fill a room 17 feet by 22 feet with gold to a height of 9 feet and to fill two smaller rooms with silver. Pizarro eagerly agreed. There were 11 tons of gold objects alone. When the task was completed, however, Pizarro had Atahualpa put on "trial" and then executed, even though Atahualpa had offered to become a Christian. Pizarro received criticism for this act from the Spanish monarch. Atahualpa on his part had seriously misjudged the Spanish and their motives, thinking they would take their treasure and leave. With Atahualpa's slaying, the Incas were left leaderless and dispirited.

Betrays Almagro

By this time, Almagro had arrived in Cajamarca with reinforcements, and the Spanish set off for Cuzco. Along the way they met Manco, a brother of Huascar, and made him the puppet ruler of Peru. They had him enthroned in Cuzco in November 1533, so it was not necessary to conquer the city. By this time the Spaniards had started to quarrel among themselves. Pedro de Alvarado, another Spanish *conquistador,* landed in Ecuador in order to conquer the country but was persuaded to leave by Pizarro. Almagro was given the lands south of Peru to conquer but returned in 1537 to put down an Inca revolt. When he tried to make himself governor he was defeated by troops led by Pizarro's brother Hernando in the Battle of Las Salinas in April 1538. Almagro had felt slighted by Pizarro as the wealth and property were being divided. Now the governor of Peru, Pizarro had his old friend and comrade Almagro tried and executed.

Killed by his own men

By this time Pizarro, who had been named the marquis of Atavillas, was an extremely wealthy member of the Spanish aristocracy. In 1535 he occupied himself with building a new capital, Lima, on the coast of Peru. However, the antagonisms of the civil war among the Spanish did not die down; the Almagro faction had complained about Pizarro's treatment of Almagro to the king of Spain.

When Hernando Pizarro, Francisco Pizarro's brother, was sent back to Madrid to report on his brother's conduct in 1539, he was imprisoned; he remained a prisoner until 1561. In the meantime, vowing revenge, the Almagrists had formed a faction under the leadership of Francisco Almagro, the son of Diego and a Native American woman from Panama. Apparently unaware of their plots, Pizarro was assassinated in his own palace in Lima by 20 Almagro supporters on June 26, 1541.

Chronology of Exploration

As an aid to the reader who wishes to trace the history of exploration or the explorers active in a particular location, the major expeditions within a geographical area are listed below in chronological order.

Africa: across the continent

1802-14	Pedro João Baptista and Amaro José
1854-56	David Livingstone
1858-64	David Livingstone
1872-73	David Livingstone
1873-77	Henry Morton Stanley
1877-80	Hermenegildo de Brito Capelo and Roberto Ivens
1884-85	Hermenegildo de Brito Capelo and Roberto Ivens
1888-90	Henry Morton Stanley
1896-98	Jean-Baptiste Marchand
1924-25	Delia Akeley

Africa: coast

1416-60	Henry the Navigator
1487-88	Bartolomeu Dias

Africa: east

1490-1526	Pero da Covilhã
1848	Johannes Rebmann
1848-49	Johann Ludwig Krapf
1848-49	Johannes Rebmann
1849	Johannes Rebmann
1851	Johann Ludwig Krapf
1857-59	Richard Burton and John Hanning Speke (with Sidi Mubarak Bombay)
1860-63	John Hanning Speke and James Augustus Grant (with Sidi Mubarak Bombay)
1862-64	Samuel White Baker and Florence Baker
1865-71	David Livingstone
1870-73	Samuel White Baker and Florence Baker

1871-73	Henry Morton Stanley (with Sidi Mubarak Bombay)
1883-84	Joseph Thomson
1905-06	Delia Akeley
1909-11	Delia Akeley

Africa: south

1849	David Livingstone
1850	David Livingstone
1851-52	David Livingstone

Africa: west

1352-53	Abu Abdallah Ibn Battutah
1795-99	Mungo Park
1805	Mungo Park
1827-28	René Caillié
1850-55	Heinrich Barth
1856-60	Paul Du Chaillu
1861-76	Friedrich Gerhard Rohlfs
1863	Paul Du Chaillu
1867	Paul Du Chaillu
1875-78	Pierre Savorgnan de Brazza
1879	Henry Morton Stanley
1879-81	Pierre Savorgnan de Brazza
1883-85	Pierre Savorgnan de Brazza
1891-92	Pierre Savorgnan de Brazza
1893	Mary Kingsley
1894	Mary Kingsley

Antarctica

1819-21	Fabian Gottlieb von Bellingshausen
1837-40	Jules-Sébastien-César Dumont d'Urville
1839-40	Charles Wilkes
1907-09	Ernest Shackleton

1910-12	Roald Amundsen
1914-16	Ernest Shackleton
1921-22	Ernest Shackleton
1928	Hubert Wilkins
1928-29	Richard Evelyn Byrd
1929	Hubert Wilkins
1933-34	Lincoln Ellsworth
1933-35	Richard Evelyn Byrd
1935-36	Lincoln Ellsworth
1937	Lincoln Ellsworth
1939-40	Richard Evelyn Byrd
1946-47	Richard Evelyn Byrd
1956	Richard Evelyn Byrd
1956-58	Vivian Fuchs
1989-90	Will Steger

Arabia

25 B.C	Aelius Gallus
1812-13	Hester Stanhhope
1854-55	Richard Burton
1877-78	Anne Blunt and Wilfrid Scawen Blunt
1879-80	Anne Blunt and Wilfrid Scawen Blunt
1913	Gertrude Bell

Arctic (*see also* North America: Northwest Passage)

1827	Edward Parry
1893-96	Fridtjof Nansen
1902	Robert Edwin Peary
1905-06	Robert Edwin Peary (with Matthew A. Henson)
1908-09	Robert Edwin Peary (with Matthew A. Henson)
1925	Roald Amundsen
1925	Richard Evelyn Byrd

1926	Roald Amundsen and Umberto Nobile
1926	Louise Arner Boyd
1926	Richard Evelyn Byrd
1926-27	Hubert Wilkins
1928	Louise Arner Boyd
1928	Hubert Wilkins
1931	Hubert Wilkins
1940	Louise Arner Boyd
1955	Louise Arner Boyd
1958	U.S.S. *Nautilus*
1986	Will Steger

Asia: interior

1866-68	Francis Garnier
1870-72	Nikolay Przhevalsky
1876	Nikolay Przhevalsky
1883-85	Nikolay Przhevalsky
1893-95	Sven Hedin
1895-97	Isabella Bird
1899	Fanny Bullock Workman
1899-1901	Sven Hedin
1900	Aurel Stein
1903-05	Sven Hedin
1906	Fanny Bullock Workman
1906-08	Aurel Stein
1913-15	Aurel Stein
1927-33	Sven Hedin
1934-36	Sven Hedin
1953	Edmund Hillary
1977	Edmund Hillary

Asia/Europe: link (see Europe/Asia: link)

Asia, south/China: link

629-45 B.C.	Hsüan-tsang
138-26 B.C.	Chang Ch'ien

1405-07	Cheng Ho
1407-09	Cheng Ho
1409-11	Cheng Ho
1413-15	Cheng Ho
1417-19	Cheng Ho
1421-22	Cheng Ho
1433-35	Cheng Ho

Australia

1605-06	Willem Janszoon
1642	Abel Tasman
1644	Abel Tasman
1770	James Cook
1798-99	Matthew Flinders
1801-02	Matthew Flinders
1801-02	Joseph Banks
1802-03	Matthew Flinders
1839	Edward John Eyre
1840-41	Edward John Eyre
1860-61	Robert O'Hara Burke and William John Wills

Aviation

1927	Charles Lindbergh
1928	Amelia Earhart
1930	Beryl Markham
1930	Amy Johnson
1931	Amy Johnson
1931	Wiley Post
1932	Amelia Earhart
1932	Amy Johnson
1933	Wiley Post
1935	Amelia Earhart
1936	Amelia Earhart
1936	Beryl Markham
1947	Chuck Yeager
1986	Dick Rutan and Jeana Yeager

Europe/Asia: link

454-43 B.C. Herodotus
401-399 B.C. Xenophon
334-23 B.C. Alexander the Great
310-06 B.C. Pytheas
1159-73 Benjamin of Tudela
1245-47 Giovanni da Pian del Carpini
1271-95 Marco Polo
1280-90 Rabban Bar Sauma
1487-90 Pero da Covilhã
1492-93 Christopher Columbus
1497-99 Vasco da Gama
1502-03 Vasco da Gama
1537-58 Fernão Mendes Pinto
1549-51 Saint Francis Xavier
1595-97 Cornelis de Houtman
1598-99 Cornelis de Houtman
1697-99 Vladimir Atlasov
1787 Jean François de Galaup,
      Comte de La Pérouse

Greenland

982 Erik the Red
1886 Robert Edwin Peary
1888 Fridtjof Nansen
1891-92 Robert Edwin Peary (with
         Matthew A. Henson)
1893-95 Robert Edwin Peary (with
         Matthew A. Henson)
1931 Louise Arner Boyd
1933 Louise Arner Boyd
1937 Louise Arner Boyd
1938 Louise Arner Boyd

Muslim World

915-17 Abu al-Hasan 'Ali al-Mas'udi
918-28 Abu al-Hasan 'Ali al-Mas'udi

943-73 Abu al-Kasim Ibn Ali al-
        Nasibi Ibn Hawkal
1325-49 Abu Abdallah Ibn Battutah

North America: coast

1001-02 Leif Eriksson
1493-96 Christopher Columbus
1497 John Cabot
1498 John Cabot
1502-04 Christopher Columbus
1508 Sebastian Cabot
1513 Juan Ponce de León
1513-14 Vasco Núñez de Balboa
1518-22 Hernán Cortés
1524 Giovanni da Verrazano
1534 Jacques Cartier
1534-36 Hernán Cortés
1535-36 Jacques Cartier
1539 Hernán Cortés
1541-42 Jacques Cartier
1542-43 João Rodrigues Cabrilho
1584 Walter Raleigh
1585-86 Walter Raleigh
1587-89 Walter Raleigh
1603 Samuel de Champlain
1604-07 Samuel de Champlain
1606-09 John Smith
1608-10 Samuel de Champlain
1609 Henry Hudson
1610 Samuel de Champlain
1614 John Smith
1792-94 George Vancouver

North America: Northwest Passage

1610-13 Henry Hudson
1776-79 James Cook
1819-20 Edward Parry

1821-23	Edward Parry
1824-25	Edward Parry
1845-47	John Franklin
1850-54	Robert McClure
1903-06	Roald Amundsen

North America: sub-Arctic

1654-56	Médard Chouart des Groselliers
1668	Médard Chouart des Groselliers
1668	Pierre Esprit Radisson
1670	Pierre Esprit Radisson
1679	Louis Jolliet
1682-83	Médard Chouart des Groselliers
1684	Pierre Esprit Radisson
1685-87	Pierre Esprit Radisson
1689	Louis Jolliet
1694	Louis Jolliet
1789	Alexander Mackenzie
1795	Aleksandr Baranov
1799	Aleksandr Baranov
1819-22	John Franklin
1825-27	John Franklin

North America: west

1527-36	Álvar Núñez Cabeza de Vaca (with Estevanico)
1538-43	Hernando de Soto
1539	Estevanico
1540-42	Francisco Vásquez de Coronado
1611-12	Samuel de Champlain
1613-15	Samuel de Champlain
1615-16	Samuel de Champlain
1615-16	Étienne Brulé

1621-23	Étienne Brulé
1657	Pierre Esprit Radisson
1659-60	Médard Chouart des Groselliers
1659-60	Pierre Esprit Radisson
1669-70	René-Robert Cavelier de La Salle
1672-74	Louis Jolliet
1678-83	René-Robert Cavelier de La Salle
1684-87	René-Robert Cavelier de La Salle
1769-71	Daniel Boone
1775	Daniel Boone
1792-94	Alexander Mackenzie
1792-97	David Thompson
1797-99	David Thompson
1800-02	David Thompson
1804-06	Meriwether Lewis and William Clark
1805-06	Zebulon Pike
1806-07	Zebulon Pike
1807-11	David Thompson
1811-13	Wilson Price Hunt and Robert Stuart
1823-25	Jedediah Smith
1824-25	Peter Skene Ogden
1825-26	Peter Skene Ogden
1826-27	Peter Skene Ogden
1826-28	Jedediah Smith
1828-29	Peter Skene Ogden
1829-30	Peter Skene Ogden
1842	John Charles Frémont
1843-44	John Charles Frémont
1845-48	John Charles Frémont
1848-49	John Charles Frémont
1850-51	Jim Beckwourth
1853-55	John Charles Frémont

Northeast Passage

1607	Henry Hudson
1918-20	Roald Amundsen
1931	Lincoln Ellsworth

North Pole (see Arctic)

Northwest Passage (see North America: Northwest Passage)

Oceans

1872-76	H.M.S. *Challenger*
1942-42	Jacques Cousteau
1948	August Piccard
1954	August Piccard
1960	Jacques Piccard
1968-80	*Glomar Challenger*
1969	Jacques Piccard

Pacific: south

1519-22	Ferdinand Magellan
1577-80	Francis Drake
1642-43	Abel Tasman
1721-22	Jacob Roggeveen
1766-68	Samuel Wallis
1766-69	Philip Carteret
1767-69	Louis-Antoine de Bougainville
1768-71	James Cook (with Joseph Banks)
1772-75	James Cook
1776-79	James Cook
1785-88	Jean François de Galaup, Comte de La Pérouse
1791	George Vancouver

1826-29	Jules-Sébastien-César Dumont d'Urville
1834-36	Charles Darwin
1838-39	Jules-Sébastien-César Dumont d'Urville
1838-42	Charles Wilkes
1930	Michael J. Leahy
1931	Michael J. Leahy
1932-33	Michael J. Leahy

South America: coast

1498-1500	Christopher Columbus
1499-1500	Alonso de Ojeda
1499-1500	Amerigo Vespucci
1501-1502	Amerigo Vespucci
1502	Alonso de Ojeda
1505	Alonso de Ojeda
1509-10	Alonso de Ojeda
1519-20	Ferdinand Magellan
1526-30	Sebastian Cabot
1527	Giovanni da Verrazano
1528	Giovanni da Verrazano
1594	Walter Raleigh
1595	Walter Raleigh
1617-18	Walter Raleigh
1831-34	Charles Darwin

South America: interior

1524-25	Francisco Pizarro
1526-27	Francisco Pizarro
1531-41	Francisco Pizarro
1540-44	Álvar Núñez Cabeza de Vaca
1541-42	Francisco de Orellana
1769-70	Isabel Godin des Odonais
1799-1803	Alexander von Humboldt
1903	Annie Smith Peck
1904	Annie Smith Peck
1908	Annie Smith Peck

1911	Hiram Bingham
1912	Hiram Bingham
1915	Hiram Bingham

Space

1957	*Sputnik*
1958-70	*Explorer 1*
1959-72	*Luna*
1961	Yury Gagarin
1962	John Glenn
1962-75	*Mariner*
1963	Valentina Tereshkova
1967-72	*Apollo*
1969	Neil Armstrong
1975-83	*Viking*
1977-90	*Voyager 1* and *2*
1983	Sally Ride
1990-	Hubble Space Telescope

Tibet

1624-30	Antonio de Andrade
1811-12	Thomas Manning
1865-66	Nain Singh
1867-68	Nain Singh
1879-80	Nikolay Przhevalsky
1892-93	Annie Royle Taylor
1898	Susie Carson Rijnhart
1901	Sven Hedin
1915-16	Alexandra David-Neel
1923-24	Alexandra David-Neel

Explorers by Country of Birth

If an expedition were sponsored by a country other than the explorer's place of birth, the sponsoring country is listed in parentheses after the explorer's name.

Angola

Pedro João Baptista (Portugal)
Amaro José

Australia

Michael J. Leahy
Hubert Wilkins

Canada

Louis Jolliet
Peter Skene Ogden
Susie Carson Rijnhart

China

Rabban Bar Sauma
Chang Ch'ien
Cheng Ho
Hsüan-tsang

Ecuador

Isabel Godin des Odonais

England

Samuel White Baker
Joseph Banks
Gertrude Bell
Isabella Bird
Anne Blunt
Wilfrid Scawen Blunt
Richard Burton
Philip Carteret
H.M.S. *Challenger*

James Cook
Charles Darwin
Francis Drake
Edward John Eyre
Matthew Flinders
John Franklin
Vivian Fuchs
Henry Hudson (Netherlands)
Amy Johnson
Mary Kingsley
Thomas Manning
Beryl Markham (Kenya)
Edward Parry
Walter Raleigh
John Smith
John Hanning Speke
Hester Stanhope
Annie Royle Taylor
David Thompson
George Vancouver
Samuel Wallis
William John Wills (Australia)

Estonia

Fabian Gottlieb von Bellingshausen (Russia)

France

Louis-Antoine de Bougainville
Étienne Brulé
René Caillié
Jacques Cartier
Samuel de Champlain
Médard Chouart des Groselliers
Paul Du Chaillu (United States)
Jacques Cousteau
Alexandra David-Neel
Jules-Sébastien-César Dumont d'Urville
Francis Garnier

Jean François de Galaup, Comte de La Pérouse
René-Robert Cavelier de La Salle
Jean-Baptiste Marchand
Pierre Esprit Radisson

Germany

Heinrich Barth (Great Britain)
Alexander von Humboldt
Johann Ludwig Krapf
Johannes Rebmann
Friedrich Gerhard Rohlfs

Greece

Herodotus
Pytheas
Xenophon

Hungary

Aurel Stein (Great Britain)

Iceland

Leif Eriksson

India

Nain Singh

Iraq

Abu al-Kasim Ibn Ali al-Nasibi Ibn Hawkal
Abu al-Hasan `Ali al-Mas`udi

Ireland

Robert O'Hara Burke (Australia)
Robert McClure
Ernest Shackleton

Italy

Pierre Savorgnan de Brazza (France)
John Cabot (Great Britain)
Sebastian Cabot (England, Spain)
Giovanni da Pian del Carpini
Christopher Columbus (Spain)
Marco Polo
Giovanni da Verrazano (France)
Amerigo Vespucci (Spain, Portugal)

Macedonia

Alexander the Great

Morocco

Abu Abdallah Ibn Battutah
Estevanico

Netherlands

Cornelis de Houtman
Willem Janszoon
Jacob Roggeveen
Abel Tasman

New Zealand

Edmund Hillary

Norway

Roald Amundsen
Erik the Red (Iceland)
Fridtjof Nansen

Nyasaland

Sidi Mubarak Bombay (Great Britain)
James Chuma (Great Britain)

Portugal

Antonio de Andrade
Hermenegildo de Brito Capelo
João Rodrigues Cabrilho (Spain)
Pero da Covilhã
Bartolomeu Dias
Vasco da Gama
Henry the Navigator
Roberto Ivens
Ferdinand Magellan (Spain)
Fernão Mendes Pinto

Romania

Florence Baker

Rome

Aelius Gallus

Russia
(*see also* Union of Soviet Socialist Republics)

Vladimir Atlasov
Aleksandr Baranov
Nikolay Przhevalsky

Scotland

David Livingstone
Alexander Mackenzie
Mungo Park
Robert Stuart (United States)
Joseph Thomson

Spain

Benjamin of Tudela
Álvar Núñez Cabeza de Vaca

Francisco Vásquez de Coronado
Hernán Cortés
Vasco Núñez de Balboa
Alonso de Ojeda
Francisco de Orellana
Francisco Pizarro
Juan Ponce de León
Hernando de Soto
Saint Francis Xavier

Sweden

Sven Hedin

Switzerland

Auguste Piccard
Jacques Piccard

Union of Soviet Socialist Republics

Yury Gagarin
Luna
Sputnik
Valentina Tereshkova

United States of America

Delia Akeley
Apollo
Neil Armstrong
Jim Beckwourth
Hiram Bingham
Daniel Boone
Louise Arner Boyd
Richard Evelyn Byrd
William Clark
Amelia Earhart

Lincoln Ellsworth
Explorer 1
John Charles Frémont
John Glenn
Glomar Challenger
Matthew A. Henson
Hubble Space Telescope
Wilson Price Hunt
Meriwether Lewis
Charles Lindbergh
Mariner
U.S.S. *Nautilus*
Robert Edwin Peary
Annie Smith Peck
Zebulon Pike
Wiley Post
Sally Ride
Dick Rutan
Jedediah Smith
Will Steger
Viking
Voyager 1 and *2*
Charles Wilkes
Fanny Bullock Workman
Chuck Yeager
Jeana Yeager

Wales

Henry Morton Stanley (United States)

Index

Bold denotes figures profiled

D

Dahar-June 787
Dahe, Qin 803
Daily Mail 492
Dakar, Senegal 426
Dalai Lama 307-309, 575-577, 753
The Dalles, Oregon 621
Damascus, Syria 76, 88, 97, 109, 157, 597
Damietta, Egypt 97
Danube River 44
Dardanelles 6
Darién 616
Darien Peninsula 625, 670
Darius I (of Persia) 434
Darius II (of Persia) 867
Darius III (of Persia) 7, 8
Darling River 145, 147
Darling, William 357
Dartmouth, England 472
Darwin, Australia 491-492
Darwin, Charles 292-305, 474
Darwin, Erasmus 292
David, Edgeworth 747
David-Neel, Alexandra 306-310
Davis, John 458
Davis Strait 472, 525
De Long, George Washington 606
Dead Sea 597
Dean Channel 564
Deccan, India 596
Deena 633
Deep Sea Drilling Project 406
Defoe, Daniel
Deganawidah 215
Deimos 587
Delaware Bay 470
Delaware River 470
Delft 487
Delhi, India 23
Denbei 42
Denver, Colorado 84
Derb-el-Haj 76
Derendingen 502
Descartes Mountains 32
A Description of New England 765

Desideri, Ippolito 576
de Soto, Hernando (see **Soto, Hernando de**)
Detroit Arctic Expedition 857
Detroit, Michigan 120, 485, 538
Devil's Ballroom 20
Devon Island 16
Dias, Bartolomeu 241, 288, **311-314,** 386, 388, 426
Dias, Dinis 426
Días, Melchor 270, 271
Dickson, James 633, 635
Diderot, Denis 127
Diebetsch, Josephine 645
Diemen, Anthony van 810
Dieppe, France 837
Dietrich, Rosine 504
Digges Island 473
Dione, moon 849
Discoverie of Guiana 715
Discovery 264-266, 464, 472-473, 830-833
District of Orleans 536
Diyarbakir 77
Djakarta, Indonesia 127, 190
Djenné, Mali 180, 579
Djibouti 580, 583-584
Dnieper River 41
Dolak Island 487
Dolphin 188, 190, 191, 257
Dominican Republic 615
Donnacona 194, 195
Donn River 41
Dorantes, Andres 165-166, 347-348
Doudart de Lagrée, Ernest 396
Drake, Francis 315-320
Druid 296
Druses 786-787
Druze 87
Dry Tortugas 697
Dubois River 530
Du Chaillu, Paul 321-324
Dudh Kosi River 752
Duifken 486-487
Duke, Charles 32
Duluth, Minnesota 142, 823
Dumont d'Urville, Jules-Sébastien-César 325-329, 511, 853

Francis of Assisi 183
François I (of France) 193-196, 837-838
Franco-Prussian War 134, 397
Franklin, Jane Griffin 367-368
Franklin, John 14, 361, **364-369,** 599, 639
Franklin Strait 16, 368
Franz Josef Land 130, 607
Fraser River 563
Fraser, Simon 563
Frederick the Great (of Prussia) 474
Freetown, Sierra Leone 180, 500
Freiburg, Germany 475
Frémont, Jessie Benton 371, 374
Frémont, John Charles 370-374
Fremont Peak 372
French and Indian War 117, 122, 508
French Congo 136
French Foreign Legion 736
French Geographical Society 182, 329
French Guiana 717
French Legion of Honor 326
French Polynesia 733
French Revolution 511
French River 142, 216
Friendship 332, 402-404
Frobisher, Martin 344, 472
Frontenac, Count de 496, 513
Frozen Strait 640
Fuchs, Vivian 375-377, 452-453, 801
Funatsu, Keizo 803-804
Furneaux Islands 360
Fury 641-642
Fury Strait 641

G

Gabet, Joseph 814
Gabon, West Africa 135, 321-322, 500
Gades, Phoenicia 710
Gagarin, Yury 378-382, 402, 559, 782, 818
Galápagos Islands 301, 303

Galfridus of Langele 68
Galileo 32, 464
Galla (tribe) 503-504
Gallatin, Albert 533
Gallatin River 533
Gallus, Aelius 383-385
Galveston Island 165, 166, 346
Gama, Paolo da 387
Gama, Vasco da 224, 288, 313, **386-392**
Gambia 55, 635
Gambia River 426, 633
Ganges River 24, 453, 462-463, 598
Ganymede 848
Garhwal, India 24
Garnier, Francis 393-399
Gaspé Bay 194
Gaspé Peninsula 194-195, 214
Gatty, Harold 700-702
Gaugamela, Assyria 8
Gauhati 463
Gaza 7
Gedrosia 12
Gemini 6 28
Gemini 8 36, 37
Genesee River 142
Genesis Rock 32
Genghis Khan 66, 67, 184
Genoa, Italy 95, 694
Geographical Magazine 755
George III (of England) 53
Georges River 360
Georgian Bay 142
Gerlache, Adrien de 15
Ghat, Libya 71
Gila River 271
Gilbert Island 326
Gilbert, Humphrey 712
Gilgit range 807
Ginuha Genoa, Italy 67
Gjöa 16-18
Gjöa Haven 16-17
Gladstone, William 105
Glenn, John 31, **400-405**
***Glomar Challenger* 406-408**
Gloster Meteor 872
Goa, India 25, 289, 636, 666, 667-668, 865-866

L

La Boussole 509, 511
Labrador 173, 338, 432, 498, 526, 652
Lacerda, Francisco José de 57-58
Lachine Rapids 142, 195, 497
La Concepción de Urbana 478
La Condamine, Charles Marie de 409-410
Ladakh, India 105, 755
La Dauphine 837-838
Lady Alice 794-795
A Lady's Life in the Rocky Mountains 104
Lae, New Guinea 520
Lagos, Portugal 239, 737
Lagrée, Ernest Doudart de 395
La Guajira 624-625
La Hogue 638
Laing, Alexander Gordon 181
Lake Alakol 185
Lake Albert 3, 43, 47-48, 50, 794, 798
Lake Athabaska 822
Lake Bangweulu 232-234, 551-552, 554
Lake Chad 69-72, 136, 737
Lake Champlain 215
Lake Chilwa 550
Lake Courte Oreille 226
Lake Dilolo 548
Lake Edward 798
Lake Erie 142, 513-514
Lake Eyre 356
Lake Huron 142, 216, 496, 514
Lake Illiwarra 360
Lake Issyk-Kul 419
Lake Itasca 662
Lake Kazembe 233
Lake Leopold 796
Lake Malawi 550-552, 826
Lake Manitoba 823
Lake Maracaibo 624
Lake Michigan 216, 496-497, 514
Lake Mweru 552
Lake Naivasha 827

Lake Ngami 544, 546
Lake Nipissing 142, 216
Lake Nyasa, Malawi 112, 231-232, 236, 505, 773, 789, 826
Lake of the Woods 823
Lake Ontario 513
Lake Parima 479
Lake Rukwa 826
Lake Simcoe 142
Lake Superior 142, 225-227, 823
Lake Tahoe, Nevada 104
Lake Tanganyika 113, 115-116, 155-156, 233-234, 236, 551-553, 774, 790, 792, 794, 826
Lake Terrens 356
Lake Victoria 3, 45, 113-114, 155-156, 435, 772, 775-777, 794, 798, 828
Lake Winnipeg 823
Lamaism 574
Lambaréné, Gabon 134, 322
Lamego, Joseph de 290
La Motte, Dominique 513
La Navidad (Limonade-Bord-de-Mer, Haiti) 246, 248
Lancaster Sound 16, 639, 642
Lanchou 691
Landells, George 145
Lander, Richard 637
Land's End, Belerium 710
Langle, Paul-Antoine de 509-510
L'Anse aux Meadows, Newfoundland 526
Laos 667
La Paz Bay 280-281
La Paz, Bolivia 654
La Pérouse, Jean-François de Galaup, comte de 326, **508-511**
La Pérouse Strait 510
La Relación y Comentarios 168
La Rochelle, France 766
La Salle, Illinois 516
La Salle, René-Robert Cavelier de 512-518
Las Conchas, Argentina 299
Las Palmas, Canary islands 244
Lassen Volcanic National Park 83
L'Astrolabe 509-511

South China Sea 222
Southern Alps 449-450
South Georgia Island 91, 749
South Island, New Zealand 259,
263, 327, 449, 810-811
South Magnetic Pole 328, 747
South Orkney Islands 328
South Pass, Wyoming 372, 485,
757
South Peak 451
South Pole 14, 18-20, 158, 160-
161, 163, 338, 377, 452-453,
744, 746-747, 804, 859
South Seas 509, 513
South Shetland Islands 92, 93, 328
Soviet Space Commission 818
Soyuz 1 382
Space Telescope Science Institute
(Baltimore, Maryland) 466
Spanish-American War 158
Spanish Armada 315, 319-320,
714
Spanish Inquisition 241
Spanish Trail 372
Sparta 870
Speke, John Hanning 45-46,
112, 113-114, 153-156, 502,
551, 580, 722, **772-777,** 794
Spencer Gulf 355, 356, 361, 362
Spencer, Herbert 358
Spice Islands 127, 174, 318, 457,
567, 570-571, 573, 733, 865
Spirit of St. Louis 539, 542
Spitsbergen Islands 130, 160, 642
Spitsbergen, Norway 21, 22, 337,
365, 611-612, 858
Spruce, Richard 481
Sputnik 26, 36, 351, 353, 379,
555, 557, **778-782**
Sri Lanka 44, 51, 79, 222-223,
596, 598, 693, 862
Srinigar, India 105, 406
Stadacona (Quebec City, Quebec)
195-196
Stafford, Thomas 29
Stag Lane 489
Stalin, Joseph 779
Stanhope, Hester 783-787
Stanislaus River 760
Stanley Falls 795

Stanley, Henry Morton 115,
134-135, 138, 233, 236, 553,
788-799, 828
Stanley Pool 134-135, 795
St. Ann's Bay 253
Station Camp Creek, Kentucky
118
St. Augustine, Florida 319, 696
St. Croix, Virgin Islands 248
Stefansson, Vilhjalmur 857
Steger International Polar Expedi-
tion 802
Steger, Will 800-805
Stein, Aurel 806-808
Stephen of Cloyes 96
Stewart, James 542
St. Helena 302, 834
St. Ignace 496
Stingray Point 764
St. John's, Newfoundland 196
St. Joseph, Missouri 483
St. Lawrence River 193, 195,
212-213, 215, 227, 255, 497-
498, 526
St. Louis, MIssouri 483-485,
530-531, 536, 539-540, 662
Stockton, Robert F. 373
St. Paul, Minnesota 662
St. Petersburg, Russia 420, 705,
708
Strabo 384
Strait of Belle Isle 194, 526
Strait of Georgia 833
Strait of Gibraltar 408, 415, 710
Strait of Hormuz 223
Strait of Juan de Fuca 832, 854
Strait of Magellan 124, 174, 188,
300, 318-319, 327, 458, 569,
600
Straits of Mackinac 514
Straits of Malacca 459
Streaky Bay 356
Stuart, John McDouall 144, 146,
149
Stuart, Robert 483-485
St. Vincent, West Indies 357
Submarine Force Museum 613
Sué River 582
Suffren 394
Sulpicians 513